AF279202

# lonely planet

ASHLEY PARSONS, STUART BUTLER, OLIVER BERRY,
STEVE FALLON, ANITA ISALSKA & NICOLA WILLIAMS

# Contents

Irish Sea
North Sea
Hamburg
DUBLIN
IRELAND
Leeds
Manchester
Liverpool
Sheffield
Lincoln
Groningen
Bremen
Elbe
Birmingham
Leicester
Norwich
NETHERLANDS
Hanover
WALES
ENGLAND
Den Haag (The Hague)
AMSTERDAM
Bielefeld
Arnhem
Swansea
CARDIFF
LONDON
Rotterdam
Dortmund
Kassel
Erfurt
Bristol
Essen
Düsseldorf
Bristol Channel
Southampton
Folkestone
Ghent
Antwerp
Cologne
GERMANY
Calais
BRUSSELS
Bonn
Brighton
BELGIUM
Frankfurt-am-Main
Plymouth
Isle of Wight
Lille
LILLE & THE SOMME p43
Würzburg
English Channel (La Manche)
Dieppe
Amiens
St-Quentin
LUXEMBOURG
Trier
Nuremberg
ATLANTIC OCEAN
CHANNEL ISLANDS
Cherbourg
Le Havre
Charleville-Mézières
LUXEMBOURG CITY
Mannheim
Rhine
Cotentin Peninsula
Rouen
Reims
Metz
Saarbrücken
Karlsruhe
Stuttgart
BRITTANY & NORMANDY p21
Caen
Seine
Nancy
Strasbourg
Danube
Brest
St-Brieuc
St-Malo
PARIS
Mulhouse
Bregenz
Lake Constance
Quimper
Rennes
Chartres
Troyes
Zürich
VADUZ
Vannes
Le Mans
Orléans
Dijon
Besançon
BERN
SWITZERLAND
Angers
Tours
Loire
Bourges
Mâcon
Lake Geneva (Lac Léman)
Lausanne
ITALY
Nantes
La Roche-sur-Yon
Poitiers
Geneva
Bay of Biscay
La Rochelle
Clermont-Ferrand
Mont Blanc (4807m)
Milan
Saintes
Limoges
Lyon
FRENCH ALPS & JURA p59
Turin
CENTRAL FRANCE p95
Périgueux
Brive-la-Gaillarde
Rhône
Grenoble
THE FRENCH ALPS
Po
Genoa
Bordeaux
Garonne
Valence
Lot
Santander
Mont-de-Marsan
Albi
Nîmes
Avignon
Nice
Gulf of Genoa
Bilbao
Biarritz
Bayonne
Toulouse
Montpellier
Cannes
MONACO
Vitoria-Gasteiz
San Sebastián
Pau
Marseille
PROVENCE & THE CÔTE D'AZUR p115
Pamplona
The Pyrenees
Narbonne
Toulon
Côte d'Azur
Bastia
Logroño
ANDORRA
Perpignan
Calvi
Burgos
THE PYRENEES p159
Pico de Aneto (3404m)
ANDORRA LA VELLA
LANGUEDOC-ROUSSILLON p139
Corsica
Valladolid
Duero
Zaragoza
Lleida
Girona
Ajaccio
CORSICA p189
MADRID
SPAIN
Ebro
Barcelona
Tarragona
Olbia
Sassari
Teruel
Tajo
Balearic Islands
Menorca
MEDITERRANEAN SEA
Sardinia
200 km
100 miles
N
Golfo de Valencia
Palma de Mallorca
Majorca
Cagliari
Valencia

# Welcome to France

From Mont Blanc and other alpine giants to the volcanic cones of the Massif Central and the visual poetry of the Pyrenees, France is blessed with wave after wave of beautiful mountain peaks. Traversing these mountain ranges is a network of high-quality walking trails that attract hikers from all four corners of the world.

But walking in France is about more than just cinematic mountain vistas. At its heart, this is a land of gentle woodlands where rivers meander past old villages surrounded by fields of vines, lavender and sunflowers.

Then, there's the salt-brushed coastline where quaint fishing villages, storm-hammered headlands and sweeping sandy beaches are linked by tranquil coastal footpaths.

All of this makes France one of the world's most diverse and inviting walking destinations. And with more than 180,000km of marked trails, you're never going to run out of new routes to explore.

**Lac de Nino (p202), Corsica**
LUKAS HODON/SHUTTERSTOCK ©

# Our Picks



## BEST HIKES WITH A VIEW

Lose your breath not only because of the steep incline – these hikes come with the best views. Across mountains, the sea, lakes, farmlands or even volcanoes, these are our favourite hikes for panoramas to remember. Stop at a *boulangerie* (bakery) before setting off to pick up a picnic filled with local specialities to enjoy when you make it to the top.

**TOP TIP**

Keep in mind that peaks or viewpoints are exposed to the wind and are usually cooler – pack appropriately.

### 15

### Pic des Mémises

Picnic while admiring nearby peaks like Dent d'Oche, Cornettes de Bise and Mont Billiat.

**P70**

### 19

### Tête de la Maye

Challenging rock faces with a big payout: a 360-degree view of the Écrins.

**P80**

### 27

### Climbing Puy de Dôme

A classic hike up to the flanks of the sleeping volcano with a view all the way to Clermont-Ferrand.

**P104**

### 41

### Pic St-Loup

On clear days you can see across Provence as far as Mont Ventoux.

**P148**

### 55

### Capu Pertusato & Bonifacio

Drenched in pink light at sunset, the cliffs of Bonifacio are emblematic of *la Corse*.

**P194**

Bonifacio (p194), Corsica

Climbing Puy de Dôme (p104)
TOP TIP
Often the sky is clearer earlier in the day in the mountains and close to urban areas.

Roussillon (p124)

TOP TIP
The selection
of baby hiking
backpacks is
enormous – you
can sometimes
rent these from
Decathlon
(decathlon.fr).

# Our Picks

DOMINIK A. SZTORC/SHUTTERSTOCK ©

## BEST FAMILY HIKES

These hikes are suitable for the whole family; they're kid-friendly but will also inspire and please teenagers and adults in the group. Wander along ravishing coastlines and historical memorials in the north, or travel back in time to castles in the south. You won't be lacking in views in the Pyrenees, and there's space for kids activities and wine o'clock on Provence's Roussillon route.

**TOP TIP**

Keep an eye on footwear and watch out for blisters; kids shoes are not always comfortable over long distances.

**02**

### La Côte de Granit Rose

Secluded bays and a wild rocky coastline lend themselves to a summer swimming session.

**P26**

**09**

### Beaumont-Hamel Newfoundland Memorial

Dotted with farming villages and war memorials, this caters to history-loving older kids.

**P48**

Lac Chambon (p94)

ELENA DIJOUR/SHUTTERSTOCK ©

**22**

### Lac Chambon & Murol Circuit

Medieval ramparts and lakeside strolls, plus side activities like swimming, cycling and kayaking.

**P94**

**44**

### Plateau de Bellevue

Get the best of the Pyrenees, overlooking the Cirque de Gavarnie, on a hike that's kid-safe.

**P162**

**33**

### Roussillon Ramble

This uncomplicated trail reveals dramatic views of the Provençal ochres, vineyards and lavender fields.

**P124**

# Our Picks



## BEST BUCKET LIST HIKES

The best of the best, the must-dos…these hikes alone are worth making the journey to France, and are simply unforgettable: mountains shimmering in icy blue lakes, pretty-as-a-picture villages, lavender fields and ancient abbeys. For some, you might have to work around the crowds – but it's a small price to pay. Charge your camera batteries and go ready to be amazed, because these hikes won't disappoint.

**TOP TIP**

The best of the best – expect crowds. Try going during shoulder seasons, or early in the morning.

 **14**

### Lac Blanc

The reflection of the EU's highest mountain shines back at you while you gaze over Lac Blanc.

**P68**

 **03**

### Giverny Impressions

Add this hike to a visit to Monet's gardens, and you'll leave totally enchanted.

**P28**

 **26**

### Stevenson's Journey

This section of the Stevenson Trail weaves through the countryside outside Le Puy-en-Velay.

**P102**

 **36**

### Gordes Loops

Visit the highlights of the Luberon region, Gordes and the Abbaye Notre-Dame de Sénanque.

**P130**

 **59**

### Lac de Nino

Amble through dense forests to one of Corsica's most beautiful lakes: Lac de Nino.

**P202**

Lac Blanc (p68), French Alps

Monet's home, Giverny (p28)

# Our Picks



## BEST WILDLIFE HIKES

There is no better way to get acquainted with French wildlife than on foot. For a single European country, you'll be amazed at the biodiversity here, in and outside of the protected areas. A pair of binoculars and some patience is usually more than enough to spot ibex, deer, stags, beavers, marmots and all the birds you can imagine – even pink flamingos!

**TOP TIP**

Wildlife, especially larger mammals, are most active at dusk and dawn – get an early or late start.

**16**

### Chalets de Bise to Lac de Darbon

Try this moderate hike to see ibex sunbathing next to a lake.

**P72**

**20**

### Lac des Vaches & Col de la Vanoise

Get in a squeaking match with the marmots and look for more ibex.

**P82**

**18**

### Cirque de Baume-les-Messieurs

Spot bats hanging in caves during a visit to the Grottes de Baume.

**P76**

**04**

### Grouin: Up to a Point

Bring binoculars and gaze at the rich birdlife that nests on the Île des Landes.

**P30**

**30**

### Wetlands of the Camargue

Spot pink flamingos in the marshes of the Camargue on this family-friendly coastal hike.

**P118**

REFLEX NATURE/SHUTTERSTOCK ©

Marmot, French Alps

# Our Picks

## BEST PRETTY VILLAGE HIKES

Love getting out in nature but still want to live out that provincial dream of Belle in her small village? These are the most beautiful villages to mix your love of hiking with your love of picturesque ancient streets. Discover northern France's half-timbered houses, abbeys that overlook woodland towns or terracotta-roofed riverside villages by trying one of these pretty hikes.

**TOP TIP**

Stay in a *gîte* (self-catering accommodation) with traditional architecture and decor; it's like trying on local life!

### Brantôme Circuit

Alongside the River Dronne, guarded by Brantôme abbey, this is woodland delight.

**P92**

### Dinan: Up & Down Town

Dinan checks all the lovely-northern-French-town boxes: cobbled squares, half-timbered houses and a busy port.

**P24**

St-Cirq-Lapopie (p99)

### Arbois to Pupillin

The historic stone centre gives a taste of the culture that makes the Jurassien *vin jaune* so special.

**P74**

### Roussillon Ramble

The blushing red houses of Roussillon contrast with the seasonal colours of the surrounding vineyards.

**P124**

### The Chemin de Halage

St-Cirq-Lapopie from all angles: get a full 360-degree experience of the terracotta-roofed riverside village.

**P98**

# When to Go

From mountains to sea, and across valleys, plains and forests, France is one of Europe's most varied hiking destinations.



### SPLITTING TIME

Ashley Parsons is a hiking and trail running enthusiast, who splits her time between the Alps and Provence. @enselle.voyage

'For me, hiking and camping go hand in hand, and I love both activities in all seasons. My favourite is when the first snow hits the Alps. The snow doesn't tend to stick, so you can still go out for a hike, and you usually have the forest to yourself. I usually don't bother with snow shoes – just a pair of waterproof socks and maybe some small chains on my trainers and I'm off into the mountains.'

Hiking is possible all year round in France, it just depends on how equipped and experienced you are! But for most of us, the main hiking season runs from April to October. In the south, summers are very hot, so consider escaping to the mountains for cooler temperatures. High mountain passes can still hold snow well into June, so find out what the situation is like from locals before you hike.

Even if the weather is nice, it's always good to bring an extra layer for unexpected breezes or showers. Brittany and Normandy can have periods of unsettled weather, with smatterings of showers, so a light raincoat is nearly always essential, just in case.

Mountain hut near Mont Blanc (p86)

## Weather Watch (Marseille)

| JANUARY | FEBRUARY | MARCH | APRIL | MAY | JUNE |
|---|---|---|---|---|---|
| Avg. daytime max: **12°C**. | Avg. daytime max: **13°C**. | Avg. daytime max: **16°C**. | Avg. daytime max: **18°C**. | Avg. daytime max: **23°C**. | Avg. daytime max: **26°C**. |
| Days of rainfall: **6** | Days of rainfall: **4** | Days of rainfall: **4** | Days of rainfall: **5** | Days of rainfall: **4** | Days of rainfall: **2** |

Hikers on the Mad Jacques Trek

## Accommodation

For popular hikes or tours, like the Tour de Mont Blanc, you might need to book months in advance. *Gîtes d'étape* (walkers' lodges) are a good budget option, as are *refuges* (huts) in high mountain areas.

## Weather Forecasts

The best local weather service in France is Meteo France (meteofrance.com) – when in the mountains, especially near the end of winter/spring, check the weather and avalanche risk on this website. Another good app for the weather, especially along the coast, is Windy.



### WINTER HIKING?

It's not out of the question! You could give Provence a try, and as long as you don't encounter a blustery mistral wind en route, you'll have all the paths in the sleepy winter light to yourself!

### MAIN HIKING EVENTS

Aubagne in the Bouches-du-Rhone region hosts an annual **Festival de Randonnées**. There are more than a dozen hikes of different difficulties and themes: night hikes, dining hikes, history hikes and cultural hikes – a real dream for hikers of all kinds! **May**

The biannual **Mad Jacques Trek** (madjacques.fr) changes locations each time but the concept is simple: turn up, hike a planned route, and after a few days you'll end up at a massive dance party! Entry gets you some swag, a support team and a few checkpoints along with the after-party. But otherwise, you'll need to be autonomous with your hiking gear and camping equipment. Think of it as a collective adventure with the option of calling for help if things get sticky. **Spring/autumn**

| JULY | AUGUST | SEPTEMBER | OCTOBER | NOVEMBER | DECEMBER |
|---|---|---|---|---|---|
| Avg. daytime max: **29°C**. Days of rainfall: **1** | Avg. daytime max: **29°C**. Days of rainfall: **2** | Avg. daytime max: **26°C**. Days of rainfall: **3** | Avg. daytime max: **21°C**. Days of rainfall: **6** | Avg. daytime max: **16°C**. Days of rainfall: **5** | Avg. daytime max: **13°C**. Days of rainfall: **5** |

# Get Prepared for France

Useful things to load in your bag, your ears and your brain

**Antoinette dans les Cévennes**
(Caroline Vignal, 2020).
A woman follows her lover and his family on holiday in the Cévennes.

**Belle & Sébastien**
(Nicolas Vanier, 2013).
A little boy and wild dog friendship film that takes place in the French Alps.

**Le Rayon Vert**
(Eric Rohmer, 1987).
A woman looking for romance on her summer hiking trip along the French coast.

**On a Marché sous la Terre**
(Alex Lopez, 2023).
Friends set out to connect an underground passage in the Vercors mountains.

**Marche à l'Étoile – Des Monts d'Ardèche à Carcassonne**
(Boris Wilmart, 2020).
An astronomer and director cross south-central France on foot.

## Clothing

**Shirts and trousers** Merino shirts and base layers are popular hiking favourites as they don't hold odour. Softshell hiking trousers can protect from the wind or thorny terrain.

**Jackets and jumpers** Unless you're certain there's nearly zero chance of rain, for example during Provençal summers, it's a good idea to have a lightweight raincoat in your pack. The key to comfort during hikes is layers – a lightweight fleece can be a lifesaver if you're walking on a cloudy day, and a windbreaker can cut the wind while you admire the view from the summit.

**Footwear** Don't let the day of your hike be the first time you try on your hiking boots! That's a recipe for blisters, as is wearing too-thin socks. Most of the hikes in this book can be accomplished with a pair of trail running shoes.

## Hats, gloves and sunglasses

A thin hat and a pair of gloves can change your outlook on life for the better if you reach the summit of a hike on a chilly day. Neck gaiters are lightweight and add comfort too. Don't forget a pair of sunglasses, especially if you're going to be seaside, lakeside or any place where there's snow.

CLOCKWISE FROM TOP LEFT: LTUMMY/SHUTTERSTOCK ©, BENIMAGE/SHUTTERSTOCK ©, OLGAGI/SHUTTERSTOCK ©, LANDSCAPEMANIA/SHUTTERSTOCK ©,

Hiking, Auvergne (p90)

MARGOUILLAT PHOTO/SHUTTERSTOCK ©

**The First 40 Miles**
(Heather Ledger, 2014).
A great podcast for new
hikers and backpackers
with tips and stories.

**The Adventure Podcast**
(2023). Worldwide
adventurers from all
walks of life guest star
in this inspiring podcast.

**Allô La Planéte Radio**
(2019). Online radio
dedicated to travel and
adventure coming out
of Ardèche.

**Paradis**
(Ben Mazué, 2020). A
French pop album with
good rhythm for hiking.

**Travels with a Donkey in the Cévennes**
(Robert Louis
Stevenson, 1879).
Beloved classic hiking
journey through
southern central
France.

**Clear Waters Rising: A Mountain Walk across Europe**
(Nicholas Crane, 1996).
A mountain walk across
Europe stretching from
western France to
Istanbul.

**First on the Rope**
(Roger Frison-Roche,
1942). French classic
about the lives of
mountain guides in the
1920s to 1930s.

**Windswept: Why Women Walk**
(Annabel Abbs, 2022).
Global story peeking
into what drives women
to walk alone in nature.

## Words

**Bonjour** Hello

**Merci** Thank you

**Parlez-vous anglais?** Do you speak English?

**Où est...** Where is…

**Les toilettes** The toilets

**Le magasin de sport** A sports shop

**Je voudrais...** I would like…

**Je voudrais reserver...** I would like to reserve…

**Chemin** Path

**Route** Road

**Sentier** Trail

**Hike/hiking** Randonnée

**Carte** Map

**Tournez à droit/gauche** Turn right/left

**Tout droit** Straight ahead

**Refuge/Cabane** Mountain hut

**C'est combien?** How much is it?

**J'ai mal au ventre** I have a stomach ache.

**J'ai une ampoule** I have a blister.

**J'ai besoin d'aide** I need help.

**Où puis-je trouver de l'eau?** Where can I find water?

**Sac à dos** Backpack/hiking pack

**Imperméable** Raincoat

**Bâtons de randonnée** Hiking poles

# EXPLORE

# Contents

ENGLAND
Barnstaple
Salisbury
Winchester
Southampton
Brighton
Folkestone
Dover
Calais
Cap Gris-Nez
Exeter
Bournemouth
Portsmouth
Hastings
Eastbourne
Boulogne-sur-Mer
Weymouth
Plymouth
Penzance
LA MANCHE (ENGLISH CHANNEL)
Abbeville
Le Tréport
Dieppe
Somme
Côte d'Albâtre
06
Cap de la Hague
Cherbourg
Alderney
03
A29
Cap de la Hève
Le Havre
Rouen
Honfleur
Colleville-sur-Mer
Baie de la Seine
Guernsey
Sark
Parc Naturel Régional des Marais du Cotentin et du Bessin
Bayeux
Ouistreham
Seine
A13
02
Jersey
St-Lô
Caen
Lisieux
Louviers
Vernon
Giverny
NORMANDY
Bernay
Évreux
Mantes-la-Jolie
04
A84
Granville
Falaise
A28
Dreux
Côte de Granit Rose
Perros-Guirec
Île Bréhat
Pointe du Grouin
Collines de Normandie
Orne
Chartres
05
Île de Batz
Paimpol
Côte d'Émeraude
St-Malo
Collines du Perche
Roscoff
Lannion
St-Quay-Portrieux
Cancale
Mont St-Michel
Parc Naturel Régional Normandie-Maine
Île d'Ouessant
Morlaix
Pontorson
Parc Naturel Régional du Perche
Brest
Guingamp
St-Brieuc
Dinan
Alençon
Pointe St-Mathieu
Parc Naturel Régional d'Armorique
BRITTANY
N12
N137
Fougères
Le Mans
Presqu'île de Crozon
Carhaix-Plouguer
A84
Vitré
Baie de Douarnenez
D769
Douarnenez
Laval
Pointe du Raz
Quimper
Locmine
N24
Ploërmel
Rennes
Sarthe
07
Quimperlé
Hennebont
Vilaine
D178
Pointe de Penmarc'h
Concarneau
Lorient
N137
Châteaubriant
Îles de Glénan
Île de Groix
Vannes
01
Carnac
Angers
Tours
Quiberon
Île d'Houat
N165
A11
Loire
ATLANTIC OCEAN
Guérande
St-Nazaire
Nantes
Belle-Île-en-Mer
Cholet
La Roche-sur-Yon
Poitiers
Niort
Vienne
La Rochelle
Bay of Biscay
Saintes
Limoges
Angoulême
N
0    100 km
0    50 miles
Périgueux

DALIU/SHUTTERSTOCK ©

**Cancale (p30)**

# Brittany & Normandy

# Brittany & Normandy

Normandy is blessed with a wonderfully varied and intensely historic coastline. The dunes and forested hills above Omaha Beach, site of the D-Day landings' most ferocious fighting, offer superb walks, while the hinterland around the impressionist village of Giverny is an easy outing. Brittany's coastline is crumpled into innumerable bays, beaches and estuaries separated by rocky headlands. There are many dramatic walks here and – most importantly – they are easily accessible.

### St-Malo

Jutting out from the Channel waters like a honey-stoned super-tanker, the walled city of St-Malo cuts one of northern France's most unforgettable silhouettes. With a plethora of great hotels and restaurants, it makes an excellent base for walks along the rugged Côte d'Émeraude and gentler Baie du Mont St-Michel. But visit in season and you won't have the streets to yourself.

The nearby (and impossibly picturesque) town of Dinan offers a slightly more chilled vibe.

### Paimpol

The busy commercial harbour of Paimpol hosts one of the area's largest fish and produce markets every Tuesday morning. It's also the launch pad for walks along the Côte de Granit Rose, where the boulders blush pink in profusion.

### Bayeux

The very attractive and historic town of Bayeux may be synonymous with the World Heritage–listed Bayeux Tapestry, which vividly depicts the dramatic story of the Norman invasion of England in 1066, but it's also a wonderfully picturesque base from which to explore the D-Day beaches, especially Omaha Beach.

It has a wide choice of places to stay and eat, and good transport links.

### Giverny

Synonymous with Monet, this small village gets swamped by visitors queuing to visit the artist's famous gardens and to pay their respects at his resting place in the little churchyard. Despite more than 600,000 visitors teeming down its one main street annually, the surrounding countryside offers gentle walks that are never overly subscribed.

### Quimper

The capital of Finistère (or 'Land's End'), village-like Quimper is the troubadour of Breton arts and culture. For walkers, it's the ideal base for the rugged trails of the Presqu'île de Crozon and the Pointe du Raz.

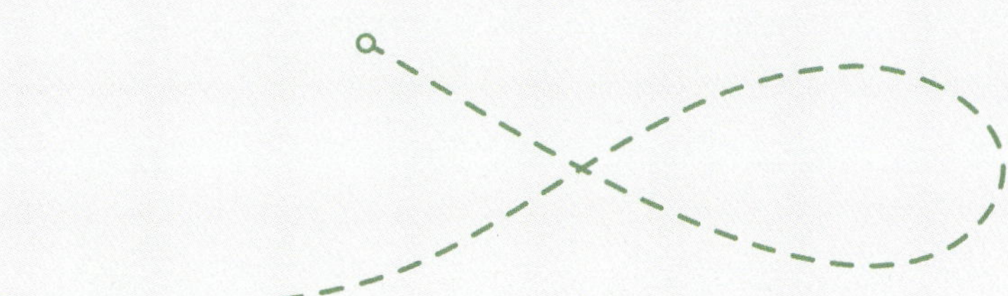

## When to Go

Villages and towns like Giverny and Dinan, where each season has its own particular beauty, are rarely quiet outside winter, though weekdays may be less crowded than weekends.

During May and June, before the crowds arrive along the coasts of Brittany and Normandy, there's a good chance of settled weather, although some camping grounds don't open until June.

Good weather is also likely in September. Spring – April and May – can be pretty wet and the days grow shorter (and the temperature drops) from October. Avoid July and August at all costs.

## Where to Stay

Whether you're looking to camp under the stars, take a room by the sea or live the high life in your very own château, you'll find something to suit in Brittany and Normandy.

Both are chock-a-block with lovely hotels and campsites, but if you really want to get under the skin of either region, *chambres d'hôte* (bed and breakfasts) are worth considering; staying with a local family is a great way of immersing yourself in the culture, and the owners are usually a great resource for local restaurant tips, sights and secret spots. Best of all, breakfast is often included in the room price.

## What's On

**Festival de Cornouaille** (festival-cornouaille.bzh; late Jul) Quimper's six-day celebration of traditional Celtic music, costumes and culture.

**Festival du Chant de Marin** (paimpol-festival.bzh; early Aug) Biannual music festival celebrating sea shanties in Paimpol.

**Fête des Remparts** (fete -remparts-dinan.com; Jul) Medieval festival in Dinan.

**Festival Interceltique de Lorient** (festival-interceltique. bzh; early Aug) A 10-day pan-Celtic festival in Lorient, 30km northwest of Carnac.

**Fêtes d'Arvor** (festival-arvor.org; 13-15 Aug) Three-day celebration of Breton culture in Vannes.

**Les Transmusicales de Rennes** (lestrans.com/le-festival; early Dec) France's biggest indie-music festival.


## Resources

**Brittany Tourism** (brittanytourism.com) Has tourist offices throughout the region.

**Normandy Tourism** (normandie-tourisme.fr) Plan your own Norman invasion.

**FFRandonnée Bretagne** (bretagne.ffrandonnee.fr) Hikes and walks within Brittany.

**Le Météo** (meteo.fr) Catch the latest weather forecasts.


**Médiévales de Bayeux** (lesmedievales.bayeux.fr; Jul) Middle Ages–themed parade and other events.

## Transport

Cities and major towns in Brittany and Normandy have good rail connections, including TGV trains to Rennes in Brittany and towards Le Havre in Normandy, though the interior remains poorly served. The bus network is extensive; however, services between smaller towns are infrequent at best.

With gently undulating, well-maintained roads, an absence of road tolls and relatively little traffic outside the major towns, driving in both regions (but especially in Brittany) is a real pleasure. Cycling is also popular, and bike-rental places are usually easy to find.

# Dinan: Up & Down Town

| DURATION | DIFFICULTY | DISTANCE | START/END |
|---|---|---|---|
| 2½hr return | Easy | 3km | Place du Guesclin |

| TERRAIN | Paved, packed-earth trail, some steps |
|---|---|

Picturesquely perched high above the River Rance, Dinan is one of the loveliest old towns in northern France. This muddle of cobbled squares, creaking half-timbered houses and snaking ramparts tumbling down to the old port, where barges and riverboats still putter along beside the old town quays, is best explored on foot.

From the **statue of Breton hero Bertrand du Guesclin** in the square of that name, walk north along rue de la Ferronerie and turn left onto the short but steep rue du Fossé. Walk along the Promenades des Petits Fossés – erstwhile moats – with the ramparts of the **Château de Dinan** on your left. Between the castle's tower and keep, pass under the **Porte du Guichet** and walk up to rue du Guichet.

Head left along rue de Léhon and past the 17th-century **Couvent des Bénédictines**. Further along on the right is the **Hôtel Kéralty** (1559), or Maison de la Harpe, with its dozen wooden sculptures in medieval dress. Further to the left is the 15th-century **Tour de l'Horloge** clock tower. At rue de l'Apport, turn left to enjoy some of the most wonderful overhanging **half-timbered houses** in Dinan.

A right onto rue de la Lainerie will take you past the sprawling **Couvent des Cordeliers** and down rue du Jerzual and its extension rue du Petit Fort, an astonishing cobbled street lined with medieval houses (pictured; don't miss the **Maison du Gouverneur**). It leads steeply downhill to the River Rance and its little port.

At the foot of the **stone bridge**, turn right on rue du Port and, just below the soaring Viaduc de Dinan, climb the switchback path (and steps) up to the lovely **Jardin Anglais**, a former cemetery behind the soaring **Basilique St-Sauveur**. Have a look at its 12th-century western portal then slip down narrow ruelle St-Sauveur and passage de l'Horloge to return to place du Guesclin.

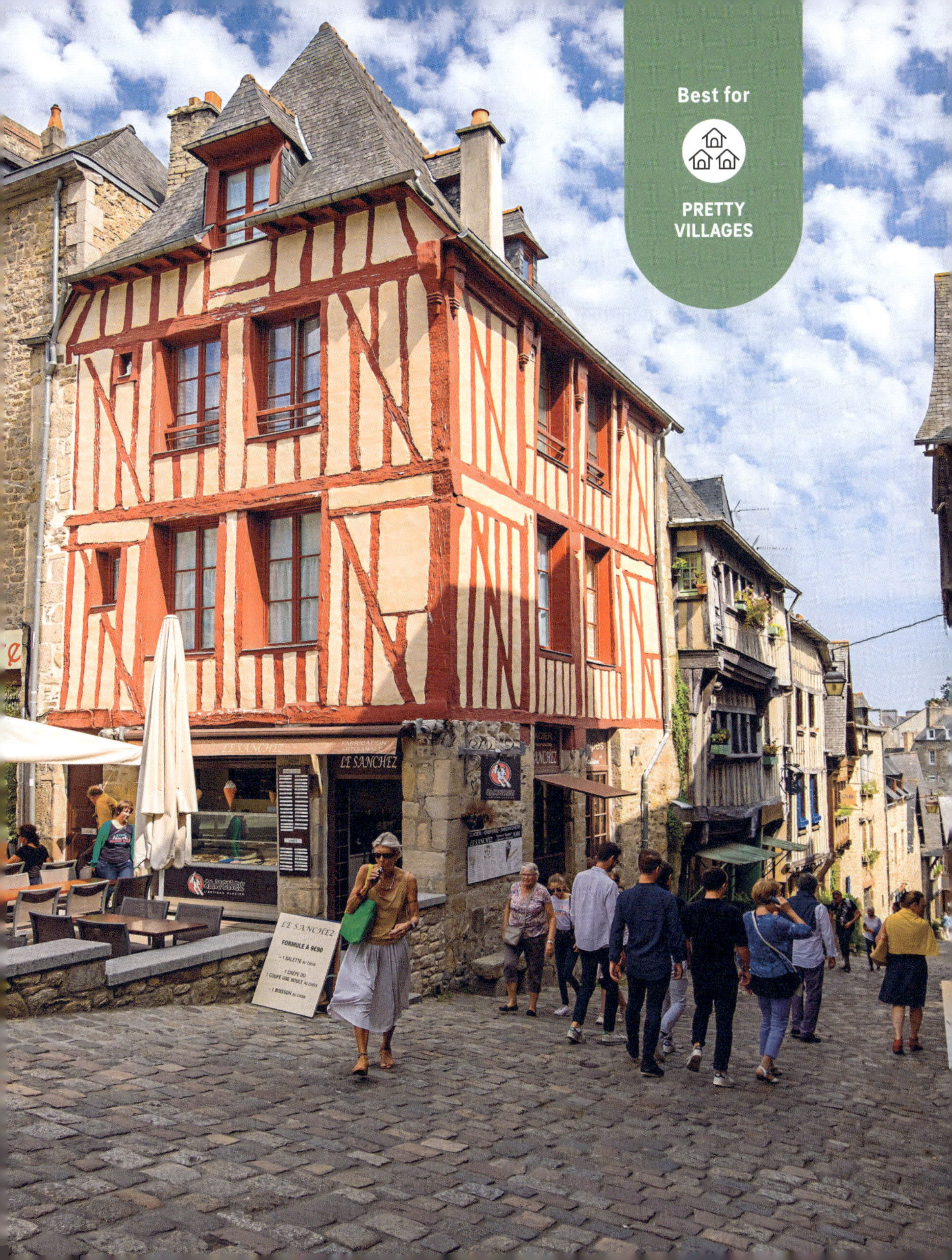
Best for
PRETTY
VILLAGES

# La Côte de Granit Rose

| DURATION | DIFFICULTY | DISTANCE | START/END |
|---|---|---|---|
| 2hr return | Easy | 5.5km | Parking du Petit Port de Ploumanac'h |
| TERRAIN | | | Road, walking trail |

This walk is one non-stop succession of secluded bays and milky-blue sea waters linked together by orange-pink granite boulders piled one upon the other like squashed strawberries. It's an ideal family walk. On a warm day, pack your swimming gear.

Walk north along the **waterfront**, and turn right along a cobbled path when you see signs for the **Sentier des Douaniers** (Customs Trail). Almost immediately, you'll be rewarded with views over melted pink-granite rock and mirror-blue waters. Meander along the clear headland path and drop down to and across the superb **St Guirec** beach.

Go uphill past an old **Breton cross** and into a giant puzzle of orange-tinted, butter-smooth boulders. Veer left off the main trail towards the **Phare de Men Ruz** (Men Ruz Lighthouse; pictured). Return back to the main route and continue eastward around the headland, where you will quickly come to a small bay with a **lifeboat station**. The lifeboat is launched by sliding down a railway track and into the sea.

Continuing east and then south, you'll pass two **rocky coves** with tempting snorkelling at high tide. At the trail junction go right, away from the coast, following red and white trail markers. Walking through gorse heath and woodland, go straight ahead at all junctions until you reach the **Parc des Sculptures**, where humanity's attempt at moulding rock is no match for nature's.

Leave the park and follow the road to the right for 100m. Turn sharp left down rue Traverse, then right at rue du Moulin. A few minutes later, you'll reach your start point.

Best for
COASTAL
VIEWS

# Giverny Impressions

| DURATION | DIFFICULTY | DISTANCE | START/END |
|---|---|---|---|
| 3-3½hr return | Moderate | 12.5km | Fondation Claude Monet car park |

| TERRAIN | |
|---|---|
| | Paved and packed earth, some steep sections |

Giverny owes its fame to Claude Monet, who was captivated by its rustic charm and peaceful atmosphere. The village has retained much of its allure, as has the surrounding countryside. Hills rise steeply from the plains through which threads the narrow Epte River, one of the painter's sources of inspiration. You'll pass through woodlands, fields and typical Normandy villages – before or after a visit to Monet's beautiful house and gardens.

## Getting Here

The springboard for Giverny is Vernon, a town 5km to the northwest served by SNCF train travelling between Paris' Gare St-Lazare (50 minutes) and Rouen (40 minutes). A *navette* (shuttle bus; €5 one way, 20 minutes) meets four to five trains a day from Easter to October.

## Starting Point

From the (free) Fondation Claude Monet car park it's a short walk to the start of the trail.

**01** With **Monet's house** (pictured) behind you, walk left along rue Claude Monet for 200m then right along chemin Blanche-Ho-schedé-Monet. Immediately veer right along rue Hélène Pillon; beyond a road diverging downhill to the right you pass villas and sloping fields. A grassy track leads uphill for about 220m; leave it to ascend a steep path with a hedge on its right.

**02** After about 150m, swing right along a path through the hedge that takes you on a contouring route through woodland and into **Bois du Gros Chêne** (Big Oak Wood). Measuring from Waypoint 02, you'll come to junctions at 240m,

# Giverny, Monet & Impressionism

In 1883 Claude Monet, the father of impressionism, established his studio in Maison du Pressoir in Giverny. He died there in 1926.

Inspired by the surrounding landscapes and gardens, he embarked on an immense artistic and botanical project in his garden. He painted his famous Nymphéas here, combining water and plants in a marvellous play of light and colour.

The house and gardens were bequeathed to the Académie des Beaux-Arts in 1966 by the painter's son and, after extensive renovation guided by the Fondation Claude Monet, opened to the public in 1980.

MSMONDADORI/SHUTTERSTOCK ©

**Best for**

## ESCAPING THE CROWDS

500m and 830m; at each, take the path that maintains your elevation. About 1.2km from Way-point 02, you'll get views of the Epte valley below and you'll exit the woodland in another 500m. Continue another 750m to a track crossing then bear right downhill.

**03** Cross the D5; turn left along the verge for 250m. Turn right down chemin du Moulin Brûlé then left on rue des Jacobins in the village of **Ste-Geneviève-lès-Gasny**. Continue to a crossroads with a church on the left; turn right along rue de l'Eau and cross two bridges over the Epte River. The road leads 450m into the village of **Gommecourt**, where you turn right

along narrow rue des Sablons. This leads eastwards for about 3.5km, initially through the **Bois des Sablons**.

**04** With vegetable plots at the village of **Limetz-Villez** on the left, turn right and follow the rue de l'Eau (D201) for 70m, then turn left down a narrow track leading west. After about 500m, the track skirts a fenced empty lot. Turn left at a road in Le Moulinet for 50m, then turn right at a T-junction to cross a small bridge over a branch of the Epte River

**05** Past an old communal laundry on the left, keep right and follow the track north for 320m, then turn right

into fields. After 280m, turn left and head north. Follow the track across fields for 750m, then turn right, soon reaching the D201. This road runs 150m, crossing the **Epte River** before meeting the D5. Here, turn left towards Giverny and then right up rue Claude Monet to the car park.

## Take a Break

**La Guinguette** ( 06 72 76 03 66; laguinguettedegiverny.com; 6 rue de Falaise, Giverny; mains €15-20; noon-2.30pm Tue-Sun, 7-9pm Thu-Sat) is idyllically situated on a branch of the Epte River.

# Grouin: Up to a Point

| DURATION | DIFFICULTY | DISTANCE | START/END |
|---|---|---|---|
| 3½hr return | Moderate | 11.5km | Plage du Verger car park |

| TERRAIN | | Sand, packed earth, some steps |
|---|---|---|

At the northern tip of the wild coast between Cancale and St-Malo, the Pointe du Grouin nature reserve juts out on a windblown promontory and into the foaming sea. It's an area begging for exploration, and one well-marked trail in particular is worth the effort. You'll be rewarded with views of the Île des Landes, a long barren outcrop and now a bird sanctuary, and on a clear day the distant outline of Mont St-Michel.

## Getting Here

Most visitors arrive by car to make the trip up to Pointe du Grouin, though **MAT** (Malo Agglo Transports; 02 99 40 19 22; reseau-mat.fr) coastal bus 9 between St-Malo and Cancale will drop you off here in July and August (€1.35, 10 minutes, every 45 minutes).

## Starting Point

The trail literally begins at the Plage du Verger car park (free).

**01** Head east along the sandy track parallel to the beach, passing a lake on the right. At the first junction, turn left and continue along a packed-earth ascending trail. The path narrows through undergrowth and then gains height; enjoy the spectacular views of the beach below. The path leads east and then due north.

**02** After passing **Pointe de la Moulière**, the path levels off and descends. Veer to the left on a narrow path and climb up to the D201. Continue for 50m, turn left and go up to **Pointe de Rochefroide**.

**03** Follow the path to a car park. Turn left and arrive at **Pointe du Grouin** (pictured), with views of Île des Landes and distant Mont St-Michel to the east. You'll pass a **decommissioned**

## Île des Landes

Separated from Pointe du Gouin by narrow Chenal de la Vieille Rivière, the wave-pounded lozenge of Île des Landes is temptingly close but has been inaccessible to the public since 1961 when it was declared a bird sanctuary.

In addition to attracting the largest colony of great cormorants in Brittany, it is also home to crested cormorants, various types of gulls, pied oyster-catchers and Belon shel-drakes, the only marine duck native to Brittany. From August to October, puffins, gannets and other seabirds also flock here. Explanatory signboards near the tip of the Point du Grouin let you know who's who. Don't forget your binoculars.

Best for

COASTAL VIEWS

WILMAR TOPSHOTS/ALAMY STOCK PHOTO ©

**lighthouse** (1861), a WWII-era German **bunker** with graffiti and ornithological signboards.

**04** From the point head south and take the first left to join the coastal path, always keeping to the left. You'll pass pine groves, an RV campground, a school, a well-preserved WWII gun battery and cottages with pretty gardens.

**05** At **Port Mer**, walk along the beachfront prome-nade and turn left, at a sign reading 'Le Port', onto rue du Chatry, which follows the outline of Pointe du Chatry as far as Port Picain.

**06** With a youth hostel on your right, walk along rue de Port Picain and follow this inland to the right. About 250m up from the port, veer left, go under a road bridge and take the second gravel path over the D201 called **La Basse Cancale** (the first path is confusingly called Impasse de la Basse Can-cale). This merges into Impasse de la Hisse before bending right to become chemin de Clairette. Zigzag across rue de la Vielle Riv-ière and continue ahead on a lane leading uphill. About 650m along this lane, pass a riding school on the left and cross the D201 again onto a paved lane, keeping the wooded **picnic area** to your left.

**07** Carry on straight ahead through the quiet hamlet of **La Gaudichais**. The path doglegs and rejoins the sandy path where you first turned left on the western coastal path. Then trace your steps in the sand back to the Plage du Verger car park.

### Take a Break

Both St-Malo and Cancale have any number of superb seafood restaurants, crêperies and cafes, but there are also a few places on the promontory itself, including, along the beach at Port Mer, **La Petite Plage** (02 99 89 81 59; 1 rue Eugène et Auguste Feyen; seafood buffet €33).

# 05

# Circling the Île d'Ouessant

| DURATION | DIFFICULTY | DISTANCE | START/END |
|---|---|---|---|
| 6hr return | Moderate | 19.5km | Lampaul |

| TERRAIN | | Road, walking track, clifftop trail |
|---|---|---|

The Île d'Ouessant is a storm-tossed and wind-battered island that feels a long way from anywhere. Covered in heathland and bounded by a magnificent coastline, at one moment it can be an inviting picture of white-sand beaches lapped by calm blue waters and the next it can be dark, rocky and imposing. Although you can walk around the entire length of the coastline in two long days, the majority of visitors only come here as a day trip. The full-day walk (make sure you get the first ferry over and the last one back) described here will show you the best of the island.

## Getting Here

Ferries for Île d'Ouessant depart from Brest and the town of Le Conquet. **Penn Ar Bed** (02 98 80 81 60; pennarbed.fr; return adult €30-35, child €20-25) has multiple daily sailings in summer from Brest (2½ hours), Le Conquet (1½ hours) and Camaret-sur-Mer (50 minutes). In low season, services are more infrequent. **Finist'mer** (0825 135 235; finist-mer.fr; adult/child return €34/24) runs high-speed boats from Le Conquet (40 minutes), Lanildut (35 minutes) and Camaret (1½ hours) one to three times per day, with more sailings in July and August.

## Starting Point

The walk starts from the church in the centre of tiny Lampaul, the island capital. Minibuses meet the ferry and will shuttle you to **Lampaul** for €2.

## Musée des Phares et des Balises

The black-and-white-striped Phare du Créac'h is one of the world's most powerful light-houses. At its base is the highly educational museum **Lighthouse & Beacon Museum** (pnr-armorique.fr/destination-parc/nos-maisons-de-parc/musee-des-phares-et-balises; adult/child €6/4), which tells the story of these vital navigational aids. There are also displays devoted to the numerous ships that have been wrecked off the island.

STUART BUTLER/LONELY PLANET ©

**Best for**

**COASTAL VIEWS**

**01** With your back to the church doors, turn left and walk downhill through the village. Turn right by the large cross. A moment later, you'll draw near to the tiny **port**. Just before this, turn left onto a grassy track, walk over the headland and past **Plage de Corz** (Corz beach). At the end of the beach, follow the road around (southwest) a short way where a minor footpath heads left (south) off the road.

**02** Just before arriving at the dinky little **port**, turn right (west) and follow the trail along low cliffs and past small coves that – on a sunny day at least – look like they could be straight out of the Mediterranean.

You'll eventually arrive at the **Penn ar Viler** headland.

**03** Follow the path around the northern side of the peninsula. You'll pass a couple of stunning white-sand, blue-water beaches. **Plage du Prat**, the second of these beaches, is particularly noteworthy. When you reach Plage de Corz retrace your steps back into Lampaul.

**04** Turn left at the church and follow the road to the point where it bends to the right. Take the small road that continues straight ahead and, a moment later, you'll find yourself on a coastal footpath again. It takes an hour to get to the **Pointe de Pern**. The most westerly point of the island (and indeed of all of

France) is a rough-edged, storm-lashed place where even the solid rock has been weathered into surreal nightmare shapes

**05** Follow the trail around to the exposed northern side of the peninsula and head to the **Phare du Créac'h** (Créac'h Lighthouse; pictured). Continue along the coastline as far as the tiny **Port de Yusin**.

## Take a Break

There are innumerable spots suitable for a picnic. If you have more time, **Ty Korn** (02 98 48 87 33; Lampaul; mains €16-22, platters from €42; 11am-3pm & 5.30pm-1am Tue-Sat; ) is a decent seafood restaurant.

# 06

# Omaha Beach

| DURATION | DIFFICULTY | DISTANCE | START/END |
|---|---|---|---|
| 4½-5hr return | Hard | 17.5km | Overlord Museum car park |
| TERRAIN | | | Packed earth, some sandy and steep sections, steps |

Omaha Beach, which saw some of the heaviest fighting and highest casualties during the D-Day landings in June 1944, may seem an unusual choice for a recreational walk. But the cliffs and the dunes running parallel to the coast offer some excellent (and sometimes challenging) trails, the views are magnificent, and the history is unforgettable. Additional bonuses include a world-class D-Day museum at the start and one of the largest American war cemeteries in Europe at the finish.

## Getting Here

Bayeux is served by trains from Caen (€5 to €8, 15 to 20 minutes, at least hourly), Cherbourg (€7 to €21, one hour, 15 daily Monday to Friday, eight to 10 daily Saturday and Sunday) and Pontorson for Mont St-Michel (€7, 2½ hours, three daily). You may have to change at Caen if going to and from coming Paris' Gare St-Lazare or Rouen. Bus 70 of the **Nomad** (☎ 09 70 83 00 14; nomad.normandie.fr) line links Bayeux' train station and place St-Patrice with Colleville-sur-Mer (€2.90, two to four daily Monday to Saturday, more frequently and on Sunday and holidays in summer, 35 minutes).

## Starting Point

Begin the walk in the car park (free) of the Overlord Museum in Le Bray, just west of **Colleville-sur-Mer**. The bus stop is at the foot of the hill up to the museum on rue des Chemins de la Liberté.

**01** We recommend visiting the **Overlord Museum** (overlordmuseum.com; adult/child €8.40/6.10; ⏱10am-5.30pm mid-Feb–Mar, Oct & Nov, to 6.30pm Apr, May & Sep, 9.30am-7pm Jun-Aug, closed Jan–mid-Feb) before setting out. It has an astonishing collection of restored WWII military equipment from both sides, and the photos, letters and personal recollections bring the human dimension of the war to life. Then, walk down to the roundabout to rte du Cimetière Militaire Américain. Follow along the verge of this road north past open fields for just under a kilometre to the cemetery's main entrance.

**02** Just past the second roundabout and with the cemetery straight ahead, turn left onto a paved track and then right at the silos. After a few minutes' walk, passing orchards on your left and houses on your right, you'll enter the **Bois Guillaume**, a protected forest, where a packed-earth track begins.

There are a few obstructions on this stretch. At the first fork, veer right, follow the trail as it descends and turn left. This soon brings you to a small bridge over a stream. Turn right here and begin your ascent. When you reach open fields turn right. The trail continues under forest cover, veers right to join another path and ascends to a clearing with wonderful views. Just ahead is a roundabout and an old aerodrome.

**03** From the plaque commemorating the Advanced Landing Ground here in WWII, head east and turn immediately left (north) onto a dirt trail. Go through the stile labelled 'Coteau du Ruquet' and continue walking with trees on the right and fields to the left. Soon you'll enjoy panoramic views of the ocean and beach.

## 6 June 1944

The most brutal fighting of the allied invasion of continental Europe, code-named 'Operation Overlord', on D-Day took place on the 7km stretch of coastline around Colleville-sur-Mer, St-Laurent-sur-Mer and Vierville-sur-Mer, 15km northwest of Bayeux, known as 'Bloody Omaha' to US veterans.

More than seven decades on, little evidence of the carnage unleashed here on 6 June 1944 remains, except for the harrowing American cemetery and concrete German bunkers, though at very low tide you can see a few remnants of the Mulberry Harbour.

For an idea of what it was like along this coast on D-Day, visit the Overlord Museum in the Le Bray area of Colleville-sur-Mer.

Ignore the waymark indicating a right turn down the hill. Instead go left, passing an **anti-aircraft gun memorial**, until you reach a set of steep and narrow wooden stairs. These lead down to rue Bernard Anquetil and the seafront in the village of **St-Laurent-sur-Mer**.

**04** From the **'Bloody Omaha' explanatory tablets** that describe the invasion of 6 June 1944, walk along the beach promenade for about 600m to the hamlet of **Les Moulins**. Along the way you'll pass rows of holiday homes and bungalows before reaching a modern memorial called **Les Braves** jutting out of the water offshore and a larger and older granite one fronting the roundabout. From here, follow ave de la Libération (rte D517) south for a short distance and turn right at a raised path called chemin de Fossé Taillis. On your right are trees and fields; on the left, you'll pass the back of the **Musée Mémorial d'Omaha Beach** (☎02 31 21 97 44; musee-memorial-omaha.com; adult/child/student €7.20/4.20/5.80; ⏱9.30am-6.30pm Apr, May & Sep, to 6pm Oct & Nov, to 7pm Jun-Aug, 10am-5pm Feb, to 6pm Mar, closed Dec & Jan). At the first junction, 650m after leaving the D517, turn right and walk up the trail, passing endless fields, till you reach a T-junction.

**05** Turn left onto rue du Hamel aux Prêtres, with the sound of crashing waves harmonising with that of the whispering pines. In the centre of the **Hamel au Prêtre** hamlet, you'll join up with rte du Port (rte D514) for a short while before turning right at rue de la

PISAPHOTOGRAPHY/SHUTTERSTOCK ©

Linière and then left at rue des Écoles, passing some provincial cottages with pretty gardens.

Turn right on rue de la Mer, which runs parallel to the D517 – along the way you'll pass the remains of an enormous **landing ship bridge** that enabled armoured vehicles to reach the shore. Rue de la Mer will lead you to the beachfront promenade in **Vierville-sur-Mer**.

**06** Begin walking east along the promenade from the cluster of **monuments** at the intersection of rue de la Mer and the D517. One is to the British RAF and another to the Americans (Secteur Charlie & Dog Green). Along the way to Les Moulins (about 2km), you'll pass several more **WWII memori-** als along the promenade, while sheep graze on the grassy cliffs above on the right. Continue along the promenade for about 1.3km until you reach **Hôtel La Sapinière**, turn right and walk up the steps to the **2nd US Infantry Memorial**. Behind it is a switchback trail of wood shavings leading back up to where you turned left to descend the steps to Omaha Beach.

**07** You're now back on familiar turf so just redo your steps in reverse. Carry on under the trees until you veer slightly to the right to join a new path; there will be open fields visible to your right. In a short while, you'll reach a T-junction. Turn left and continue till you come to that small bridge over

a stream. Cross it and continue upward. At the first fork go right and follow the trail as before, climbing over that tree trunk again, before reaching the Bois Guillaume then orchards and farmhouses. Turn left at the silos and, within minutes, you'll be at the roundabout with the main entrance to the cemetery on the left.

**08** The **Normandy American Cemetery and Memorial** (abmc.gov; ◷9am-6pm Apr-Sep, to 5pm Oct-Mar) **FREE** is well worth a visit. The visitor centre on the eastern side has an excellent multimedia presentation on the D-Day landings, told in part through the stories of individuals' courage and sacrifice.

On the western side, Stars of David and white-marble crosses (pictured) stretch off in seemingly endless rows on a now-serene bluff overlooking the bitterly contested sands of Omaha Beach. Some 9387 American soldiers, including 33 pairs of brothers, are buried here.

Between the graves and the visitor centre is a large colonnaded memorial centred on a **statue** called *The Spirit of American Youth,* maps explaining the order of battle, and a wall honouring 1557 Americans whose bodies were not found. A small, white-marble chapel stands at the intersection of the cross-shaped main paths through the cemetery.

## Bayeux Tapestry

'Operation Overlord' was not the only cross-Channel invasion that gave Bayeux a front-row seat. An equally pivotal moment took place here some nine centuries before. The Norman invasion of England in 1066 changed the course of European history, and the dramatic and bloody story is told in 58 vivid scenes by the astonishing Bayeux Tapestry, embroidered just a few years after William the Bastard, Duke of Normandy, became William the Conqueror, King of England. Particularly incredible is its length – nearly 70m – and fine attention to detail. See it in all its glory at the **Bayeux Museum** (La Tapisserie de Bayeux; bayeuxmuseum.com; adult/child €9.50/7.50) in Bayeux.

**09** After your visit, walk south along rte du Cimetière Militaire Américain to the roundabout, the Overlord Museum and the start of the walk.

## Take a Break

Bayeux has some superb restaurants and cafes; one of our favourites is **L'Alcove** (☎02 31 92 30 08; facebook.com/lalcovebayeux; 31 rue Larcher; lunch menus €18-25; ◷noon-1.30pm & 7-9pm Tue-Sat).

# Pointes du Raz & Van

| DURATION | DIFFICULTY | DISTANCE | START/END |
|---|---|---|---|
| 6hr return | Hard | 20km | Baie des Trépassés car park |

| TERRAIN | Road, walking track, clifftop trail |
|---|---|

The most westerly point of mainland France, Pointe du Raz, and its neighbour just to the north, Pointe du Van, are places of elemental beauty. On every side, gorse-cloaked cliffs plummet to the waves far below and gulls trace lazy arcs overhead. On a stormy day, with giant waves hurling themselves at the cliff faces, it feels like the end of the world. But on a warm and clear day it can feel more like heaven.

## Getting Here

In high season only, BreizhGo bus 53 from Quimper goes to the Baie des Trépassés (€2.50, three daily Monday to Saturday, 1¼ hours), but it's easier and more sensible to visit with your own wheels.

## Starting Point

The walk starts in the Baie des Trépassés car park for which there is a fee of €6.50.

**01** Walk south along the back of the beach and at the **war bunkers** turn left and follow the yellow waymarkers signed for La Tour de la Pointe du Raz. When you reach the dirt road, turn right and carry on uphill into the village of **Kerherneau**. Continue to follow yellow waymarkers around and then back into the village. Eventually, you will come to a small **stone chapel**. Turn left here and walk through countryside of low hedges and stumpy trees. When you come to a road and a big grey wall turn right. After a couple of hundred metres turn right again.

**02** When the road ends, veer left onto a walking trail and head towards the edge of the cliff. You will meet another trail, this one with red and white GR markers. Turn right and it's now

STUART BUTLER/LONELY PLANET ©

simply a case of following this cliff-edge trail all the way up to the end of France. It's a dramatic hike with the high cliffs crashing down into the turbulent ocean below. Watch for dolphins and seals playing in the waters below. It takes around an hour to walk to the Pointe du Raz.

**03** Walk back along the northern side of the headland (pictured), following the red and white way-markers. The views of the **Baie des Trépassés** keep getting bigger and brighter. You'll arrive back where you started. You could call it a day here, which makes for a three-hour walk.

**04** Walk north towards the **Relais de la Pointe du Van Hotel**, and turn right down a track leading from the beach to the road. Follow the road to the point where it bends left and goes uphill. Take the trail leading left (north). At the farmhouse turn right, cross the main road and follow small farm roads signed with yellow waymarkers. Take the track to the left of the Breton and cross into woodland. Emerging from the woods go straight, past an old windmill, and then left as you enter the village of **Kerléodin**. Walk for 10 minutes to the busy D7 road. Turn right and 15m later turn left onto a small side road.

**05** Passing a car park continue straight to the cliffs. Turn left and follow red and white waymarkers to **Pointe du Van**. On the way, you'll pass several glorious but forbidding-looking bays. From the point, bend south and pass a lonely chapel on a heather-stained headland. Take the right trail fork behind the chapel and follow the dramatic coast past several bays to the car park.

## Take a Break

There are two hotels offering full meals by the Baie des Trépassés, but rather than eat inside have a picnic while you take in glorious sea views.

# Also Try...

JULIA KUZNETSOVA/SHUTTERSTOCK ©

## Mont St-Michel

| DURATION | DIFFICULTY | DISTANCE |
| --- | --- | --- |
| 7½hr one way | Moderate | 30km |

The renowned rock-top abbey of Mont St-Michel beckons continuously on an unusual route along the shores of Baie du Mont St-Michel, past vast grazing meadows and historic towns.

This walk starts at Avranches in the northeast corner of the bay and follows the shore of the estuary of the Sée and Sélune Rivers, making use of quiet roads and paths on the edge of the grassland, part of the waymarked GR223 trail. It ends at the Mont itself (pictured). Although the open grass-lands seem to offer easy walking, they're riven by surprisingly deep, soft-sided channels; finding safe crossings can be time-consuming.

Take very seriously notices warning about venturing onto the tidal flats around the bay.

## Côte d'Albâtre

| DURATION | DIFFICULTY | DISTANCE |
| --- | --- | --- |
| 4-4½hr one way | Moderate | 15.5km |

Quiet rural roads lead to breathtaking paths above sheer white limestone cliffs, extraordinary natural arches and slender wave-washed pinnacles of Normandy's remarkable Côte d'Albâtre (Alabaster Coast).

The walk described here links the two popular coastal towns of Fécamp and Étretat, and includes a vertigo-inducing clifftop path past the finest examples of geological fantasy. The route follows part of the waymarked GR21 trail, making use of quiet roads, tracks and footpaths.

A scenic side trip that takes you from Étretat to a prominent lighthouse offers some quieter paths, which were originally used by customs officers chasing smugglers.

CARLOS MARTIN DIAZ/SHUTTERSTOCK ©

## Carnac Megaliths

| DURATION | DIFF. | DISTANCE |
|---|---|---|
| 3½hr return | Easy | 10km |

The countryside around Carnac contains the world's largest gathering of more than 3000 ancient standing stones.

Starting from the edge of the coastal town of Carnac, the route, which is well marked with yellow waymarkers and direction panels, takes you first to the famed Ménec standing stones (pictured) and then to the Kermario collection. You'll also visit a couple of ancient water fountains and a chapel as well as walk through a charmed rural landscape of fields and forests. The Carnac tourist office can provide detailed maps and route descriptions.

## Presqu'île de Crozon

| DURATION | DIFF. | DISTANCE |
|---|---|---|
| 5hr return | Moderate | 13km |

The coastline between Morgat and Cap de la Chèvre on the Crozon Peninsula is striking. Beyond the marina at the southern end of Morgat's beach, the coastal path (part of the GR34) follows the sea cliffs to scenic Cap de la Chèvre.

The route takes you past an old fort and pine forests overlooking numerous little coves. Be sure to pause at Plage de l'Île Vierge, an idyllic cove lapped by turquoise waters and framed by lofty cliffs. Finish at Cap de la Chèvre on the windy western side of the peninsula.

## Île de Batz

| DURATION | DIFF. | DISTANCE |
|---|---|---|
| 3½hr return | Easy | 10km |

Lying in the Channel waters just off Roscoff, the Île de Batz is a low-lying and lightly inhabited island fringed by white-sand beaches and crisscrossed by quiet country lanes and walking tracks.

A delightful half-day walk, beginning and ending by the ferry dock from Roscoff, allows you to circumnavigate the island. There are no signed waymarkers but it's simple to just follow the coastal trails around the island. With minimal elevation gains and plenty of beachy excuses to stop, it makes for a good family walk.

ENGLAND
Deal
Dover
North Sea
Ostend
Bruges
Channel Tunnel
Nieuwpoort
Bray Dunes
Veurne
Strait of Dover
Dunes Flamandes
Diksmuide
Dunkirk
Sangatte
Gravelines
Malo-les-Bains
Calais
Bergues
BELGIUM
Cap Blanc-Nez
A16
Roeselare
Cap Gris-Nez
Wissant
IJzer
D940
A25
Poperinge
Audresselles
Ypres
Kortrijk
Ambleteuse
10
Parc Naturel Régional des Caps et Marais d'Opale
St-Omer
Arques
Menen
Wimereux
FLANDERS
Mouscron
Boulogne-sur-Mer
N42
Leie
Tourcoing
Hazebrouck
Roubaix
La Manche (English Channel)
N43
Armentières
Lille
Béthune
Villeneuve d'Ascq
Fromelles
N41
D901
A26
La Bassée
A23
C_anche Estuary
Carvin
A1
Le Touquet Paris-Plage
Étaples
Artois
Agincourt (Azincourt)
Lens
Montreuil
St-Pol-sur-Ternoise
Hénin-Beaumont
Berck-sur-Mer
A16
Douai
Authie Estuary
Hesdin
N39
Avesnes-le-Comte
Arras
Parc du Marquenterre Bird Sanctuary
Crécy-en-Ponthieu
D939
St-Quentin-en-Tournon
Rue
Authie
08
Cambrai
Le Hourdel
N17
Le Crotoy
Doullens
Bapaume
N30
Cayeux-sur-Mer
Noyelles-sur-Mer
Auchonvillers
09
A26
St-Valery-sur-Somme
D40
HAUTS-DE-FRANCE
Hamel
Thiepval
D917
Mers-les-Bains
Abbeville
Pozières
Somme
A16
11
Albert
Fricourt
Le Tréport
A28
Hargicourt
D1001
Bray-sur-Somme
D6
Gamaches
Péronne
Blagny-sur-Bresle
Corbie
D1029
N29
Amiens
St-Quentin
N29
Villers-Bretonneux
Harbonnières
NORMANDY
A16
A1
Nesle
Neufchâtel-en-Bray
Ham
Royalty
N
0    20 km
0    10 miles
Breteuil
Montdidier
Roye
Noyon

Beaumont-Hamel Newfoundland Memorial (p48)

# Lille & the Somme

**08 Thiepval Loop**

A walk through the Somme battlefields surrounding the Thiepval Memorial. **p46**

**09 Beaumont-Hamel Newfoundland Memorial**

A melancholy amble through some of the last surviving WWI trenches. **p48**

**10 Baie St-Jean**

Varied coastal walk along windswept beaches and unusual dune habitats. **p50**

**11 Lochnagar Crater**

Ponder the waste of war as you walk through no-man's land. **p52**

# Lille & the Somme

There are two sides to a walking holiday in this northern region. The first gives the enjoyment of striding through the wide horizons of beaches washed by giant tides. But where there is pleasure, there is also sadness. And inland, away from the beaches, are the bloodied WWI Somme battlefields, and walking here is nothing less than a pilgrimage.

### Boulogne-Sur-Mer

The beautiful Opal Coast – named for the interplay of greys and blues in the sea and sky – features lofty chalk cliffs, rolling green hills, windswept beaches, scrub-dotted sand dunes and charming seaside towns that have been a favourite of British beach lovers since the Victorian era.

The largest – and most enticing – of these seaside towns, and an ideal base for walks in this region, is Boulogne-sur-Mer. Its largely redeveloped waterfront is home to **Nausicaá** (03 21 30 99 99; nausicaa.fr; bd Ste-Beuve; adult/child €26/19; 9.30am-6.30pm, closed 3 weeks Jan), one of the world's largest aquariums.

### Albert

The small town of Albert was almost totally destroyed in WWI, but today it's a bustling little place with reasonable facilities for walkers taking on the trails around the nearby war memorials.

Albert is linked by train to Amiens (€7, 25 minutes, up to two per hour) and Arras (€8, 25 minutes, every two hours). You'll need a car to reach most of the village trail heads.

### Amiens

One of France's mightiest Gothic cathedrals is reason enough to visit Amiens, the former capital of Picardy. The mostly pedestrianised city centre, tastefully rebuilt after WWII, is complemented by lovely green spaces along the Somme River.

Amiens is an ideal base for visits to many of the Battle of the Somme memorials, although you definitely need your own car to get from Amiens to most of the villages where the walks begin.

The St-Leu Quarter is lined with riverside restaurants and pubs, many with terrace views of the cathedral.

### When to Go

With no high mountains covered in winter snows and no punishing summer heat, you can walk in the Somme region at any time of the year. However, the coast of England is within eyesight and like that famously drizzly and wet country, this far-northern corner of France can sometimes feel as if the drizzle will never ease off.

Winter is, of course, the wettest, coldest and darkest time of year to visit, but if you hit a rare dry period then it can be a pleasant time to walk (though be aware that many rural hotels might be closed). Autumn is similar to winter.

On paper summer (June to August) should be the driest, sunniest time, but it can vary wildly from year to year. Some summers can have wall-to-wall sunshine and the mercury in the thermometers can soar; other years, it can blend into autumn in an unceasing curtain of rain.

Spring is an often overlooked time to walk here but, in recent years, it's often been graced by long periods of dry, stable weather and ideal walking temperatures.

Whatever time you come though, do yourself a favour and pack an umbrella!

## Where to Stay

Boulogne-sur-Mer has plentiful accommodation options. One highly recommended bed and breakfast is **Les Terrasses de l'Enclos** (☎ 03 91 90 05 90; enclosdeleveche.com; L'enclos de l'Évêché, 6 rue de Pressy; r/f from €90/150; 📶), which has five spacious rooms with hardwood floors and contemporary furnishings.

In Amiens there are lots of hotels aimed at business travellers. A wonderful place to thank aching après-walk muscles is the **Hôtel Marotte** (☎ 03 60 12 50 00; hotel-marotte. com; 3 rue Marotte; r from €175; P❄📶), where modern French luxury is at its most romantic.

## What's On

**ANZAC Day Ceremony** (🕑around 25 Apr) Held at the New Zealand Memorial in Longueval.

**Ceremonies of the Battle of the Somme** (🕑1 Jul) Commemorating the start of the Battle of the Somme. Events are held in numerous places including La Boisselle, Contalmaison, Thiepval, Beaumont-Hamel and Fricourt.

**Ceremony at the South African Memorial** (🕑5 Jul) Held in Longueval.

**Armistice Day** (🕑11 Nov) 'Lest we forget' ceremonies marking the signing of the Armistice are held at war memorials throughout the region.



## Resources

**Remembrance Trails** (remembrancetrails -northernfrance.com) Info on travelling set routes around the war-grave sites.

**Commonwealth War Graves Commission** (cwgc.org) Website of the Commonwealth War Graves Commission.

**Visit Somme** (visit-somme. com) Tourist board of the Somme region.

**Great War** (greatwar.co.uk) Everything you need to know about WWI.

## Transport

Transport connections from Paris, Lille and other big northern cities to Boulogne-sur-Mer and Amiens are generally good with frequent trains and some buses. To get from these towns to village and beach trailheads using public transport is considerably more challenging. We would highly recommend hiring a car in Amiens or, better, Paris or Lille.

The coastal roads around Calais can be very busy, but otherwise most roads are quiet and the driving much less frenetic than in southern parts of France.

# 08

# Thiepval Loop

| DURATION | DIFFICULTY | DISTANCE | START/END |
|---|---|---|---|
| 2½hr return | Easy | 8km | Thiepval Memorial |

| TERRAIN | | Farm track, road |
|---|---|---|

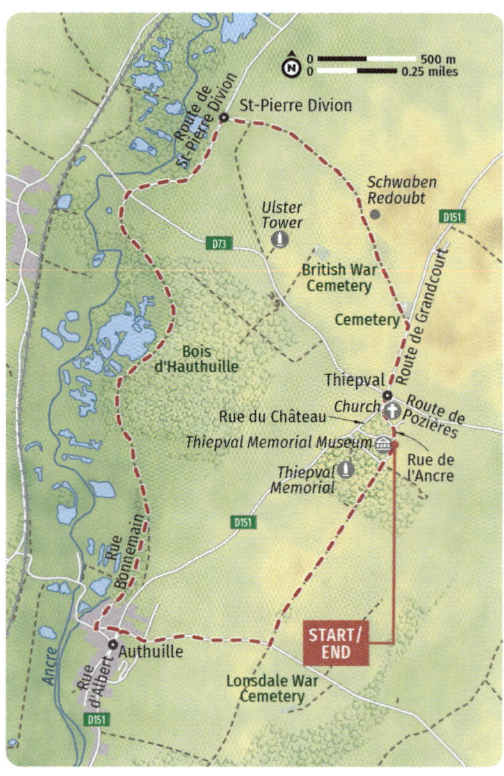


The imposing red-brick Thiepval Memorial is perhaps the most powerful memorial to the waste that was the Battle of the Somme. It is dedicated to the estimated 72,000 British and South African soldiers who died in the fields of France during WWI and have no known grave. This short circular walk starts and ends at the memorial and heads past battle sites, along pretty riverbanks and over fields that once rang with violence, but today stand silent and peaceful.

We recommend visiting the **Thiepval Memorial & Museum** (historial.org; memorial free, museum adult/child €6/3; ◷ 9.30am-6pm Mar-Oct, to 5pm Nov-Feb) before you start this walk, but save the memorial itself for afterwards. From the car park outside the museum, walk down to the village, past the church and along the D151 signed Grandcourt. Around 400m later, turn left by the village cemetery and follow yellow markers across fields. This area is the **Schwaben Redoubt**, a German defensive line that was the scene of a bloody battle on the first day of the Battle of the Somme.

Turn left at the village of **St-Pierre Divion** and follow the river to the junction of the D73. Cross straight over and follow the trail into broadleaf woodland. Eventually, you will hit a dirt road. After 200m, take the very discreet turn-off right and head back into forest (there are faded orange markers and two metal poles). Continue to the church in the village of **Authuille** (look for the peacocks in village gardens!). Cross the D151 and follow signs for **Lonsdale War Cemetery**. At the crest of the hill, turn left and walk through a copse of woodland and then over fields for a dramatic approach back to the memorial.

Best for
EXPLORING
HISTORY

# Beaumont-Hamel Newfoundland Memorial

| DURATION | DIFFICULTY | DISTANCE | START/END |
|---|---|---|---|
| 2¾hr return | Easy | 9km | Auchonvillers |

| TERRAIN | | Road, walking trail |
|---|---|---|

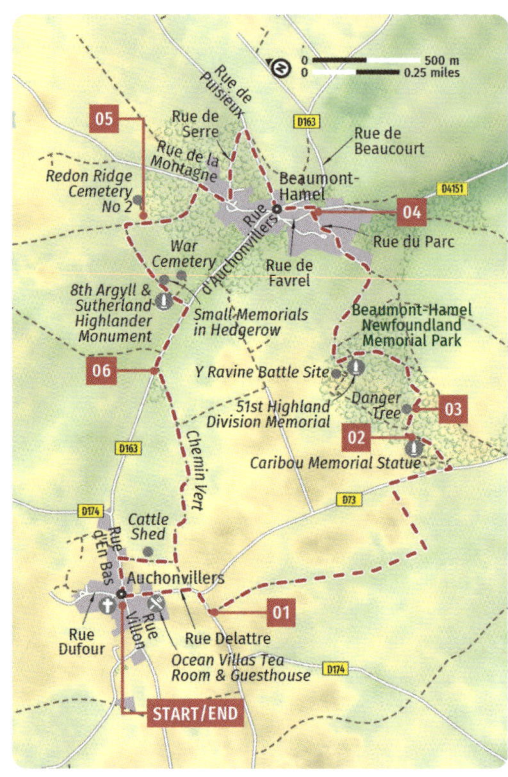


On the morning of 1 July 1916, the volunteer Royal Newfoundland Regiment, made up of 780 men, climbed out of their trenches and advanced towards the German lines. Within 30 minutes almost the entire regiment had been wiped out. The next day the commander of the 29th British Division said, 'The assault only failed of success because dead men can advance no further.' This walk takes you through melancholic battlefield sites, where the trenches are still visible, through now quiet and peaceful farming villages, and past numerous war memorials.

## Getting Here

The walk begins in Auchonvillers, 35km northeast of Amiens along the D919. Public transport is very limited.

## Starting Point

There are no shops in the village but there is a guesthouse and tea rooms.

**01** From the village **church**, cross the main road and follow signs to the Beaumont-Hamel Newfoundland Memorial. At the far end of the village, swing right down the D174 at the junction signed for Mesnil-Martinsart (the Newfoundland Memorial is left); 100m later, a **farm track** veers left across fields before a sharp left turn leads to a quiet road. Turn right here.

**02** A moment later, you will reach the **Beaumont-Hamel Newfoundland Memorial** (pictured p43). It's one of the few places where the web of **trenches** still exists (pictured). The no-man's land that separates the Allied and German lines is still a blistered mess of **bomb craters**.

**03** Walk towards the far northern end of the site, past the **Danger Tree**. Sitting in the middle of no-man's land, this shattered tree was used as a landmark and gathering point for the Newfoundland Regiment as they marched towards their death. Continue over to the **51st Highland Division Memorial**, which commemorates those who died here in a fierce battle on 13 November 1916. Just past this is the **Y Ravine battle site**, and next to this is a gate and exit from the memorial site. Follow the trail across fields and down into Beaumont-Hamel village.

**04** Turn right in front of the **memorial** dedicated to villagers killed by the Germans. Almost immediately afterwards turn left and follow the farm road. You will soon come to a road junction. Turn right and head uphill. At a fork, swing left, re-enter the village and turn right at the junction.

**05** Follow the trail signed **Redon Ridge Cemetery no 2**. After a few minutes, you'll see the cemetery off to your right. Our route bends left and heads downhill. At the bottom of the hill is a **hedge**: look for small crosses and **poppies** left by those paying their respects to the 165 men who died here on 1 July 1916. At the base of the hill, just past a **memorial** to the 8th Argyll and Sutherland Highlanders, is the D163 road. Turn right here.

**06** One hundred metres later, veer left down a waymarked **farm track**. Where the gravel track bends left, take a small grassy trail heading straight (southwest). A few hundred metres later, leave the main track and take a smaller trail that passes a grey **cattle shed**. When you reach the road, turn left back into Auchonvillers and the village church.

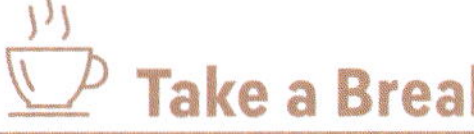

## Take a Break

The **Ocean Villas Tea Room & Guesthouse** (☎ 03 22 76 23 66; avrilwilliams.eu; 10 rue Delattre; mains €8-12; ⏰ 9am-5pm), on the edge of Auchonvillers, serves English breakfasts, cakes and soup.

SERIOUSREINDEER/ALAMY STOCK PHOTO ©

# 10

# Baie St-Jean

| DURATION | DIFFICULTY | DISTANCE | START/END |
|---|---|---|---|
| 3hr return | Moderate | 10km | Pointe aux Oies car park |

| TERRAIN | Road, walking trail |
|---|---|

This varied coastal walk takes in lofty clifftop views, an unusual dune habitat, wetlands, a beautiful wide beach dotted with war bunkers and an enjoyably old-fashioned seaside resort. Generally flat, and with plenty of opportunities for little people to dunk their toes in the sea, this is a good family walk for older kids.

## Getting Here

The small seaside town of Wimereux is 7.5km north of Boulogne-sur-Mer. Multiple trains connect the two towns (€1.80, five minutes). Buses (€1, 11 minutes) run less frequently.

## Starting Point

The walk begins from the Pointe aux Oies car park, a couple of kilometres north of the town centre. There

are hiking information boards here but no other facilities. You could also start the walk from outside the tourist office in Wimereux, but the advantage of starting from the Pointe aux Oies car park is that it turns the walk into a neat figure-of-eight route with your car at the centre, which means that you could easily do just half the walk.

**01** Walk north along the headland following yellow trail markers. Veer right at the first junction. Slide through low, scrubby dunes to the next junction where you again turn right at a car park, cross the busy road and then go left a few metres before veering off into the dunes by the yellow waymarker. A moment or two later you will come to a raised wooden **viewing tower**.

**02** The trail soon snuggles down into a woodland of **stunted trees**. Around 45 minutes from the start, you reach a raised **wooden viewpoint** overlooking a large pond covered in water plants.

STUART BUTLER/LONELY PLANET ©

**03** The trail carries on through a mix of open dunes and woodland (pictured) before bending to the west along a raised boardwalk through a marshy area. Cross the main coastal road and head down the cobbled track towards the sea. Next to you are extensive reed beds that are good for bird-watching. Up ahead is the Fort Vauban d'Ambleteuse, which sits on a small island in the bay.

**04** When you reach the beach, turn left and walk down its length back to the car park. You can either call it a day (two-hour walk) or carry on to **Wimereux**.

**05** The yellow trail markers lead south from the car park along the edge of 80m-high cliffs with memorable sea views. After 20 minutes you will come to the football pitch on the northern edge of Wimereux. Turn left at the far end of the pitch, then right and down rue du Tennis.

At the road junction by the mini-golf, go straight ahead down rue Pierre-André Wimet and then right into the **Jardins de la Baie St-Jean**. After passing the duck pond and exiting the gardens, turn left and descend to the town centre.

**06** Turn right and walk towards the **seafront**, where you turn right again and pass lots of wooden **beach huts**. At the end of the row of huts, veer off to the right and up a set of steps. At the top of the steps, go right and meet up with rue du Tennis. You now simply retrace your steps back along the cliffs to the car park.

## Take a Break

Grab an ice cream from one of the seafront places in Wimereux and enjoy it while building a sand castle on the beach.

# 11

# Lochnagar Crater

| DURATION | DIFFICULTY | DISTANCE | START/END |
|---|---|---|---|
| 3½hr return | Moderate | 12km | Fricourt |
| **TERRAIN** | | Road, walking trail | |

This walk takes you straight through the heart of a WWI battlefield. As well as the vast crater that still marks the spot where the mine that started the Battle of the Somme exploded, you will walk quietly down the no-man's land that once separated the opposing sides, along the now buried Allied trenches, past a number of war cemeteries and through some attractive farming countryside.

This walk is best done before or after the crops are planted in the fields. Just after harvesting in late summer is a good period, and if the fields have been ploughed keep an eye peeled for war debris, which is frequently dug up – don't pick anything up, though, and stick to the trail.

## Getting Here

The walk starts from the car park next to the church in the small red-brick village of Fricourt, which is 6km east of central Albert. There's just one bus a day in either direction between Albert and Fricourt, and it's really just a school bus. It's better to bring your own car!

## Starting Point

There are no special facilities for walkers at the start point of this walk and not much in the way of facilities for passing travellers of any type in Fricourt, although there is a bakery just down the road from the church.

**01** Walk north uphill along the small road to the right of the church. Continue to rue du Haut Bois. Turn left (west) here, and go past the water tower. Turn right at the bigger D147 road. There are occasional yellow waymarkers. Continue a couple of hundred metres uphill and go into the **German War Cemetery** on your right. The German flying ace, Manfred von Richthofen, or '**The Red Baron**', who shot down 80 allied aircraft between 1916 and 1918, was buried here. Today, his remains are in Germany.

**02** Descend back down the D147 towards Fricourt. Just at the entrance to the village, turn right (west) down rue de la Boisselle following the signs for the **Fricourt New Military Cemetery** (pictured) and Peake Wood Cemetery. You're now on a farm track. Two hundred metres later, at the trail junction, go right (ignoring the sign left to the cemetery). Then turn right again at the next trail junction and follow the trail through cropland (you're likely to startle plenty of pheasants as you walk down here).

**03** You'll reach a small **copse of woodland**. Technically, the public right of way continues straight ahead, but the farmer often plants crops over the trail. If you can, carry on straight ahead, until the trail bends right and joins the D147. If the trail is blocked then cut straight down to the D147 where you can.

**04** Turn left and walk 50m up the road. You'll see a clear farm track on your left. Head down this. There are yellow waymarkers. You will soon see a **Commonwealth War Cemetery** to your right, but it can't be reached from this trail.

After walking for 20 minutes you will come to the D20 and the village of **La Boisselle**. Turn left (south) and descend downhill through the village. At the far end of the village turn left by the road sign for Becordel-Bécourt, then immediately left again following the sign for the Grande Mine.

## Lochnagar Crater

The Lochnagar mine was a huge underground explosive charge secretly planted just in front of the German trenches by the Tunnelling Companies of the Royal Engineers. It was one of 19 mines that were planted by the British and set to go off early on the morning of 1 July 1916.

At the time, these were the largest mines ever detonated but, although they did wipe out a section of the German trenches, for all their flash and bang, they failed to neutralise the German defences. The British were supposed to capture the village of La Boisselle within 20 minutes, but by the end of the day, there were 11,000 Allied casualties on the battlefields around La Boisselle.

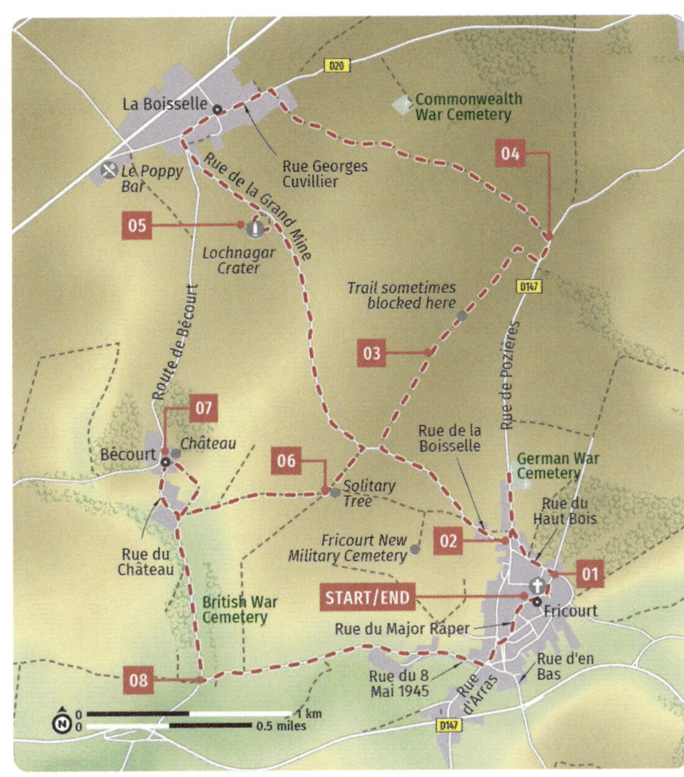


BROWN/ OW BROTHERS/ALAMY STOCK PHOTO ©

**05** Take your time exploring the **Lochnagar Crater** site (pictured). It's more than just a huge hole in the ground; there are the graves of some of those who died here and numerous information panels reveal the moving stories of those involved in the battle.

**06** Leaving the crater, follow the road downhill. It becomes a farm track after 100m. You are now on a path right down the middle of the **no-man's land**. When you get to the trail junction, turn right and walk towards the **solitary tree** that marks the line of the **Allied trenches**. Turn right and you are now walking through the mud where men once fought and died.

**07** Ten minutes later you will arrive on the edge of **Bécourt village**. Turn right by the statue of Christ and a small war memorial, wander through parkland for a few minutes and up to the village **château**, and then descend back down the hill via the rue du Château. At the road junction turn right. After a few minutes, you will come to a **British War Cemetery**, which is worth a visit.

**08** Continue on down the road, then take the first left up a minor road that climbs slightly and bends to the right before turning into a gravel farm track. Follow this for 10 minutes back towards **Fricourt**. At the road junction, carry on straight and back uphill to the church.

STUART BUTLER/LONELY PLANET ©

## Battle of the Somme

With close to a million people losing their lives over the space of four and a half months, it's hardly a surprise that the Battle of the Somme has become a byword for the waste of war.

The First Battle of the Somme (1 July to 18 November 1916) was an Allied offensive designed to relieve pressure on the beleaguered French troops at Verdun. On 1 July 1916, Allied troops 'went over the top' along a 34km front. But German positions proved virtually unbreachable and instead of the predicted fast gains, the battle dragged on for four and a half months.

When this particular act of WWI came to a close, the British had advanced just 12km and the French 8km.

## Take a Break

Just south of the turn-off for the Lochnagar Crater, **Le Poppy Bar** ( 03 22 75 45 45; 4 rte de Bapaume, La Boisselle; menus from €17; noon-2pm & 7-9pm Mon-Fri) looks very basic from the outside, but it actually serves pretty decent, traditional French dishes that are good value.

# Also Try...

ARTERRA PICTURE LIBRARY/ALAMY STOCK PHOTO ©

## Les Crocs

| DURATION | DIFFICULTY | DISTANCE |
|---|---|---|
| 5½hr one way | Hard | 16km |

To understand the vast Somme estuary (which has some of the world's biggest tides), march through this long, loop walk.

Along the way you'll experience an impressive array of environments, from towering desert-like sand dunes (known as *crocs* in Picard, the local language), to a beach as wide as the horizon at low tide, a fertile water-logged bird reserve, and gentle rural countryside. Keep your eyes peeled and you might spy seals, herons, spoonbills and a wealth of other wildlife.

The walk begins at the beach car park near St-Quentin-en-Tournon. Follow the sandy path through the dunes for 3.6km to the beach. Turn left (south) and march all the way down the beach and then follow the banks of the estuary inland until you hit the road again. At this point, head north to the village of Le Bout des Crocs and then carry on back to where you parked.

## Armistice Memorial Circuit

| DURATION | DIFFICULTY | DISTANCE |
|---|---|---|
| 3hr one way | Easy | 8½km |

When, after four long years, WWI finally came to an end, it did so at the 11th hour of the 11th day of the 11th month inside a train carriage in an obscure wooded corner of northern France. This walk, which meanders through those woods and along the banks of the pretty Aisne River, will show you where that most momentous of moments happened and is the perfect place in which to finish off a walking holiday in the Somme.

The walk begins at the Mémorial de l'Armistice (pictured), not far from the little town of Compiègne. Following a clear trail waymarked in yellow and red and white, you will walk in a roughly circular route down small farm tracks to take in the best of this countryside. Save visiting the replica train carriage (the first was destroyed in Germany in the closing stages of WWII) until the very end of the walk.

MAELICK/SHUTTERSTOCK ©

# Cap Blanc-Nez

| DURATION | DIFF. | DISTANCE |
| --- | --- | --- |
| 2½hr return | Easy | 7½km |

This is an enjoyable, family-friendly walk to the summit of the 158m high Cap Blanc-Nez cliffs.

These chalky-white cliffs (pictured) mark the closest spot between mainland Europe and the British Isles, and are an ideal spot from which to watch the ferries crisscross between the two lands. The walk begins from the village of Escalles and follows a clear trail down to the beach. The hard part is the haul up the slopes of the cliff before an easier descent and then a loop back via the villages of Mont d'Hubert and Haute Escalles.

# Le Hourdel

| DURATION | DIFF. | DISTANCE |
| --- | --- | --- |
| 2¾hr return | Easy | 8km |

Walking the exposed sandspit of Le Hourdel, between sea and lagoon, can feel like you're at the end of the world.

But there's life at the world's end: masses of seabirds and lots of grey seals. In fact, this is one of the better places in France to commune with these playful aquatic mammals. This walk, which begins from the Somme village of La Mollière, sweeps through bleak, sandy countryside and then down the long narrow sandspit in one enjoyable half-day walk. Don't forget your binoculars!

# Faÿ: The Lost Village

| DURATION | DIFF. | DISTANCE |
| --- | --- | --- |
| 3hr return | Easy | 9km |

In the summer of 1916, the village of Faÿ found itself right on the front line between opposing sides in a chilling example of the destruction of WWI.

At the end of the war, Faÿ had been almost completely destroyed. All that remained was part of the church and a bit of a farm building. Rather than rebuilding, the inhabitants chose to leave the old village as a memorial of what had happened. This easy stroll (marked with yellow waymarkers) around what remains of Faÿ will certainly live long in the memory.

0 50 km
0 25 miles
N
Dijon
Besançon
Biel
BERN
Auxonne
Ornans
Morteau
Neuchâtel
Fribourg
Thun
A36
Dole
N83
N57
Lac de Neuchâtel
SWITZERLAND
Doubs
N5
Pontarlier
Yverdon-les-Bains
Arbois
17
Frasne
Lac St-Point
Poligny
Malbuisson
Métabief
Château-Chalon
Champagnole
Mouthe
Vallorbe
JURA
Seille
Baume-les-Messieurs
Mouthe
Lausanne
15
BOURGOGNE FRANCHE-COMTÉ
18
Doucier
Lac de Joux
Lons-le-Saunier
Morbier
Lake Geneva (Lac Léman)
Montreux
Louhans
Clairvaux-les-Lacs
Parc Naturel Régional du Haut-Jura
Les Rousses
Évian-les-Bains
Creusaz
Cornettes de Bise (2432m)
Sion
Saône
Lac de Vouglans
Lamoura
Col de la Faucille
Nyon
Thonon-les-Bains
Vacheresse
16
Charchilla
Yvoire
Châtel
Tournus
Moirans-en-Montagne
St-Claude
Mijoux
Gex
Rhône
St-Jean-d'Aulps
Morzine
Martigny
Ferney-Voltaire
Avoriaz
N1
N5
Les Gets
Oyonnax
Lelex
Annemasse
Vallorcine
Mâcon
Geneva
Bonneville
Cluses
Col des Montets
Argentière
Bourg-en-Bresse
Nantua
A40
Arve
N205
Les Praz-de-Chamonix
Mont Dolent (3819m)
14
Bellegarde-sur-Valserine
N201
La Clusaz
Sallanches
Chamonix
Aiguille du Midi (3842m)
Ain
N508
St-Gervais-les-Bains
Tunnel de Mont Blanc
Ambérieu-en-Bugey
Annecy
Megève
Mont Blanc (4808m)
Courmayeur
Aosta
Artemare
Lac d'Annecy
Talloires
Les Houches
A41
Parc Naturel Régional du Massif des Bauges
N212
Roc du Vent (2360m)
Col du Petit St-Bernard
Belley
Lac du Bourget
Albertville
12
Lac de Roselend
Bourg-St-Maurice
ITALY
AUVERGNE RHÔNE-ALPES
Aix-les-Bains
Les Arcs
Gran Paradiso (4061m)
Lyon
La Feclaz
N90
La Plagne
Val d'Isère
Chambéry
Moûtiers
Tignes
Bourgoin-Jallieu
Tarentaise
Brides-les-Bains
Le Praz
Courchevel
Grande Casse (3855m)
Bonneval-sur-Arc
A47
A43
Meribel
Parc National de la Vanoise
Bessans
Vienne
N75
St-Martin de Belleville
Val Thorens
Lanslebourg
La Côte-St-André
A48
Pralognan-la-Vanoise
20
Col du Mont Cenis
Voiron
Les Menuires
Lac de Mont Cenis
Susa
Col de la Croix de Fer (2061m)
N6
Isère
FRENCH ALPS
Arc
Modane
A49
Parc Naturel Régional de Chartreuse
Vinay
Méaudre
Grenoble
Oulx
St-Marcelin
Vaujany
Col du Galibier (2645m)
13
N91
Alpe d'Huez
Le Monêtier-les-Bains
Cesana Torinese
Rhône
Villard de Lans
N85
La Grave
Barre des Écrins (4102m)
Col du Montgenèvre
Romans-sur-Isère
Les Deux Alpes
Venosc
Briançon
Parc Naturel Régional du Vercors
Parc National des Écrins
La Bérarde
19
PROVENCE ALPES CÔTE D'AZUR
Valence

Col de la Vanoise (p82)

# French Alps & Jura

# French Alps & Jura

No part of France is more synonymous with walking than the French Alps. The Golden Age of Alpinism was born here amid Europe's highest mountain peaks in the 1850s. The region's iconic hamlets and alpine pastures, soul-soaring cols (mountain passes) and glacier-carved valleys, shark-toothed summits and spellbinding blue lakes have seduced visitors ever since. Nearby are the gently rolling Jura Mountains.

## Chamonix

Mountains loom large everywhere you look in Chamonix, the mythical heart and soul of the French Alps dominated by Europe's highest peak, snowy domed Mont Blanc (4808m). A packed schedule of seasonal events in the small, dynamic town ensures ample off-trail entertainment: outdoor yoga, forest baths, guided walks and trail runs, traditional alpine arts and crafts, and so on. Dining, drinking and shopping options in town are equally generous and varied.

## Besançon

An important stop on Gallo-Roman trade routes linking Italy, the Alps and the Rhine, laid-back Besançon is today a springboard for the brooding landscapes of the sparsely populated Jura Mountains. Tucked in a bend of the Doubs River, the town is capped with a museum-filled citadel built by Vauban in the 17th century, and enjoys active contemporary arts and local music scenes.

## When to Go

The walking season is short in the French Alps. Snow can linger on high mountain passes, summits and steep, serpentine access roads well into May and return again in October. This makes June to September the best time to hit the trail: daylight hours are at their longest, weather conditions are warm and sunny with little risk of storms, uneven mountain footpaths are dry and subsequently less slippy, and views as you climb – of soaring mountain peaks blitzing a cloudless, crystal-clear horizon – simply don't get better. Lower elevations in the Jura Massif extend the walking season by a few weeks.

Popular walking routes get busy on July and August weekends; set out early or overnight in a *refuge* (mountain hut) on the trail to bag ethereal views of mirror lakes, icy summits and sunbathing ibex all for yourself.

In larger resorts cable cars and chairlifts take out some of the legwork between late June and mid-September. Bureaux des Guides (mountain guide offices offering guided walks) in resorts share the same seasonal hours.

Alpine wildflowers are at their most exquisite in June, although each summer month sports its own distinctive blooms. Crocuses and snowbells are among the first to emerge from

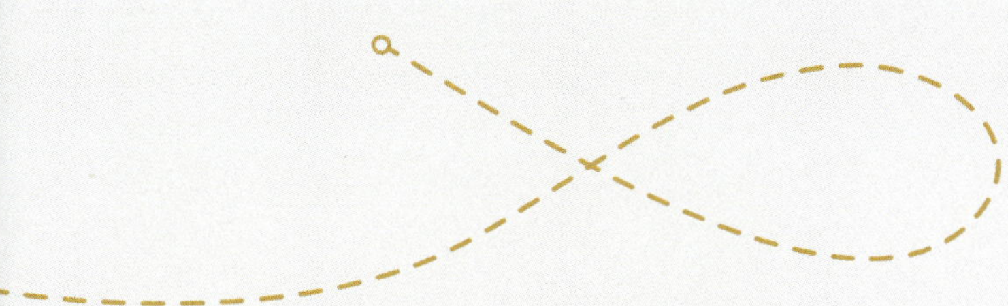



## Resources

**Savoie Mont Blanc** (savoie-mont-blanc.com) Walking itinerary suggestions, accommodation links and mountains of other practical information for Savoie and Haute-Savoie.

**Isère Tourisme** (isere-tourisme.com) Practical trail information for Grenoble and surrounding mountain resorts.

**Jura Tourisme** (jura-tourism.com) One-stop shop for information on the French Jura, including 55 suggested walks with trail maps.

**Chamonix Tourist Office** (04 50 53 00 24; chamonix.com; 85 place du Triangle de l'Amitié; 9am-7pm mid-Jun–mid-Sep & mid-Dec–Apr, shorter hours rest of year; ) Excellent source of information on accommodation, activities and mountain conditions for the entire Chamonix Valley.



winter hibernation, carpeting grassy pastures in a blaze of white and purple. Tiny blue forget-me-nots pepper hillsides well into July, as do yellow archangels and blue bugles. Eye-catching blue and yellow gentians flower June to August, alongside wild orchids. August and early September is the time to forage for wild blueberries, strawberries and raspberries.

## Where to Stay

From campgrounds, tree houses and self-catering *gîtes* (self-catering cottages and villas) in remote valleys to pleasure-palace hotels in celebrity ski resorts, the French Alps sport every stratum of accommodation. The choice in the Jura is more low-key.

Summer accommodation is easier to bag than in winter's ski season; hotels open mid-June to mid-September. Advance booking is essential for *refuges*, strategically located on long-distance GR trails and other walking routes.

Tourist offices in major ski resorts run an accommodation service with online booking.

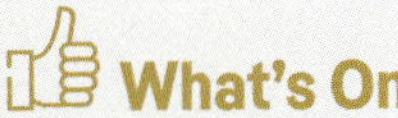

## What's On

**Cosmo Jazz Festival** (cosmojazzfestival.com; late Jul) Open-air jazz concerts on village and town squares, up mountains and at other exhilarating outdoor venues for nine days in the Chamonix Valley.

**Fête du Lac** One of Europe's largest pyrotechnic displays showers Annecy's lake in magic, 'oohed' and 'aahed' at by some 200,000 spectators. Spectacular music, lighting and special effects accompany the one- to two-hour firework display on the first Saturday in August.

**Le Tour de France** (letour.fr; Jul) The world's most famous cycling race always zips up and down a couple of torturous cols in the French Alps during its mammoth three-week, 3500km journey around France.

## Transport

Car is the easiest way of getting around. Many walkers fly into Lyon (lyonaeroports.com), Grenoble (www.grenoble-airport.com) or Geneva (gva.ch) in Switzerland and rent a car.

Within France, train services to the Alps are decent. Buses link railhead Moûtiers with Les Trois Vallées and Bourg St-Maurice with Val d'Isère. Modane is the rail stop for the Vanoise, linked by bus to Bonneval-sur-Arc. For Chamonix, change to the Mont Blanc Express at St-Gervais-les-Bains. Besançon is the main railhead for the Jura Mountains, with services to/from Paris-Gare de Lyon and Dijon.

# 12

# Lac de Roselend & Lac de la Gittaz

| DURATION | DIFFICULTY | DISTANCE | START/END |
|----------|------------|----------|-----------|
| 3hr return | Easy | 10.5km | Lac de Roselend |

| TERRAIN | Gravel road, forest and field footpaths |
|---------|------------------------------------------|

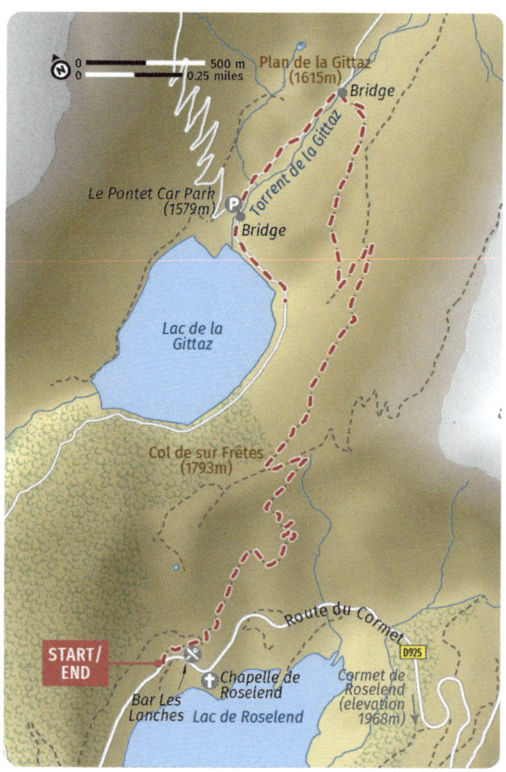



The road trip to Lac de Roselend – over the 1968m-high mountain pass of Cormet de Roselend – is as stunning as the lake views accompanying walkers on this lake-to-lake walk. Find the trail (min/max altitude 1562/1793m) in Savoie's eminently peaceful, pastoral, Beaufortain region.

Park by Chapelle de Roselend on the northern shore of **Lac de Roselend** (pictured). Tour de France cyclists whizz around this lake wedged between mountains, and views are picture-postcard. Walk downhill past **Bar Les Lanches** to the roadside 'La Gittaz' waymarker. Follow the gently winding, gravel road uphill, past fields of bell-clanging cows. North, the craggy peak of Roc du Vent (2360m) looms large. Lake views get dreamier, the higher you climb.

After 40 minutes (1.6km), the gravel road flattens onto **Col de sur Frêtes** (1793m) – actually a grassy cow field. Continue straight, traversing a short section of enclosed pasture (duck beneath the electric wire) before dropping down to the 'Col de sur Frêtes' waymarker on the right. The milk from these red Tarentaise cows goes into AOP Beaufort, Tome des Bauges and Reblochon cheese.

Now narrow and cowpat-splattered, the footpath weaves downhill to farmland. Views of artificial **Lac de la Gittaz** from above steal the show. Lower down, the path circumvents a hillock and crosses Torrent de la Gittaz over a footbridge to arrive on a tarmac road at **Plan de la Gittaz** (1615m). Turn left to 'Le Pontet & Col de la Gittaz' and follow the road for 700m to **Le Pontet car park** (1579m). Bear left, recrossing the river, and follow the road for 500m to a lay-by with a footpath that plunges to the shore. Return to Roselend the same way.

# 13

# Les Chalets d'Arsine & Lac de la Douche

| DURATION | DIFFICULTY | DISTANCE | START/END |
|---|---|---|---|
| 5hr return | Moderate | 11.6km | Le Casset |

| TERRAIN | |
|---|---|
| | Forest paths, mountain trails, occasional rocky sections |

A family-friendly classic in the Parc National des Écrins, the hike up to Les Chalets d'Arsine is the right balance of challenge and reward. The path ascends slowly at first, giving hikers time to warm up their legs before climbing to the milky blue Lac de la Douche. Finish with a view over a small plateau where small rivers of glacier melt weave their way downhill. Admire 3000m-plus peaks, or turn your gaze down to soak up the beauty of the lake; wherever you look, you're sure to spot something special.

## Getting Here

From Le Monêtier-les-Bains, drive towards Col du Lautaret and turn left onto the D300 to Le Casset. Park here, and head to the south of the village.

## Starting Point

Start on the south side of Le Casset, at the bridge over the Guisane river. Cross it to follow the red-and-white GR54 trail markers.

**01** From the bridge over the Guisane, you'll see yellow hiking signs for the Lac de la Douche, which is your first objective. Follow the path uphill through the forest, admiring the milky blue Torrent du Petit Tabuc that runs along the trail. This brook, mainly glacier runoff, is the first hint that the landscapes will change from lush valley prairies and pine forests to rocky glaciers over the course of this hike.

BERTRAND LOUIS/SHUTTERSTOCK ©

**02** The path is wide and shaded by a rich forest as you pass the small private hamlet called **Clos du Gué**, after about 1km. Cross a small rustic bridge without handrails to continue onwards. From here on, you'll climb up through what may feel like an enchanted forest: water flows everywhere, in small waterfalls, with loud gurgles as the soundtrack.

**03** You're not imagining things – the path is getting steeper. Expect an average 13% incline as you hike up to a possible resting spot: **Le Grand Pré**. The clearing is at the intersection of the Torrent du Glacier du Casset and the Torrent du Petit Tabauc. Stop here for a break, a snack or a gulp of water, especially if you're hiking with children, but save the picnic for later, at the Lac de la Douche.

**04** Another kilometre after leaving Le Grand Pré, you're still following the GR54 signs and the Torrent du Petit Tabuc up the trail. The trees thin out a bit and become older, with small clearings left and right to enjoy the scenery. In autumn, mushrooms spring up across the forest floor, but harvesting them is forbidden as this trek lies within the boundaries of the Parc National des Écrins. The forest is full of larch trees, whose leaves turn bright gold in autumn.

**05** The last kilometre to the **Lac de la Douche** (pictured) is the steepest, but what a view! You'll have to walk between some rocks and across some small bridges to reach the shores. Benches dot the banks for meditative reflection. This small lake is encased by mountains and is the perfect spot for a picnic. Despite its name, translated as 'the shower lake', it's not recommended to swim in these (very cold) waters, which are home to a fragile mountain ecosystem. Instead, take a dip in the rivers or a *plan d'eau* (swimming hole) on the valley floor, where the moving water better disperses the traces of chemical products and bacteria left by human skin.

# GR54

This hike follows a section of the GR54, the Grand Tour des Écrins, which is a 10- to 15-day hike that does a loop through the Parc National des Écrins. Come back and try your hand at the full GR54! In France, there are more than 200,000km of trails that make up the country's network of Grande Randonnée de Pays. One of the more difficult, but also one of the wildest, the GR54 attracts hikers and trail runners from all over. It's less crowded than more-famous trails like the Tour de Mont Blanc or the GR20 in Corsica.

**06** Continue on the trail upwards after the lake, following the signs for Col d'Arsine. While hiking up the steep zigzags, turn around: this is the best photo of the lake you can get: the **Roche des Agneaux** (2925m) and the surrounding glaciers tower above the lake. Late afternoon is the best time to get a sun-splashed photo of the lake and the mountains behind it. But early-morning photoshoots, before other hikers turn up, can produce photos that exude tranquility and peace.

**07** The rocks here are somewhat brittle, and as they erode into the streams they make *farine glacière* (glacier flour). This mix is what gives the glacier runoff streams and lakes their milky-blue to turquoise colours. As the trail steadily climbs up, look across the Petit Tabuc at the Roche Baron. Depending on the time of day, the colour of the water changes in this spot that receives the full-afternoon sun.

**08** You'll arrive on a small plateau where you'll find several bridges; this place is known as **Les Chalets d'Arsine** (2250m). Explore the bright blue waters, and photograph the Pic d'Arsine (3240m), the Pic du Dragon (3188m) and the Pics de Chamoissière (3208m). Here your journey ends, and you'll follow your footsteps back to the car park. Or if you have the energy, continue on up an extra few kilometres to the **Col d'Arsine** (pictured) for even more views.

BERTRAND LOUIS/SHUTTERSTOCK ©

## Serre Chevalier

Stretching from Briançon to the Col du Lautaret, the Serre Chevalier valley is the main winter hub in this part of the Écrins. The region is less crowded all year round than fancier ski areas, such as Chamonix or Val d'Isère, and these advantages feel multiplied in the summer. For hiking, mountaineering, rock climbing or wildlife watching, this Serre Chevalier hike to Les Chalets d'Arisine is a great starting point for mountain adventures in the Écrins. The night train from Paris to the valley is back in action, so reserve a sleeper car and wake up in the Alps!

 ## Take a Break

Grab an ice cream at the summer **ice-cream stand** in Le Casset. It's not an official restaurant, but you'll find it at the corner of rue du Lauzet and rue du Conchamp. You'll find the classics, but also some local flavours, such as mountain blueberry and genepi (the sweet mountain liqueur often enjoyed after meals). Try an ice cream made from bright orange sea buckthorn! It's full of vitamin C and will cool you down after a hike.

# 14

# Lac Blanc

| DURATION | DIFFICULTY | DISTANCE | START/END |
|---|---|---|---|
| 3½-4hr return | Moderate | 8.5km | Top of Flégère cable car |

| TERRAIN | Rocky footpath with steep ascent |
|---|---|

Admiring razor-sharp reflections of Europe's highest peak in Chamonix's famous lake is what this classic loop is about. The celebrated trail (min/max altitude 1877/2352m) gets packed on summer weekends, so plan ahead – start early or overnight in Lac Blanc's lakeside mountain hut to gorge on sumptuous sunrise views in splendid isolation.

## Getting Here

From Chamonix, follow the Martigny road 3km north to Les Praz-de-Chamonix. Park at the bottom station of the Télécabine de la Flégère and ride the gondola (single/return €15/19) up to 1877m.

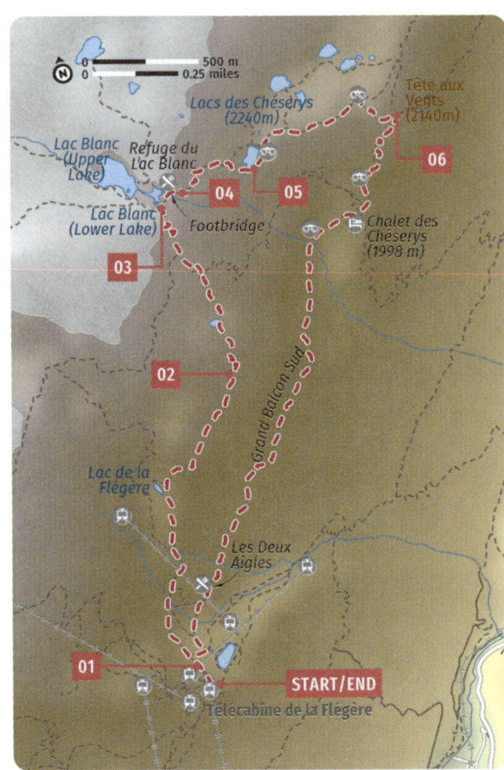


## Starting Point

Exit the cable car's top station and bear right to pick up the trailhead clearly signposted 'Lac Blanc'. A gravel road briefly dips downhill before morphing into a mountain path.

**01** Soon after the Lac Blanc trailhead, the rocky path steepens as it zigzags between blueberry bushes and limestone boulders coloured lime-green with lichen.

**02** Wooden walkways ensure dry feet across the occasional stream and metal handrails assist walkers on a tight but short rocky corridor. Turn back to admire **snowy Mont Blanc** (4808m) across the valley – a hypnotic constant throughout the 3.2km, 1½-hour ascent.

**03** **Postcard views of Lac Blanc** (2352m) reward at the top (pictured). Cross the **footbridge** and follow the lakeshore path directly beneath Refuge du Lac Blanc's terrace deck

## Two Lakes

Buried in snow for some eight months of the year, high-altitude Lac Blanc (White Lake) seduces summertime walkers with its startling turquoise water and occasional pale-pink-breasted water pipit foraging for food on the lake shores.

The lake comprises two bodies of glacial water split by a narrow channel. Even in July and August the larger upper lake, 9m deep, retains a chilly polar vibe with its year-round patches of snow. The smaller lower lake is 3.2m deep and has shallower, crystal-clear water.

ROBERTO MOIOLA/SYSAWORLD/GETTY IMAGES ©

to marvel at Mont Blanc reflections in the lake.

**04** Avoid the late-morning crowd labouring up to Lac Blanc by returning to La Flégère cable-car station via Lacs des Chéserys – a 5km descent. From Lac Blanc, continue past Refuge du Lac Blanc and follow the 'Sentier Piétons' sign between rocks. Almost immediately the path turns into a series of steep but unchallenging wooden steps and metal ladders. Leave 20 minutes to reach the first of several tiny lakes known as **Lacs des Chéserys** (2240m).

**05** Skilfully crafted stone cairns mark the **Aiguilles Rouges nature reserve**, named after the ginger crags shaped like 'red needles' that dominate here. About 1km after the first lake, the trail arrives at **Tête aux Vents** (2140m) – the furthest point north on this walk, from where you head back south to La Flégère along a section of Chamonix's **Grand Balcon Sud trail**. A magnificent panorama of (left to right) the Tour, Argentière, Mer de Glace and Boissons glaciers dominates the return walk.

### Take a Break

**Refuge du Lac Blanc** (☎ 06 02 05 08 82; refuge-lac-blanc.fr; dm incl half-board adult/child €56/50; ⏱ mid-Jun–Sep), with dorms and cafe terrace sensationally overlooking Lac Blanc, serves drinks with Mont Blanc view. Lunch at mountain restaurant **Les Deux Aigles** (☎ 07 67 15 23 37; ⏱ mid-Jun–Sep; 🚼), on the trail 10 minutes from the end of this walk. *Croûte au fromage* (oven-baked bread smothered in ham and gooey Comté and raclette cheese) is the house speciality, while *tartelette aux myrtilles* (blueberry tart) and ice cream (fiery génépi, honey, blueberry) are local sweet temptations.

# 15

# Pic des Mémises

| DURATION | DIFFICULTY | DISTANCE | START/END |
|---|---|---|---|
| 3hr return | Moderate | 6.5km | Col de Creusaz, Bernex |

| TERRAIN | Forest/mountain tracks and a 12m-high ladder |
|---|---|

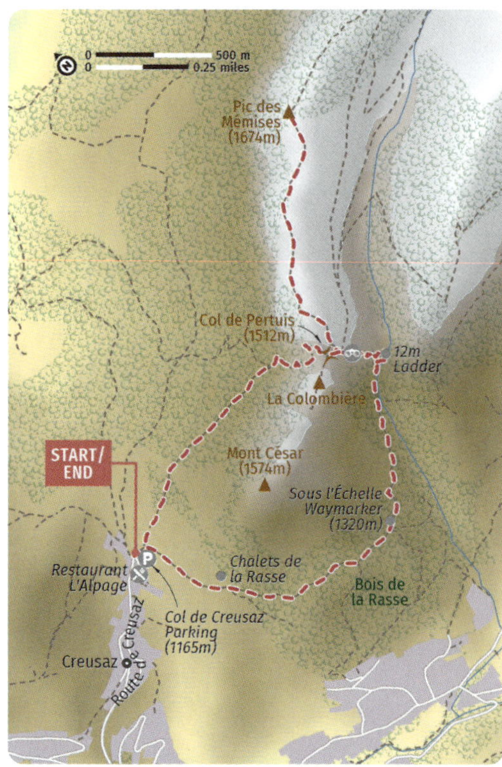



Grassy pastures and coniferous woods bookend this circular walk in Haute-Savoie's Bas-Chablais region. Panoramic views of Europe's largest alpine lake – Lake Geneva – and a vertiginous ladder are highlights (min/max altitude 1165/1674m).

From Bernex, drive 4km northeast to Creusaz. Park in the **Col de Creusaz parking** (1165m) in front of Restaurant L'Alpage. From the yellow waymarker at the end of the car park, follow the footpath right to 'Sous l'Échelle'.

Enjoy rural views of the tiny ski resort of Bernex as the wide gravel track gently climbs past grassy pastures along the southern flank of craggy **Mont César** (1574m). The path narrows as it winds through **Bois de la Rasse** (1250m) – forest stitched from conifers and boulders cloaked in emerald-green moss.

At the **Sous l'Échelle** waymarker (1320m), fork left to 'Échelle'. The stream-side trail dives sharply uphill between rocks and tree roots. The final 10m to the foot of this walk's famous 12m-high iron ladder (*échelle*) is an agile clamber across boulders. At the top of the ladder, follow the path up to **Col de Pertuis** (1512m), with sweeping views. Continue straight to Pic des Mémises – a 25-minute walk along a scree slope then grassy ridge path.

A 5.5m-tall oak cross signals **Pic des Mémises** (1674m; pictured). Picnic over a sublime panorama of subalpine peaks (including Dent d'Oche, Cornettes de Bise and Mont Billiat in France, the Swiss Jura across the lake and the snowy Swiss Alps). The big blue waters of Lake Geneva shimmer far below. For the descent, backtrack to Col de Pertuis then turn right to follow a well-signed path downhill for 45 minutes back to Col de Creusaz.

# 16

# Chalets de Bise to Lac de Darbon

| DURATION | DIFFICULTY | DISTANCE | START/END |
|---|---|---|---|
| 3½hr return | Moderate | 6.5km | Chalets de Bise, Vacheresse |

| TERRAIN | | Rocky mountain path with several mountain climbs |
|---|---|---|

This spectacular circular walk climbs from grassy alpine pastures to a trio of mountain passes peppered with sunbathing ibex in summer. Find it in Haute-Savoie's cheese-fuelled Val d'Abondance (min/max altitude 1500/1955m).

## Getting Here

From Châtel in ski area Les Portes du Soleil, drive 19km west along the D22 to Vacheresse. Turn left in the village towards 'Site de Bise', left again after 4.4km, then follow the wiggly, single-paved road to the end (another 4.7km).

## Starting Point

From Chalets de Bise car park, stroll with serenading goats past chalet-restaurant Les Cabrettes to the farm shop and *refuge* La Ferme de Bise. Swing through the wooden gate in front to pick up the trailhead.

**01** Follow the path uphill, admiring (right) the natural stone masonry of **Cornettes de Bise** (2432m), Val d'Abondance's highest peak.

**02** Clanging cow bells will entertain as you traverse alpine pastures peppered with monk's rhubarb, yellow gentians, purple harebells and alpine crocuses. At the **La Salle** waymarker (1535m), take the left fork towards Col de Floray.

**03** The uneven footpath becomes rockier as it zigzags up towards the crags of **La Pointe des Pavis** (2052m), looming large ahead. Listen out for – and spot – whistling marmots at the foot of the huge rocks. In August linger to pick wild petrol-blue bilberries.

**04** The final leg up to **Col de Floray** (1940m) is steep and can be slippy when wet. At the top turn right, enjoying head-spinning **360-degree mountain views** as you walk along the ridge towards **Lac de Darbon** (1813m).

## Alpage de Bise

A protected nature reserve at the foot of the imposing Cornettes de Bise (2432m), this remote alpine hamlet – snowed in and inaccessible in winter – is inhabited for just four months of the year by farmers who bring their Abondance cows up from the valley in June to graze here on higher summer pastures. Their milk goes into the valley's signature Reblochon, Abondance, Tome de Bauges and Beaufort cheeses, which have Appellation d'origine contrôlée (AOC; certification of origin).

NICOLA WILLIAMS/LONELY PLANET ©

**05** **Bird's-eye lake views** come into view as the crest path drops off to the left and snakes downhill towards the crystal-clear water. Enjoy lake reflections of surrounding rocks and the spiky, needle-like **Aiguilles de Darbon** (2043m). Snow patches linger around the shore until June and, in early summer, **herds of shaggy ibex** lounge lakeside and in the rocks.

**06** Follow the footpath (signposted Col de Parvis) around the eastern side of **Lac de Darbon** and bear right (east) uphill along the narrow footpath to **Col de Parvis** (1944m). Ibex often laze on steep sun-baked slopes here.

**07** Cross the col's grassy plain sprinkled in late summer with **violet crocuses** and, on clear days, admire the **magnificent panorama of Lake Geneva** languishing far below.

**08** The path, washed away in parts, swiftly descends to Montagne de Neuteu Est (1870m) and, five minutes further, Montagne de Neuteu Sud (1834m). Brace yourself for more visual high drama as it climbs gently back up past tiny **Lac de Neuteu** to **Col de Bise** (1915m).

**09** Take a breather on the col's grassy banks with sweeping views of the tooth-like **Tête de Charousse**

(2094m) and **Dent du Velan** (2087m).

Leave 45 minutes for the straightforward descent down to La Salle (1535m) and beyond to Chalets de Bise.

## Take a Break

Grab an ice cream made with fresh cow's milk at the local farm (known as **La Ferme de Bise**) or reserve a table at **Les Cabrettes** (☎ 09 88 18 47 77; Chalets de Bise; ⏲ Jun-Sep; P ). Deep-fried *beignets de pommes de terre* (potato fritters) with local cheeses and charcuterie is the restaurant's wildly popular house speciality.

# Arbois to Pupillin

| DURATION | DIFFICULTY | DISTANCE | START/END |
|---|---|---|---|
| 4-5hr return | Moderate | 13km | Arbois |

| TERRAIN | |
|---|---|
| | Paved lanes, vineyard tracks and forest footpaths |

This serene vineyard loop in the Jura is for gourmets. Tasting opportunities at *caves* (wine cellars) in honey-coloured Arbois and yellow-brick Pupillin are highlights.

## Getting Here

Arbois is a 50-minute drive (40km) southwest of Besançon along the N83. SNCF trains also link the two towns (€12, 40 to 50 minutes, hourly).

## Starting Point

The trail begins by **Église St-Just**, opposite the tourist office on main street rue de l'Hôtel de Ville. Leave 20 minutes on foot from Arbois train station.

**01** From the 'Arbois St-Just (293m)' sign by the church, follow rue du Souvenir Français to the cemetery, then turn right onto chemin de la Platière (signposted 'Sentier Pédestre') – a river-side footpath with sweet views of the Cuisance River and the 18th-century **Moulin de la Bourre** mill.

**02** After 500m the path veers left onto rue Pointelin. At the next fork, turn left onto chemin des Loups and follow the road uphill onto a grassy footpath between vines. As the N83 pops into view, turn left.

**03** Follow the cemetery wall, turn right through a tunnel under the N83, then turn left to follow a paved lane past vineyards for 1.2km to La Maladrerie. The **wrought-iron sculpture** of a glass and 6m-long bottle of *vin jaune* mid-pour (2012) is by Arbois artist-winemaker Freddy Wood.

**04** From **La Maladrerie** enjoy 1.9km of mellow vineyard walking along country lanes to **Paradis** (328m). At the Paradis waymarker, fork sharp right to Pupillin, 4.1km south. Vineyards and fruit orchards groan with grapes, cherries, pears, apples and autumnal quince – *paradis* (paradise) for France lovers.

## Vin Jaune

*Vin jaune* (literally, 'yellow wine') – a slowly fermented, golden wine – is legendary, and was France's first to gain an AOC in 1936. Savagnin grapes – unique to *vin jaune* – are harvested late and their sugar-saturated juice left to ferment at least six years and three months in oak barrels: 100L of grape juice ferments down to just 62L of *vin jaune*, then is bottled in a chubby 0.62L bottle called a *clavelin*. Prime vintages keep for more than a century.

NICOLA WILLIAMS/LONELY PLANET ©

**05** The lane climbs gently up to **Domaine de la Pinte**, one of the first estates to plant savagnin grapes in the 1950s. Admire the *cabane de vigne* (vineyard hut), used to store tools. At the road junction, continue straight to spaghetti downhill through vineyards.

**06** At **La Ronde** (333m), continue straight ahead uphill – still between vines – and after 200m, at the top, turn sharply right. The vineyard panorama remains joyous now for the next 2km.

**07** When the vineyard trail hits the tarmac road, turn left and climb up to **Pupillin** village. Several winemakers offer *dégustation* (tasting). From the main street, rue du Ploussard, walk 200m north, turn right uphill along rue Bagier, and further uphill along rue de la Croix Bagier into woods.

**08** Arriving amid fields at the **Croix Bagier** (504m) waymarker, next to a wooden cross, turn left towards Allée du Roi de Rome and follow the grassy footpath into the forest.

**09** At the **Allée du Roi de Rome** waymarker, turn left towards Ermitage and Arbois–St-Just. Tramp through woods for another 300m, then turn left downhill along the road (D469).

**10** Arriving on **Plateau de l'Ermitage**, savour the village panorama from the lookout platform in the park. Continue 150m downhill to 17th-century **Chapelle de l'Ermitage** (closed), then follow stone steps and a forest track back to Arbois–St-Just, 1km away.

## Take a Break

Reserve a table at **Auberge de Grapiot** (☎ 03 84 37 49 44; legrapiot.com; 3 rue Bagier; menus €25-75; ⏱ noon-1.30pm & 7-9.30pm Thu-Mon) in Pupillin. Chef Samuel Richardet cooks up an inventive cuisine from local produce.

# 18

# Cirque de Baume-les-Messieurs



| DURATION | DIFFICULTY | DISTANCE | START/END |
|---|---|---|---|
| 5-6hr return | Moderate | 13km | Abbaye de Baume-les-Messieurs |

| TERRAIN | Forest footpaths, rocky steps with two short steep sections |
|---|---|

The thickly forested Jura is known for its *reculées* or *cirques* (steep-head or blind valleys), formed 200 million years ago by glacial erosion – and Cirque de Baume-les-Messieurs is the region's finest specimen. This circular day walk (min/max altitude 307/510m) takes you from Baume-les-Messieurs, sunken in the imposing limestone amphitheatre, up to its vertiginous limestone cliffs, and through fields and forests atop its horseshoe brow. Crashing waterfalls and bat-filled caves provide high-drama entertainment.

## Getting Here

Leave 90 minutes to drive from Besançon to Baume-les-Messieurs (pictured), 82km south via the N83 and N193. En route, drive through cheese-fuelled Poligny and wine town Château-Chalon. The final approach, from the northwest along the D70, brings you past Baume's village cemetery, right across the bridge (D70E1), left along the left bank of the River Seille to Pont de l'Abbaye, and back across the river to Parking de l'Abbaye by Baume's iconic abbey (p78).

## Starting Point

From the abbey car park, walk into the village along main street rue Guillaume Poupet, past the 'Fontaine (308m)' waymarker in front of the tourist office. After the *mairie* (town hall), turn immediately left down chemin du Gyp Bega, cross the river, and when you hit the tarmac road, turn left. Continue for about 10 minutes, past Pont de l'Abbaye, until you reach the 'Échelles de Sermu (Bas) 307m' waymarker.

**01** Head uphill for 700m to **'Échelles de Sermu (Haut)'** – not an *échelle* or ladder at all, but several short flights of steep, irregular stone steps interspersed with scrubby footpaths fringed by wild blackberry bushes and piles of fallen rock.

As you climb, lovely village views unfold – of Baume's 13th- to 16th-century Benedictine abbey and its surrounding patchwork of ancient stone-tiled roofs. Arriving on the plateau atop the limestone cliff, turn left towards Sermu.

**02** The footpath – now delightfully flat and tree-shaded – snakes along the crest of Baume's trademark cliffs for 1.1km. Admire the sheer drop down to Baume-les-Messieurs on your left and grassy fields of grazing cows divided by crumbling dry-stone walls on your right.

After about 10 minutes, the path emerges from the trees to unveil a 180-degree panorama of rocky limestone cliffs holding spectacular sentry on the other side of the deep blind valley – a mirror image of those you're standing on!

**03** A line-up of beehives and tractors parked up in a barn herald your arrival in the tiny farming hamlet of **Sermu**. The footpath now joins a tarmac road; carry on straight, following signs for Belvédère des Roches (1.6km) and Grottes de Baume (2.4km).

**04** Where the road forks to the right, continue straight and enjoy the peace and quiet of the country for another 10 to 15 minutes until you reach **Belvédère de Crançot** – a viewpoint at the valley's southern end. Bear left, following the road for another 100m to **Belvédère des Roches** (507m), where more dramatic views of the cliff-ensnared, horseshoe valley unfold.

## Grottes de Baume

Spawned during the Jurassic period, the spectacular **Grottes de Baume** (baumelesmessieurs.fr; adult/child €9.50/6.50) were uncovered in 1610.

In the 19th century, music concerts were held in the stalactite-laced cave chambers with soaring 71m-high ceilings.

Today, niphargus (blind white cave shrimps with no eyes) swim in the cave lake and 5000 bats hibernate here for six months in winter. Watching 800-odd resident summer bats circle wildly overhead is a tour highlight.

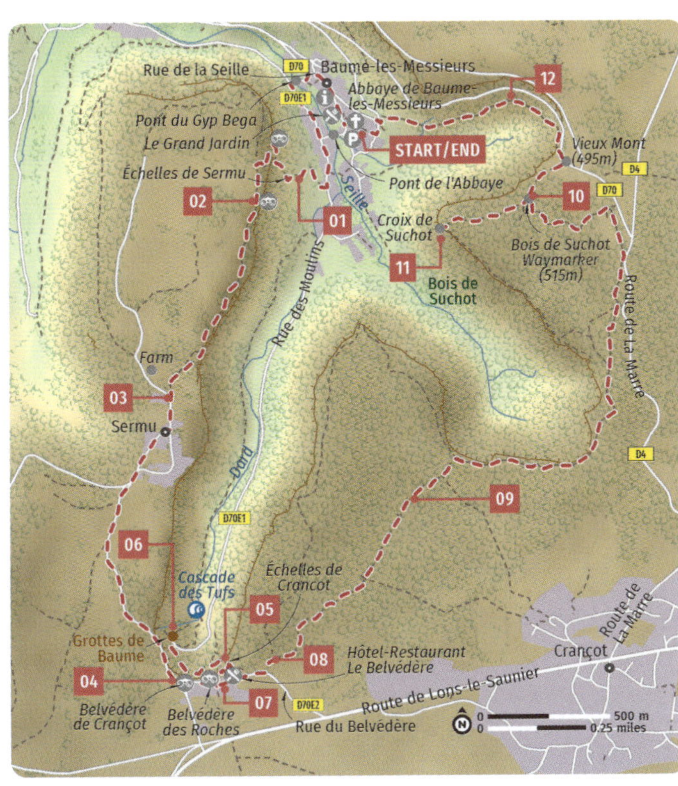

**05** Turn left, following signs to Grottes de Baume (800m) and Échelles de Crancot (400m). The trail now leaves the road and descends sharply between trees to caves hidden in the cliffs via the **Échelles de Crancot** (irregular stone steps) slicing through woods. Mules laboured up and down here in the 19th century, carrying grains and freshly milled flour between farm and mill.

**06** Break for a 55-minute **guided tour** of a 450m stretch of the sprawling 3km-long caves followed by a picnic perhaps – at tables in front of the cave ticket office or on the grass overlooking the neighbouring **Cascade des Tufs**, a huge mushroom-shaped waterfall where the Dard River dramatically crashes down over bulbous tuff beds. Later, retrace your steps up the Échelles de Crancot and back to the Belvédère des Roches waymarker by the road (D70E2).

**07** Turn left towards Croix de Suchot, 3.6km away, and walk about 100m along the road (the D70E2), past **Hôtel-Restaurant Le Belvédère**, then turn left onto a gravel road marked with a small 'Croix Suchot' sign nailed on a tree.

**08** When the road forks, bear right into the forest. At the next fork, continue straight, always following the single yellow horizontal stripe painted on trees that now marks the leafy forest trail (actually part of the GR59). At the next couple of forks, simply follow the yellow stripe – ignore forks marked with a yellow cross.

**09** Enjoy a mellow amble along the shaded forest path, flat and carpeted with golden leaves in autumn. The occasional picnic table in a sun-dappled clearing encourages lingering. Watch out for the odd mountain biker tearing along the same dirt track.

**10** After about an hour don't be surprised to hear the faint rumble of motorised traffic as the path strays towards the forest edge. Arriving at the **'Bois de Suchot (515m)' waymarker**, turn left towards the Croix de Suchot, 400m away. Almost immediately the footpath forks – bear right.

**11** At the **Croix de Suchot** – a large wooden crucifix atop a hillock at 510m – the 11km you have walked are rewarded with a beautiful panorama of Baume village and its rock amphitheatre spreadeagled far below.

**12** The final 2km to the village is a well-posted stroll back through the forest and past a field of beehives. Upon hitting the road (D70) after 700m at **Vieux Mont** (495m), turn left downhill, round the bend and pick up another forest footpath on your left (look for the same single yellow stripe and a sign indicating horses are forbidden to use the path). Zigzag along the narrow path between trees until the stone-spired abbey pops into view. End with a serene walk around the abbey's elegant trio of historic courtyards. In 16th-century **Cour du Cloître**, dip your hands in the central fountain.

## Abbaye Impériale

Baume-les-Messieurs' **Benedictine abbey** (baumeles messieurs.fr; adult/child €8/5) grew in the 7th century. In 910, its abbot, Bernon (c 850–927), set out with six monks from Baume to establish western Europe's most influential monastical abbey at Cluny in Burgundy.

Guided visits at the abbey include the church, with its 15th-century sculpted doorway, 71m-long arched nave and exquisite polychrome Flemish altarpiece in the choir (pictured) dating from the 16th century (the period when the abbey was at its apogee). In 1759, Pope Clement XIII signed a bill turning the abbey into a secular chapter house.

## Take a Break

Footsteps from the main abbey entrance in the village, **Le Grand Jardin** (03 84 44 68 37; legrandjardin.fr; 6 place Guillaume de Poupet; menus €22-40; closed Tue & Wed Sep-Jun; P) serves regional dishes prepared with a personal touch, such as rabbit stuffed with *saucisse de Morteau* (sausage) and char (a type of fish) with absinthe. The artisanal ice cream (absinthe, apricot or violet anyone?) is among the Jura's finest. There are a handful of B&B rooms above for overnighting in style.

# 19

# Tête de la Maye

| DURATION | DIFFICULTY | DISTANCE | START/END |
|----------|-----------|----------|-----------|
| 4hr return | Hard | 7km | La Bérarde |

| TERRAIN | Steep rocky path; vertiginous sections with cables |
|---------|---------------------------------------------------|

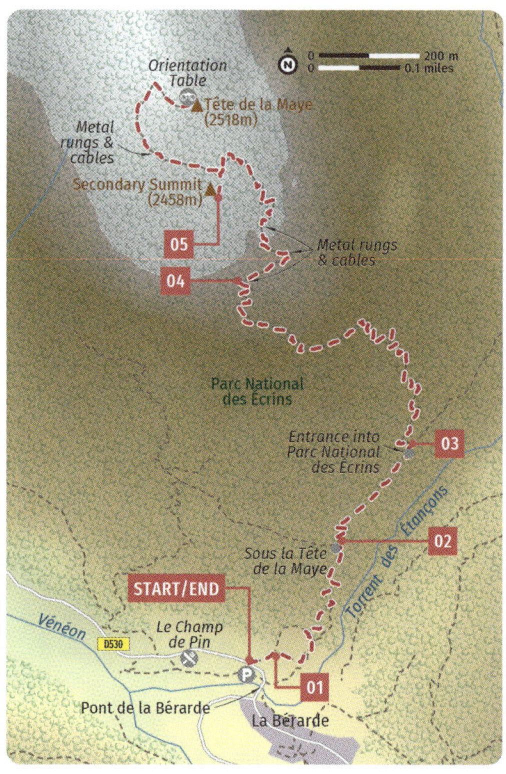


It isn't the highest peak in the park, but on clear days the 2518m-high summit of Tête de la Maye rewards with a 360-degree panorama of France's second-largest national park. The way up is steep (min/max altitude 1719/2518m) and challenging rock faces make it unsuitable for children.

## Getting Here

From Grenoble it is a 1½-hour drive (85km) southeast, via Le Bourg d'Oisans, to La Bérarde. This wildly remote hamlet lies at the end of the narrow, sinuous D530 in the dead-end Vénéon Valley.

## Starting Point

Follow the only road (D530) through the hamlet to the car park immediately before the green bridge across the crashing glacial water of Torrent des Étançons. The yellow **Pont de la Bérarde** (1719m) trail marker is on the left.

**01** The rocky footpath up to Tête de la Maye – signposted 2.8km but a little over 3km – climbs mercilessly from the second it leaves the roadside. Basic chalet huts with metal-sheet roofs and scant decorative frills hint at how harsh life is in this remote alpine valley. Dangerous rockfalls in winter force the few who live here to abandon the valley from October to May.

**02** As the path zigzags up the mountain past pine, birch and mountain ash trees that blaze with cherry-red berries in late summer, admire the forbidding 3421m-high peak of **Grande Aiguille de la Bérarde** across the valley. This is the giant of a mountain that the low winter sun fails to eclipse, depriving the hamlet of direct sunlight for several months of the year. After 10

# Parc National des Écrins

Glacial action and the thrashing Durance and Drac rivers carved out France's second-largest national park (ecrins-parcnational.fr). An awe-imposing 918-sq-km expanse of mountains and steel-grey moraines stretching between the towns of Le Bourg d'Oisans, Briançon and Gap, the Écrins National Park showcases 100-plus peaks, climaxing with the Barre des Écrins (4102m). Some 700km of walking trails follow in the footsteps of shepherds and yesteryear smugglers, passing en route glaciers, beech forests, waterfalls, wild blueberry fields and summer meadows sprinkled with flowers.

NICOLA WILLIAMS/LONELY PLANET ©

minutes, at the **'Sous la Tête de la Maye' waymarker**, follow the path around to the right.

**03** Ten minutes on (or 800m into the walk), a French flag painted on a boulder and information panel marks your entrance into the **Parc National des Écrins**. About 30m further, at the fork, bear left to follow 'Tête de la Maye'. Peer down to see gushing Torrent de Bonne Pierre fed by the Bonne Pierre glacier.

**04** At the 1.85km mark, **metal rungs and cables** drilled into the rock help walkers safely cross a 250m-long wall on the mountain's austere south face. Three more sections of steps and cables follow. The final assisted rock climb up a short dramatic gully rewards with dizzying views of the glacier-gouged valley below.

**05** After two hours of walking, **Tête de la Maye's secondary summit** (2458m) appears, recognisable by its flat stoney dome. Continue for almost another kilometre to the summit – red and white stripes on the rocks and cairns left wayside by other walkers mark the way. A ceramic orientation table identifies surrounding peaks. Return to La Bérarde the same way.

## Take a Break

Squirrelled away roadside at the western end of La Bérarde, friendly hotel-*refuge*-restaurant **Le Champ de Pin** ( 04 76 79 54 09; lechampdepin.com; lunch & dinner May–late Sep; P ) is a delicious spot for refuelling post-hike on traditional *gratin de crozets au sarrasin* (buckwheat pasta with wild spinach, cheese and potatoes), *tartiflette* (oven-baked cheese, bacon and melted Reblochon) and mixed charcuterie platters. Produce is strictly local and artisanal. Summer dining is alfresco beneath a mountain ash tree, and a wood-burning stove keeps the rustic interior warm and cosy.

# 20

# Lac des Vaches & Col de la Vanoise

| DURATION | DIFFICULTY | DISTANCE | START/END |
|---|---|---|---|
| 5-7hr return | Hard | 15.2km | Les Fontanettes car park |

| TERRAIN | |
|---|---|
| | Forest trails, gravel roads and rocky mountain paths |

A cinematic stone walkway across water, spectacular lakes and gargantuan glaciers are highlights of this challenging walk in Savoie's Massif de la Vanoise. Ensnared within France's oldest national park, the trail today (min/max altitude 1650/2516m) piggybacks part of the celebrated GR55.

## Getting Here

The trail begins in the low-key mountain village of Pralognan-la-Vanoise on the western fringe of the Parc National de la Vanoise. Leave 1½ hours to drive from Chambéry (105km west) and an hour from Albertville (50km northwest) or Bourg St-Maurice (55km northeast). Approaching the village from the north along the D915, turn left at the roundabout before the village centre and head uphill for 2.5km, following signs for 'Les Fontanettes'.

## Starting Point

Park in Les Fontanettes' car park, which services a trio of ski lifts at 1650m. The trail starts by the yellow 'Parking des Fontanettes' waymarker opposite the Télésiège de l'Eidelweiss (chairlift).

**01** Walk uphill along the gently inclined footpath through **pine forest and grassy ski pistes**, following signs for 'Refuge et Col de la Vanoise'. The first drag lift whisked winter skiers up the picturesque slopes here in 1937 and Pralognan-la-Vanoise has been an enchanting family ski resort ever since.

**02** After 650m the forest path emerges onto a gravel road. Cross it and follow the footpath back into the forest, past the yellow **'Dou de l'Ecu' waymarker** at 1770m. About 200m further, don't get confused when the path briefly crosses a mountain-bike track – simply continue uphill.

**03** Emerging from the forest onto another gravel road, turn right and follow it briefly. At the yellow 'GR55' marker, follow 'Col de la Vanoise' signs back into the woods, arriving about 20 minutes later beneath a chairlift. Continue uphill for another five to **Refuge des Barmettes** at 2000m.

**04** The trail continues up behind the *refuge*, winding right over a bridge to cross the crystal-clear **Torrent de la Glière**. Ahead, spellbinding views of the Massif de la Vanoise's mightiest peaks distract: the shark fin of **Aiguille de la Vanoise** (2797m) with its legendary north face and, to the left, the massif's highest peak Grande Casse (3855m).

**05** The path curves gently uphill between dry-stone walls. These beautifully crafted walls trace part of the historic Salt Road across **Plateau de la Glière**. Underfoot is rocky now. To the right (east) rises the flat stoney crown of **Le Moriond** (2298m).

**06** After passing the abandoned shepherds huts of **Chalets de la Glière** (2060m) the trail steepens. Waterfalls crash down the mountainside ahead. Tall wooden poles sticking out of the path-side scrub every few metres were planted in the 1830s to guide early alpinists up to the **Col de la Vanoise**; many poles conveniently remain.

**07** About 3.5km into the walk, the path steers closer to the banks of Torrent de la Glière. Cross the thundering glacial water using wooden footbridge **Pont de Canton** and continue up the rocky path towards Grande Casse and its glacier.

**08** **Lac des Vaches** (Lake of Cows) is cradled in an amphitheatre at 2318m and is stunning. Giant stone slabs (pictured) form a spectacular 210m-long walkway across the lake which, when shallow enough

## Route du Sel

The Col de la Vanoise has been a vital link between the high-altitude Maurienne and Tarentaise valleys since the Bronze Age.

The Romans used it to flit between Rome and Lyon, and in the 11th century the Dukes of Savoy travelled across it from Chambery to Turin.

In the 18th century mules laboured across the high mountain pass, carrying salt from the Royal Saltworks in nearby Moûtiers to Piedmont, Italy; they returned laden with spices and fabrics. Local Beaufort cheese, tanned leathers and mountain honey were likewise exchanged for potatoes, rice and corn on the strategic trade route.

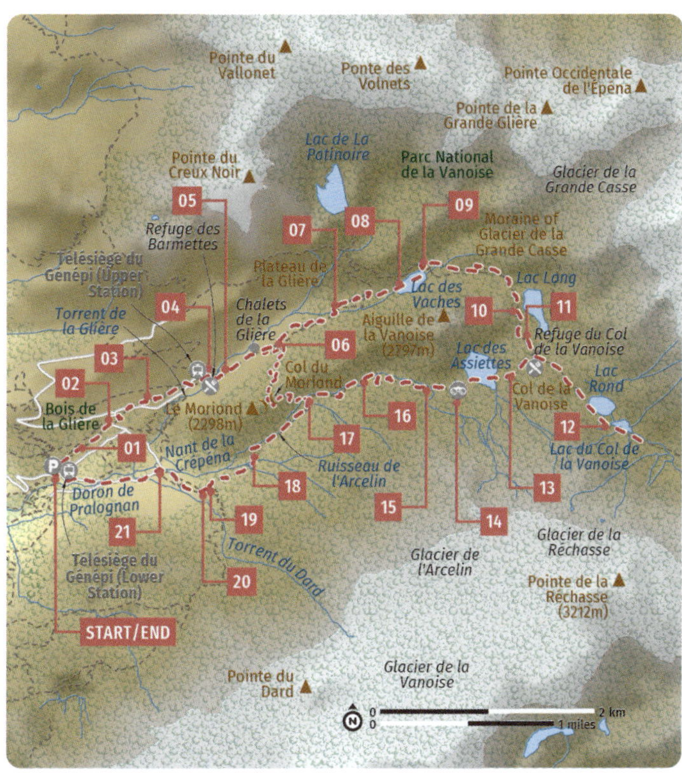

in August and September, doubles as boggy pasture for grazing Abondance cows.

**09** From the lake, a rubble path zigzags steeply up the slate-grey moraine of the **Glacier de la Grande Casse**. Specks of glacier-white quartz in the grey dirt glitter in the sun, and fuchsia-pink cornflowers and yellow star-shaped stonecrops add colour to the desolate grey landscape.

**10** Listen to the echoing voices of climbers dangling from the limestone crags of Aiguille de la Vanoise as you approach **Lac Long**, a lake right beneath the Glacier de la Grande Casse's icy tongue. You are now 6km into the walk.

**11** The footpath flattens as it heads towards the grassy plain of **Col de la Vanoise** (2516m), 700m from Lac Long. Walkers on the long-distance GR55 trail bask on the sun-drenched terrace of **Refuge du Col de la Vanoise**, a historic mountain hut from 1902 completely rebuilt with solar panels and other ecological frills in 2014. Views of Grand Casse's western face are awe-inspiring.

**12** Walk past the refuge on your right and follow the footpath for another kilometre across the flattish col and gently down through tufty alpine grass to bijou **Lac Rond** and, 200m further, **Lac du Col de la Vanoise**. Wedged between the mammoth peaks of Grand Caisse (left) and Pointe de la Réchasse (right), these two lakes are a sublime picnic spot.

DABOOST/SHUTTERSTOCK ©

**13** Return to the *refuge* and bear left (southwest), past the helipad behind the modern building, to pick up the return trail to **Lac des Assiettes**, a 15-minute walk. Bear right at the fork and descend across rocks and boulders down to the lake bowl – as dry as a bone in summer.

**14** Cross the flat-as-a-pancake bottom of the 'lake', admiring, on the right, huge views of **Aiguille de la Vanoise**'s southern face. Scale the bank to the other side to enjoy a new panorama of **Aiguille du Fruit** (3048m), **Petit Mont Blanc** (2680m) – named for its Mont Blanc–like rounded dome coloured white with gypsum – and other peaks.

**15** Follow the path gently downhill, enjoying dramatic views down the valley. Continue straight, crossing the summer-dry stream bed of the **Ruisseau de l'Arcelin**. Take it slow where the path scrambles across rocks.

**16** The path now closely follows the course of the Arcelin. Marmot whistles warn of your descent past the rocky **Aiguilles de l'Arcelin**.

**17** At the 11.8km mark the trail splits: right to **Col du Moriond** (30 minutes) and back to Refuge des Barmettes (one hour) along a family-friendly trail; or straight ahead via a more challenging descent only recommended on dry summer days. This walk tackles the latter.

## Parc National de la Vanoise

France's first national park, created in 1963, is a 529-sq-km protected zone packed with 100-plus peaks over 3000m in the Massif de la Vanoise. High-altitude glaciers, moraines and lichen-spattered rock rise above alpine meadows and spruce forests. Marmots, chamois and France's largest colony of bouquetins (alpine ibexes) – around 1800 – graze freely beneath larch trees and 125 bird species wheel overhead. Find information in situ at **Maison de la Vanoise** (pralognan.com).

**18** The path descends sharply, crossing the hillside to arrive on the rocky right bank of the **Nant de la Crépéna**. After five minutes or so, follow the trail over the wooden bridge to the left bank of the dramatic rock-creviced stream. In late summer it can be completely dry.

**19** Continue along the trail; yellow plaques emblazoned with a stubby arrow ensure you stay on track. A brief section between trees provides shade. Where the path splits, ignore the left-hand path signposted 'Col du Grand Marchais & Refuge de la Vallette' and continue downhill.

**20** At the national park sign the path forks again; bear left and continue downhill, don't miss the dramatic view of the **Torrent du Dard** waterfall gushing out of the rocky mountainside high above on the left.

**21** Arriving on a gravel road at the bottom of the **Cirque de l'Arcelin** (1720m), admire, to your right, the ice-blue river of **Nant de la Crépéna** thundering under a wooden-plank bridge. Don't cross it. Rather, head left along the gravel road for 15 minutes to the car park at **Les Fontanettes**.

## Take a Break

An enchanting wood-decking terrace with mountain views and love hearts carved in its wooden balustrade lend **Refuge des Barmettes** (☎04 79 08 75 64; lesbarmettes-refuge.com; Pralagnon-la-Vanoise; ⏱late Dec-Mar & Jun-Sep; 👥), atop the Génépi chairlift, instant sex appeal. Higher up, **Refuge du Col de la Vanoise** (☎04 79 08 25 23; refugecoldelavanoise. ffcam.fr; dm €25.50, mains €8-12; ⏱Mar-late Sep) serves salads, sweet and savoury crêpes, sandwiches to take away and irresistible blueberry tarts. Bookend stops at either address with shots of local génépi.

# Also Try...

HUANG ZHENG/SHUTTERSTOCK ©

## Tour du Mont Blanc

| DURATION | DIFFICULTY | DISTANCE |
|---|---|---|
| 10 days return | Moderate/hard | 170km |

Hands-down the most revered multiday walk in the French Alps, the TMB takes you right around – literally – western Europe's highest peak.

Beginning and ending in the Chamonix 'suburb' of Les Houches via drop-dead gorgeous trails in neighbouring Italy and Switzerland, the celebrated Tour du Mont Blanc is a 10-day loop encircling Mont Blanc. The classic 10-day, 170km-long, anticlockwise route involves 7km to 21km walking a day; many cut the trek into shorter multiday chunks and it is also possible to mix-and-match walking with public transport. The trail never climbs higher than 3000m in altitude, meaning walkers don't require special equipment – anyone with a decent fitness level can walk it (pictured above). Find maps, route suggestions, accommodation lists, trail conditions, bus/train and cable-car timetables and other useful information at autourdumontblanc.com.

## Aiguille de la Grande Sassière

| DURATION | DIFFICULTY | DISTANCE |
|---|---|---|
| 6hr return | Hard | 14km |

Hanging out with the birds at a heady 3747m, this high-altitude summit in the Réserve Naturelle de la Grande Sassière is an epic invitation to stand on top of the world.

Unlike other mountain peaks of similar heights in the French Alps, Aiguille de la Grande Sassière can be summited without setting foot on its glacier – making a steep walk up to its panoramic summit (elevation gain 1510m) accessible to anyone with a decent fitness level. The weather (strictly sunny bluebird days only) and the time of year (late-June to August) is also crucial. The memorable trail climbs from the car park on the shore of Lac du Saut, 25 minutes' drive from the big-name ski resorts of Tignes and Val d'Isère, through grassy alpine pastures and barren rocks, to the icy edge of the Sassière glacier and beyond.

HEMIS/ALAMY STOCK PHOTO ©

# The GR5

| DURATION | DIFF. | DISTANCE |
|---|---|---|
| 32-46 days one way | Hard | 650km |

Walkers eager to 'do' the French Alps should consider this legendary long-distance trail.

This GR5 or 'Grande Traversée des Alpes Françaises' (Great French Alps Crossing) crosses the Alps en route from Thonon-les-Bains or St-Gingolph on Lake Geneva's southern shore to Nice or Menton on the Med. It tackles peaks and passes up to 3000m, wild valleys and glaciers in Haute-Savoie, Savoie, Chamonix, Parc National de la Vanoise and south to Haute-Provence and beyond. Leave 20 days to walk to Briançon – in one trek or chunks of approximately 20km a day.

# Cirque du Fer-à-Cheval

| DURATION | DIFF. | DISTANCE |
|---|---|---|
| 3hr return | Easy | 9km |

Accessed from Sixt-Fer-à-Cheval in the Grand Massif ski area, this circular walk plunges walkers into an amphitheatre of limestone cliffs spring-loaded with shimmering waterfalls.

This classic trail leads families to Le Bout de Monde – 'the end of the world'. Highlights include a Himalayan bridge across the river (pictured above) and snow fields well into early summer. June is the best month to admire the spectacular waterfalls crashing 500m down from the cliffs into the valley below.

# Cirque des Évettes

| DURATION | DIFF. | DISTANCE |
|---|---|---|
| 6-7hr return | Hard | 9km |

Discovering one of France's most beautiful villages and the Alps' highest mountain-pass road are thrilling add-ons to this high-altitude loop in Parc National de la Vanoise.

A good one to tackle after Lac des Vaches & Col de la Vanoise (p82), this day walk (elevation 700m) begins near gorgeous Bonneval-sur-Arc (1850m) at the southern end of the world-famous Col de l'Iseran (2764m) road pass. It climbs from L'Écot up through gorges to the Reculaz waterfall and beyond to the glacial scape of Col des Évettes (2561m) with lake and *refuge*.

Châteauroux
Le Blanc
Argenton
La Châtre
A71
Moulins
N79
Digoin
Lussac-les-Chateaux
Chauffailes
Vienne
Creuse
A20
Montluçon
La Souterraine
Gouzon
N145
Vichy
Roanne
Guéret
Bellac
Aubusson
27
A71
Confolens
Pontaumur
Riom
Thiers
A89
St-Junien
Limoges
Parc Naturel Régional de Millevaches en Limousin
Puy de Dôme
(1465m)
Clermont-Ferrand
Courpière
Feurs
Eymoutiers
A89
Montbrison
21
A20
Châlus
Le Mont-Dore
Murol
22
Issoire
Ambert
St-Étienne
Parc Naturel Régional Périgord-Limousin
St-Yrieix-la-Perche
Ussel
28
Puy de Sancy
(1886m)
Ardes
Parc Naturel Régional du Livradois-Forez
Firminy
Thiviers
Égletons
Neuvic
Bort-les-Orgues
Lac Pavin
Brioude
La Chaise-Dieu
Uzerche
A89
Condat
Yssingeaux
Brantôme
Isle
Tulle
Mauriac
Riom-ès-Montagnes
Parc Naturel Régional des Volcans d'Auvergne
Massiac
Le Puy-en-Velay
Périgueux
Brive-la-Gaillarde
Dordogne
Argentat
A75
Moissac
Langeac
A89
23
Le Lardin-St-Lazare
Vézère
Plomb du Cantal
(1855m)
Murat
St-Flour
Sauges
Mt Mézenc
(1753m)
La Rogue St-Christophe
Sarlat-la-Canéda
Martel
Aurillac
St-Chely d'Apcher
26
Bergerac
Beynac
Souillac
St-Céré
Monbazillac
Dordogne
Castelnaud
Belvès
Domme
Rocamadour
Gramat
25
Marvejols
Mende
Mt Lozère
(1699m)
Monpazier
Figeac
Lot
Villeréal
Parc Naturel Régional Causses du Quercy
Sévérac-le-Château
Florac
Fumel
Vers
Lot
St-Cirq-Lapopie
Aveyron
Rodez
Lac Pareloup
A75
Alès
Villeneuve-sur-Lot
29
Cahors
24
Villefranche de Rouergue
Meyrueis
Mt Aigoual
(1567m)
Anduze
Agen
Caussade
Carmaux
Millau
Parc Naturel Régional des Grands Causses
Ganges
Valence
Moissac
A20
Garonne
Aveyron
Montauban
Albi
Lodève
Gignac
Hérault
Montpellier
Castelsarrasin
Gaillac
A68
Bedarieux
Clermont l'Herault
Beaumont-de-Lomagne
Tarn
St-Suplice
A62
Auch
Parc Naturel Régional du Haut-Languedoc
Pezenas
Frontignan
Sète
Toulouse
Castres
Mazamet
Béziers
A9
Agde
Mediterranean Sea
Muret
Revel
Ariège
Garonne
A61
Castelnaudary
50 km
25 miles

Basilique de St-Sauveur (p101), Rocamadour

# Central France

# Explore

# Central France

Central France – the Dordogne, Lot and Auvergne regions – is the heart and soul of la belle France with lands of dense oak forests, ancient volcanoes and chains of cinder cones, winding rivers, emerald-green fields, fairy-tale châteaux and picture-perfect villages. Walking through this area offers the quintessential French experience.

### Brantôme

Enchanting Brantôme's visual centrepiece is its impressive abbey sandwiched between a cliff face and a bend of the River Dronne. The town is a big tourist destination and has lots of places to stay and eat as well as good transport connections to other towns in the region.

### Sarlat-la-Canéda

The beautiful old-town heart of Sarlat-la-Canéda boasts some of the region's best-preserved medieval architecture and it makes an ideal base for walks 23 and 29. The start point for both of these walks is only around a 15-minute drive from Sarlat.

### Rocamadour

It's hard to resist a little gasp as Rocamadour first swings into view, its rooftops and shrines clamped dramatically to a plunging rock face of the Alzou Gorge. Most magical at sunset, the scene is topped by a dainty little 14th-century château on the overhanging clifftop above.

### St-Cirq-Lapopie

Magical St-Cirq-Lapopie is the sort of place people take one look at and decide they'd like to stay forever. While you might not be in a situation to do this, if you do walk 24 then you'll at least have to spend a day here. As a small and very popular place it can be hard to get accommodation here in summer: book well in advance.

### Murol

Bisected by a gargling river and enclosed by forests, the stone village of Murol slows the pulse. There are a few two-star hotels and campgrounds near Lac Chambon, while Murol village has several B&Bs and *gîtes* (self-catering accommodation), which must be booked ahead.

### Le Puy-en-Velay

With two volcanic pillars looming craggily above its rooftops, it would be impossible to mistake Le Puy-en-Velay for anywhere else in France. Topped with a 10th-century church and a vermillion statue of the Virgin Mary, these stone pinnacles tower hundreds of feet high, like two sacred rockets in the middle of blast-off.

There's a good choice of accommodation in all price ranges as well as *gîtes* and *chambres d'hôte* (B&Bs) in the surrounding countryside.

### Le Mont-Dore

The Auvergne's most elegant mountain resort has a glint of 19th-century glamour among its fondue restaurants and gear-hire shops. Nestled in a narrow valley 42km southwest of Clermont-Ferrand, and 4km north of Puy de Sancy (1886m), the town originally rose to prominence as a spa resort. Today it's an ideal base for walkers taking on the nearby trails.

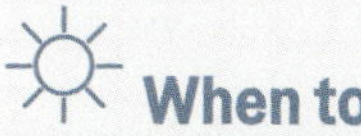

## When to Go

The Dordogne and Lot regions have a gentle climate that's rarely too hot and only truly cold for a few short weeks in midwinter. This means that you can hike in this area at pretty much anytime of the year. But winter and spring can see a lot of rainfall and many hotels and guesthouses close.

In summer the sheer popularity of the region can be an issue. Accommodation can be hard to come by and honeypot villages such as Brantôme and St-Cirq-Lapopie can be unpleasantly busy. May and June are great times to hike here, but the best period by far is September and early October. Time it right and you can get idyllic temperatures, blue skies and an autumnal colour show in the extensive chestnut and oak woodlands.

The Massif Central has a much more extreme climate and winters at altitude are cold indeed, with snowfall common. Avoid hiking here from late October to the end of April. Spring can be wet one year, perfect the next. The ideal period is May through to September.

## Where to Stay

Central France offers a full range of places to stay from historic châteaux to farmhouse bed and breakfasts, camping grounds and many holiday-home rentals. Wherever you stay, it is usually essential to book ahead in July and August. From November to April much closes down, but what stays open is often great value.

## What's On

**La Ringueta** (ringueta-sarlat.fr) Traditional sports and games of the region held in Sarlat over the Whit-Sunday weekend of even-numbered years.

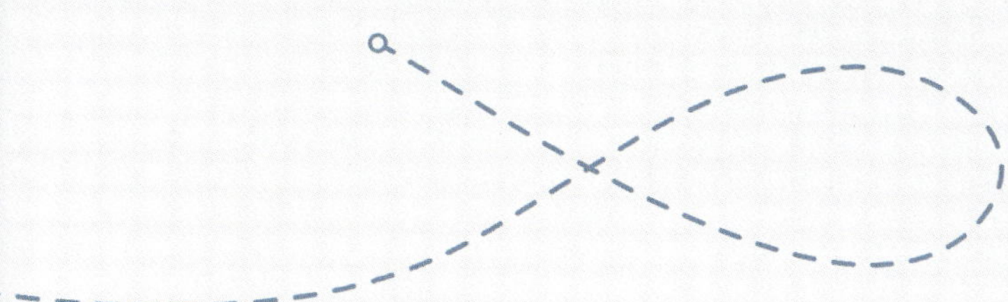

## Resources

**Auvergne** (auvergne-destination-volcans.com) Tourist-board site that covers the Massif Central.

**Dordogne** (dordogne-perigord-tourisme.fr) Tourist-office website that includes walking route suggestions.

**The Lot** (tourisme-lot.com) The official tourist-board website has plenty of walking suggestions.

**Festival des Jeux du Théâtre** (festival-theatre-sarlat.com; ⏱mid-Jul–early Aug) Held in Sarlat, this is one of the most important theatre festivals in France.

**Semaine Mariale** (⏱early Sep) Held in Rocamadour, this week-long religious festival is dedicated to the Virgin and includes pilgrimages and a torchlit procession.

**Rassemblement Européen de Montgolfières** Major hot-air balloon festival held in Rocamadour on the third weekend in September.

## Transport

Bergerac, Limoges and Brive-la-Gaillarde have domestic and international flights. Bordeaux and Toulouse are also nearby hubs. Local train service in the region is limited. This, coupled with limited bus service keyed to school timetables, makes much of rural Central France a good place to hire a car.

# 21

# Brantôme Circuit

| DURATION | DIFFICULTY | DISTANCE | START/END |
|---|---|---|---|
| 3hr return | Easy | 10km | Brantôme Abbey |

| TERRAIN | Road, walking trail |
|---|---|

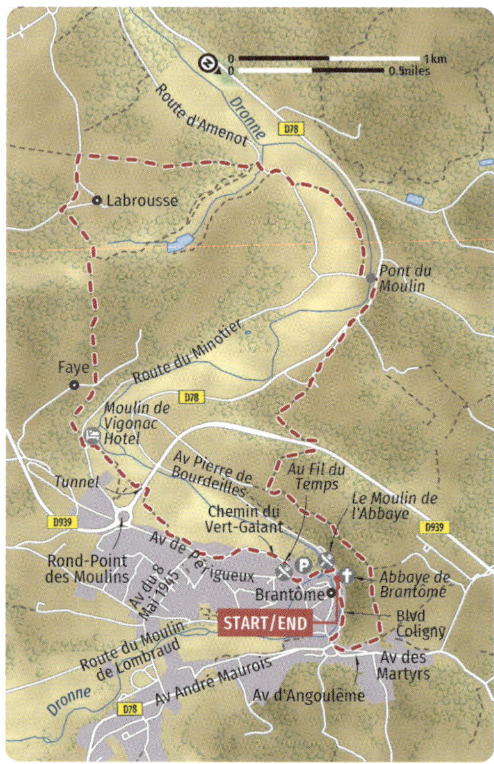


Built on a great bend of the River Dronne and overlooked by an enormous abbey, Brantôme is one of the most alluring towns in the Dordogne. This walk takes in the abbey as well as the patch-work of fields, woodlands and farming hamlets that surround the town.

With your back facing the **abbey** turn right and cross the **stone bridge** next to the Michelin-starred restaurant, **Le Moulin de l'Abbaye**, a much-photographed riverside delight. Cross through the park and right onto **chemin du Vert-Galant**. Just before the traffic lights, turn right down a track. After five minutes go through a tunnel under the D939 road. On the other side turn left and then immediately right. Walk past the **Moulin de Vigonac hotel**. Turn right by the stop sign and then left onto a walking trail through woodland.

Climb uphill to the village of **Faye** and then straight ahead on a forest trail. On reaching a road at the entrance to the village of **Labrousse**, turn right and go uphill.

Fifty metres after the last house, turn right and stroll across the fields into **oak woodlands**. Turn right along a quiet road and after 100m take the trail leading off left across **fields**. At another small road, turn left and cross the **metalled Pont du Moulin**. At the main road, turn right and after 200m you will see two roads turning off left. Take the **second road**. At the junction continue straight ahead down a track. At the fork go right and cross the D939 road via a **bridge**. Go left at the junction and walk for 15 minutes through a mix of woodland and farmland. At a meeting of junctions go right and then right again at the **T-junction** and re-enter Brantôme.

Best for
PRETTY
VILLAGES

# 22

# Lac Chambon & Murol Circuit

| DURATION | DIFFICULTY | DISTANCE | START/END |
|----------|-----------|----------|-----------|
| 2hr return | Easy | 8km | Tourist office, Lac Chambon |

| TERRAIN | Level boardwalks and paved uphills |
|---------|-------------------------------------|

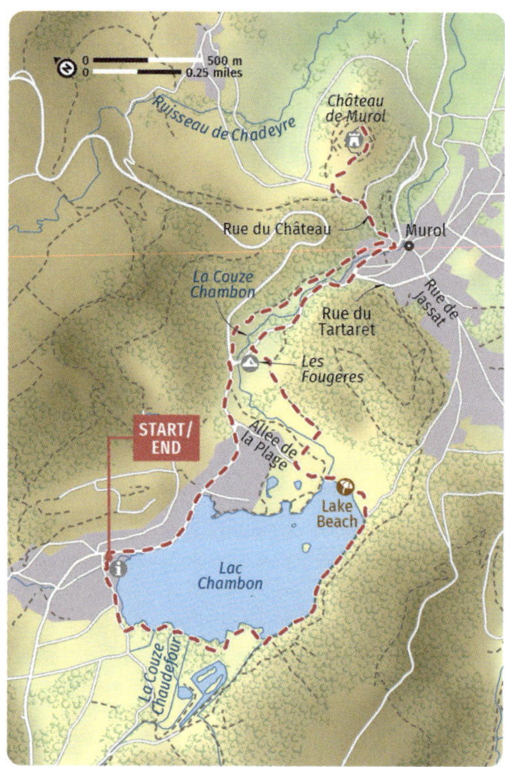


Admire a hilly panorama from Château de Murol, then meander along tranquil lake shores. This family-friendly walk (min/max altitude 876/1050m) unites quaint streets, watery views and medieval ramparts that kids will love to clamber.

From the tourist office car park, turn left and stroll along Lac Chambon's north shore, heading east towards the village of Murol. To your right is the glass-still **crater lake** (altitude 876m). To the left, holiday homes and restaurants snooze by the water. At the second roundabout, follow tree-shaded rue de Levat along the north bank of the river. Continue for 15 minutes, past stone houses lining the babbling **Couze Chambon**.

Take a left uphill along rue du Château, weaving through beech forest to **Château de Murol**. A sweeping panorama of the Auvergne's volcano-sculpted terrain is the reward for the final ascent.

These 12th-century ramparts overlook the town from a basalt perch. Give your calf muscles a rest by staying awhile to tour the castle. Château de Murol (pictured) hosts glinting medieval weaponry and audiovisual displays to entrance the kids.

Descend from the castle, your head swirling with images of sparring knights. This time, at the foot of the hill take rue d'Estaing west through the village. Turn left into **Les Fougères** campground and continue south to the shore of Lac Chambon. Join the lakeside trail clockwise around Lac Chambon; **wooden boardwalks** guide your way. In winter, the shore is fringed with frost – watch your step on the slippery planks!

As you ramble the eastern shore, look across the water to see the **Massif de Sancy**, whose peaks are dusted with snow well into spring. Along Lac Chambon's pike-filled waters, signposts point back to the car park. A playground and summer kayak rental might prolong your stay.

# Beynac Castle Loop

| DURATION | DIFFICULTY | DISTANCE | START/END |
|---|---|---|---|
| 3½hr return | Easy | 10km | Beynac |

| TERRAIN | Road, farm track, walking trail |
|---|---|

Fairy tales come true along the banks of slow-flowing rivers in Central France. Hoisted atop a beach-yellow cliff and with a honeycomb of wobbly medieval houses at its feet, the Château de Beynac is straight from a Hans Christian Anderson story. And this walk (suitable for families) will take you through dense wood where the big bad wolf once lived and down trails where knights in armour might once have searched for dragons to slay, before finally arriving at the old gates of this magical village and castle.

## Getting Here

Beynac is 12km southwest of Sarlat; there is no public transport. Various parking lots cost €3.50 per day April to October, but are free out of season.

## Starting Point

The walk begins from the riverfront at the bottom of the village. There are plenty of parking areas here, but in summer it's still hard to find a space.

**01** Go up the main village street, **rue de la Balme**. Take the first narrow, **cobbled road** on the left. Go through the wooden barrier and into the woods.

**02** When you reach a quiet road turn right. The road turns into a dirt track and loops left past a clutch of **stone houses**. Keep going straight.

**03** After 35 minutes, you'll come to a road junction. Go left. Shortly afterwards, you'll see some walking signposts. The main route continues straight ahead, but turn right and walk 150m over the field to a fine view over Beynac castle. Return back to the main trail and carry on straight (northeast) past a horse-riding centre.

## Château de Beynac

The 12th-century **Château de Beynac** (chateau-beynac.com; Beynac-et-Cazenac) towers gloriously above the village (pictured).

The views from its battlements are a big draw and the interior retains a sparse, medieval feel with decor limited to carved fireplaces, wooden coffer-trunks and the odd tapestry.

OSTILL IS FRANCK CAMHI/SHUTTERSTOCK ©

**04** Immediately after is a road junction. Yellow walk arrows tell you to turn right and double back on yourself. Ignore these and instead carry on straight for another 200m to another junction. Go sharp right here and descend down a **quiet country lane**. You will soon pass a row of houses. At the road junction go right. After about 350m take the small country road veering off left. There's a yellow walk sign.

**05** Turn right when you hit a bigger track and walk through some lovely woodland.

**06** Go right when you hit the road again and pass a mill with donkeys and peacocks in a field beside it. A moment later the **Château de Beynac** makes a dramatic appearance on the cliffs ahead. Continue uphill.

**07** At the junction, go right and then right again at the fork. As you reach the houses go left down a grassy track. When the road bends left and goes downhill, take the walking trail leading off to the right through woodland.

**08** Go left on reaching the road and then right at the junction. A moment later the castle will reappear, this time towering above the village houses right in front of you. Walk past the **cemetery** and through the old town gates. Fork right and you'll come to the **castle entrance**. Allow a couple of hours for a visit. Afterwards drop steeply down through the pretty village until you get back to the river. Walk a short way along the river past the campsite for postcard-worthy views.

## Take a Break

**La Petite Tonelle** (📞 05 53 29 95 18; la-petite-tonnelle.fr; menus €20-45; ⏱ noon-2.30pm & 7-9.30pm Fri-Tue) serves an array of seasonal, local specialities (truffles, duck, lamb).

# 24

# The Chemin de Halage

| DURATION | DIFFICULTY | DISTANCE | START/END |
|---|---|---|---|
| 4hr return | Easy | 16km | Parking de la Plage |

| TERRAIN | | Road, farm track, walking trail |
|---|---|---|

Teetering at the crest of a sheer cliff, high above the River Lot, St-Cirq-Lapopie is a beautiful braid of terracotta-roofed houses and vertiginous streets that's rightly known as one of the most beautiful villages in France. This walk gives you a variety of different views of the village, takes in a memorable boat towpath carved into a leering cliff face and rambles through extensive oak forests before finishing up back in the enchanted village of St-Cirq-Lapopie.

## Getting Here

St-Cirq-Lapopie is 25km east of Cahors and 44km southwest of Figeac. There are irregular buses from Cahors and Figeac.

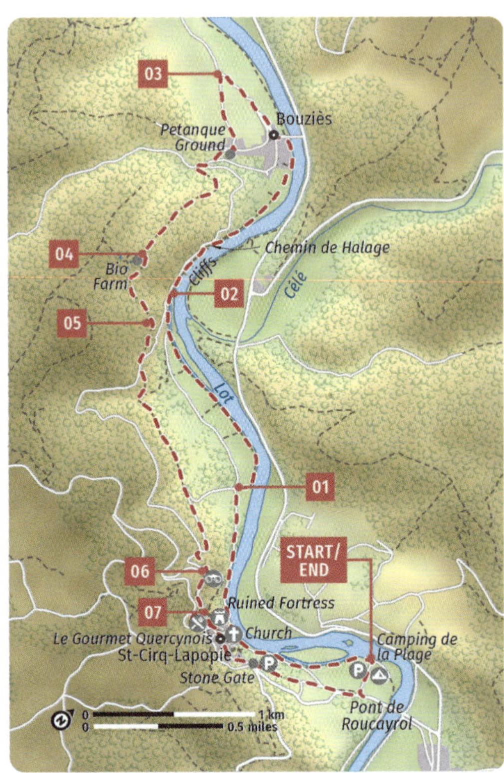


## Starting Point

The walk begins from the Parking de la Plage, next to the Camping de la Plage and just east and downhill of St-Cirq-Lapopie. There are no facilities.

**01** Follow the footpath along the River Lot in a downstream direction. The trail merges onto a country lane. The views of St-Cirq-Lapopie up ahead will put a wow in your step. After a good 40 minutes swerve right off the road and onto a **walking trail**, following signs for the Chemin de Halage. After 20 minutes the enjoyably easy riverside trail leads to the point where the sheer cliff face stands straight up against the river.

**02** An amazing engineering feat, the **Chemin de Halage** (pictured) is a footpath carved into the side of the cliff face like a half-tunnel. After 300m pass an iron **train bridge** and a few minutes later enter the village of **Bouziès**. Continue along the river up to another iron bridge.

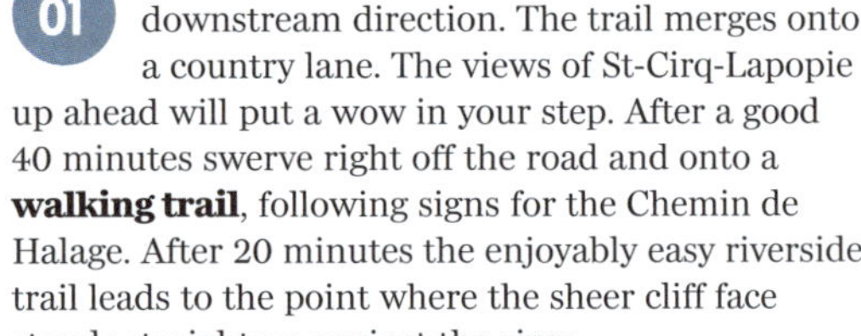

SCULPTOR: DANIEL MONNIER; STUART BUTLER/LONELY PLANET ©



**03** At the walk signs, turn left and head up to the main village road. Turn right and then at the fork go left and then left again. When you come to the stone cross bend left. Fifty metres later, in front of the **petanque ground**, turn right and then right again following the route to **Combe de Bouziès**. One hundred metres on, turn left sharply and, following yellow waymarkers, embark on a 20-minute haul uphill.

**04** Just before the **bio farm**, take the footpath that leads off left. Pass through three gates.

**05** After the final gate follow the footpath through oak forest. After 15 minutes cross a road and back onto the footpath, which continues its woodland descent.

**06** On reaching a **small road**, follow it uphill and after five minutes take the walking trail that leads off left. A moment later, you will pass the first of the St-Cirq-Lapopie car parks. At the far end of the car park is a **viewpoint**.

**07** Take the signed walkway next to the car park and a water tower. Follow this down to another set of car parks, turn left and drop down into **St-Cirq-Lapopie**. Climb up the crumbling **fortress walls** for aerial views. Go past the **church** and follow the road downhill right through the village before exiting through a stone gate. Keep going straight and start a slow drop to the river, and back to the car park.

## Take a Break

**Le Gourmet Quercynois** (☏ 05 65 31 21 20; restaurant-legourmetquercynois. com; rue de la Peyrolerie; lunch/dinner from €14/23; ⏰ noon-1.30pm & 7-9pm mid-Feb–Dec) serves well-prepared local classics. The village of Bouziès has a few snack bars. There are also riverside picnic tables here.

# 25

# Pilgrimage Around Rocamadour

| DURATION | DIFFICULTY | DISTANCE | START/END |
|---|---|---|---|
| 3¾hr return | Moderate | 12km | Le Château car park, Rocamadour |

| TERRAIN | Road, farm track, walking trail |
|---|---|

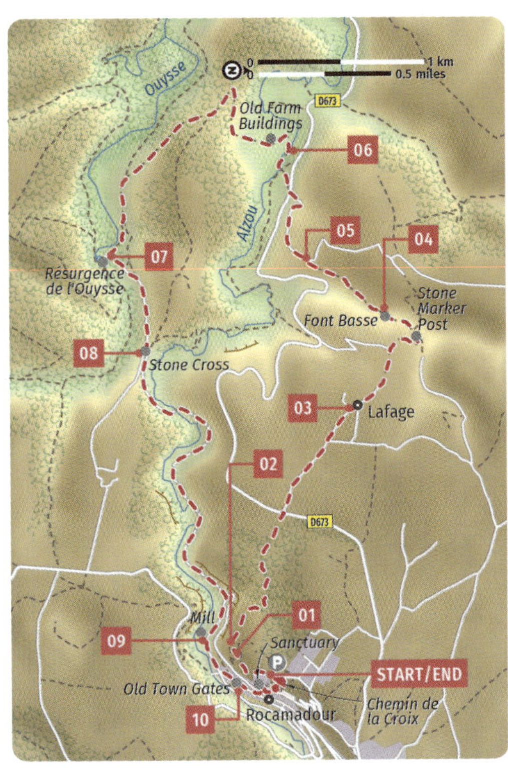



This walk, up and along canyon ridges and across farmland, follows in the footsteps of medieval pilgrims bound for the cliff-side village of Rocamadour. Today, Rocamadour sits precariously on the very edge of sheer cliff walls and is one of the biggest tourist draws in Central France, but by walking this circuit around the village you can escape the crowds and recreate the sense of awed wonder that must have swept over pilgrims when they first sighted the village.

## Getting Here

Rocamadour-Padirac train station on the Figeac–Brive line is 5km northeast. By car, Rocamadour is 59km north of Cahors, 51km east of Sarlat.

## Starting Point

The walk starts from the P2/Le Château car park, which is the uppermost car park.

**01** Take the track heading south between dry-stone walls. Pass an old electrical transformer building and 50m later veer left off-trail onto a **narrow track** that goes downhill.

**02** Go right at the fork and through a wire gate. Tiptoe along the lip of a **gorge** and into woodland. Go through another wire gate.

**03** Twenty minutes from the start, cross a road and walk past vineyards towards **Lafage** village. Walk straight through, past a *chambre d'hôte* (B&B), and the tar road fades into a dirt road.

**04** At the walking signs, go downhill towards Combe des Fontaines. Two hundred metres later turn left at the **old stone marker post**. Continue straight ahead at the next stone

Best for

ESCAPING THE CROWDS

JUANJE PEREZ PHOTOGRAPHY/SHUTTERSTOCK ©

marker post. Shortly after you'll pass a water source, **Font Basse**.

**05** An hour from the start you'll reach a country lane. Follow the indistinct trail on the left through scrubby grass. It runs parallel to the road. The trail wends around the weathered canyon slope until it reaches a bigger road. Turn right and walk 30m before dropping left onto a minor walking track heading southwest.

**06** Cross the normally dry **Alzou** riverbed and follow a farm track steeply uphill for 10 minutes. After the path levels out, go right at the fork and then left at the meeting of farm tracks.

**07** A few minutes later, take the small trail that drops towards the river. The waters here form an enchanted natural pool known as the **Résurgence de l'Ouysse**.

**08** Follow a tarmac road away from the river and then turn right a moment later where roads meet. You're now following red and white GR trail signs. At the trail junction on the crest of the hill go left past the **stone cross**. The road drops down to the canyon floor and crosses a **bridge**.

**09** Forty-five minutes from the stone cross, turn right and walk down the tarmac road back into Rocama-

dour. Pass an old, towered **mill** and take the small cobbled road going diagonally uphill past an ivy-covered house.

**10** Stroll through the **old town gates**, then left up the steps to the Sanctuary (pictured p89). Walk through the tunnel and then follow the winding **Chemin de la Croix** (Stations of the Cross) up to the ramparts and back to the car.

## Take a Break

There are plenty of places to eat in Rocamadour, but none of them are very memorable. The Résurgence de l'Ouysse makes a delightful picnic spot.

# 26

# Stevenson's Journey

| DURATION | DIFFICULTY | DISTANCE | START/END |
|---|---|---|---|
| 7hr one way | Moderate | 19km | Le Puy-en-Velay/ Le Monastier-sur-Gazeille |

| TERRAIN | Road and meadows, hilly in places |
|---|---|

Experience a journey infused with literary history. *Treasure Island* author Robert Louis Stevenson immortalised his 12-day solo hike in *Travels with a Donkey in the Cévennes* (1879) and this walk (min/max elevation 645/952m) links two way stations of his journey. Experience a glimpse of the Scottish writer's travels on this day walk or use it as a springboard for the full route.

## Getting Here

Le Puy-en-Velay is linked to Clermont-Ferrand by SNCF bus and train (2½ hours). From Lyon or Paris, travel via St-Étienne. The hike is one way: prearrange onward transport, or a lift back to Le Puy, with La Malle Postale (lamallepostale.com).

## Starting Point

Begin in Le Puy-en-Velay, the striking town of volcanic plumes and sacred chapels where Stevenson stayed ahead of his hike through the countryside, accompanied by his cantankerous donkey, Modestine.

**01** From **place de la Mairie**, follow rue Chaussade east, then rue Crozatier south, turn left and cross the main road. Turn right along av Georges Clemenceau and, after about 180m, cross the junction and continue along rue Farigoule. Then, turn right and follow the av d'Ours Mons.

**02** At the Centre Nautique, turn right and follow the GR430 as it cuts into meadows, before rejoining chemin de Bel Air. After crossing rte du Couderc, the route snakes into a field. Continue along chemin du Vallon, a sleepy tree-shaded road flanked on either side by farmland.

## Chemin de Stevenson

For adventurous hikers, the full Chemin de Stevenson (Stevenson Trail; GR70) continues from Le Monastier-sur-Gazeille, first to the village of Goudet – see chemin-stevenson.org. The full route between Le Puy-en-Velay and Alès spans 272km of rugged hills, sweeping heathland and remote villages. Highlights of the full trek are the crater lake of Le Bouchet-St-Nicolas, attractive Pradelles and the lost-in-time village Le Pont-de-Montvert.

The author took 12 days to make this journey, but allow two full weeks to do this route justice. It is still possible to hire a donkey, just as Stevenson did, but most travellers go without an animal companion or tackle the route by mountain bike (be warned, it's a bumpy ride!).

**Best for**

**EXPLORING HISTORY**

PHILIPPE DESMAZES/AFP VIA GETTY IMAGES ©

**03** Take the pedestrian crossing over the N88. When across, the path dips south. Follow it through the meadows for around 2km. A right turn leads you on to chemin de Lachamp, after which another right-hand bend directs you west.

**04** Turn left at the T-junction at **chemin de Chaubon**, where the path leads downhill. You'll see a spectacular unfurling of velvety green scenery.

**05** After around 1.5km you'll cross the River Loire and stride into **Coubon**. This sleepy village has 10 centuries of history and a brick church with three crowning bells — you'll see it on the road to the right as you cross the bridge.

**06** Leave Coubon by walking south along rte Dempeyre. Go right following rte de l'Olme, a narrow ribbon of pitted tarmac lined by trees. After 1.5km you'll walk through a cluster of houses where you'll turn left, taking you southeast.

**07** After 4.5km, you'll reach pleasantly secluded **L'Herm**. GR430 signs guide you south and then east through a French pastoral fantasy with sweeping views of distant evergreens.

**08** A final 2km leads to **Le Monastier-sur-Gazeille**. Arriving here in 1878, Stevenson marvelled at the beauty of the setting, comparing it to his native Scottish high-lands. Look for the plaque at Chez Morel (now a pharmacy) commemorating his time in this quaint stone village.

## Take a Break

**Le Ré Bémol** ( 04 71 03 87 16; 39 rue St-Jean, Le Monastier-sur-Gazeille; mains from €12) has gregarious staff, and regulars tuck in to tartines, meaty daily specials and regional wines. A few simple, clean guest rooms ensure there's only a few steps between dinner and bed, if you wish to linger in Le Monastier.

# 27

# Climbing Puy de Dôme

| DURATION | DIFFICULTY | DISTANCE | START/END |
|---|---|---|---|
| 2½–3½hr return | Moderate | 4.9km | Panoramique des Dômes lower station |

| TERRAIN | Gravel, ungroomed meadows, occasional wooden steps |
|---|---|

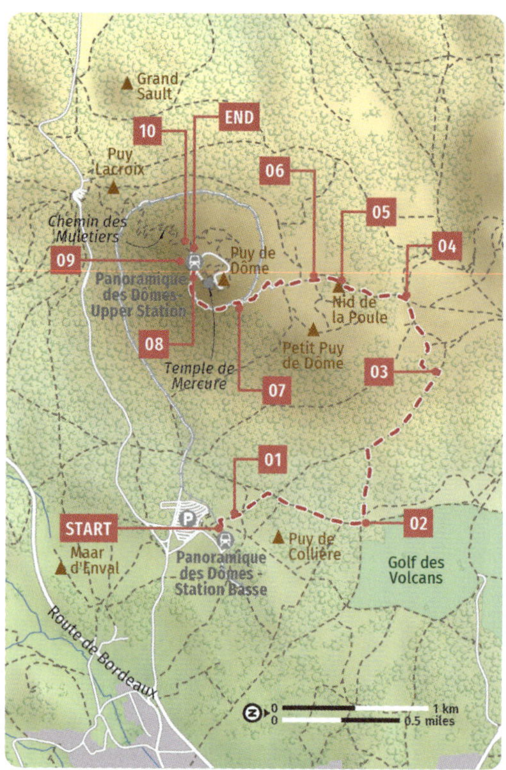


Trek to the top of Puy de Dôme, an ancient lava dome in the Auvergne. The Chemin des Chèvres (Chèvres Trail, min/max altitude 904/1465m) bestows mesmerising views from the peak's north face: a panorama of meadows, valleys and slumbering volcanoes.

## Getting Here

The foot of Puy de Dôme is 9km west of Clermont-Ferrand. Car or taxi is easiest but, in July, August and during French school holidays, a twice-daily shuttle bus links the train station to Puy de Dôme. A scenic cog railway, the Panoramique des Dômes, rattles to the summit – even though you're walking to the top, you can ride the rails back down!

## Starting Point

At Panoramique des Dômes lower station visitor centre, you can get walking advice, buy snacks and (for convenience) purchase your return train ticket in advance.

**01** Outside the **Panoramique des Dômes lower station**, set out towards the mountain. Get directions from inside the station if you're unsure – signposting is scant at first, other than yellow markings on some trees. Where the trail divides, go right (signed 'Sommet Puy de Dôme').

**02** After around 20 minutes of walking through silver birch trees, the path curves left and slightly uphill. Keep following the yellow dots as it rises up the flank of Puy de Dôme.

**03** Around 45 minutes in, the path gets more exposed, affording views across the ashy peaks. After a **wooden hut** and rough stone marker, the trail veers left through a stately birch grove.

LUCENTIUS/GETTY IMAGES ©

**04** Take the wooden stair-well, which appears through the forest as if by magic! Follow signs for Circuit Boucle des Dômes, along a trail with brick-red soil.

**05** Beyond the trees it gets blustery, but it's a painterly scene: in winter the charcoal-coloured path contrasts with snow; in summer you'll see wildflowers beneath a blazing blue sky.

**06** Around 1¼ hours in, follow another set of wooden stairs. Take time to marvel at the volcanic peaks behind you. Higher up is a **lookout point**; on clear days you can see Clermont-Ferrand's twin-spired cathedral.

**07** The path curves uphill, following the rail track. You're only a few minutes' walk from the summit.

**08** When the train station is in view, take the right-hand path for a quick detour to the **Temple de Mercure**, a mysterious Gallo-Roman ruin.

**09** Continue in the direction of the train station – you've made it! Time to gaze out at volcanic cones.

**10** You can retrace your steps or tackle the alternative path – its name, Chemin des Muletiers (the Mule Track), is a good descriptor. But descending via the **Panoramique des Dômes train** is infinitely more relaxing. Sit on the right-hand side for views of the pine-furred panorama.

## ☕ Take a Break

There's a canteen at the foot of Puy de Dôme and a restaurant up top, but the richest culinary rewards are in Clermont-Ferrand. The town has an abundance of restaurants serving rich *cuisine auvergnate*. In Clermont's old town **L'AOC** (☎ 04 73 19 12 12; restaurant -aoc-clermont.fr; 4 rue des Petits Gras; mains from €10/14; ⏱ noon-2pm & 7.30-10pm Mon, Tue & Thu-Sat) chalks up a daily menu of prized produce.

# 28

# Ascent to Puy de Sancy

| DURATION | DIFFICULTY | DISTANCE | START/END |
|---|---|---|---|
| 3½hr return | Moderate | 7km | Station de Mont-Dore car park |

| TERRAIN | Grassy uphills, wooden stairs |
|---|---|

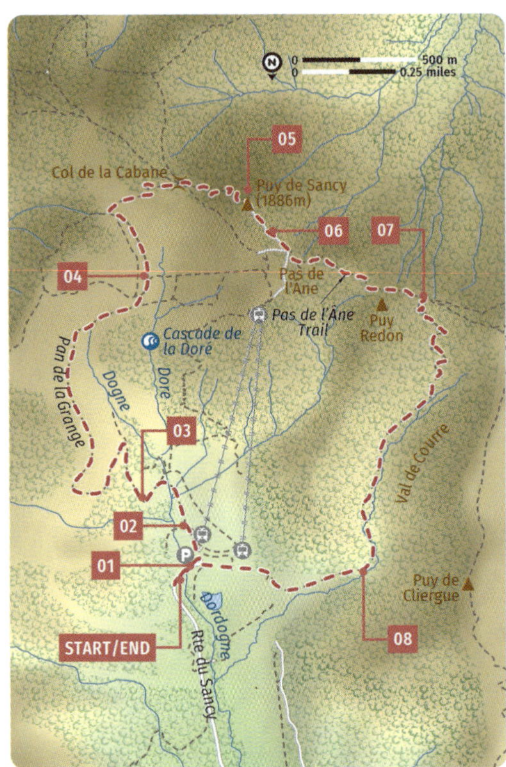


From the peak of Puy de Sancy, gaze at saw-toothed mountains, glacier-scoured plains, and valleys where wild goats scamper. Journeying to the top of this ancient stratovolcano (min/max altitude 1329/1886m) reveals sublime views of the Auvergne. A popular trail wends clockwise around the mountain, darting up wooden stairs to dizzy heights before threading the scenic Val de Courre back down.

## Getting Here

By public transport, reach Le Mont-Dore by daily direct SNCF buses from Clermont-Ferrand (€15.20, 1½ hours). Station de Mont-Dore is 3km south of Le Mont-Dore town – take a shuttle bus.

## Starting Point

The walk begins from Station de Mont-Dore's car park, which fills early in high summer.

**01** From the roundabout on rte du Sancy, take the left-hand road to the short tunnel beneath the ski slope. Follow the trail as it curves to the right, past a few piste-side businesses.

**02** Follow the trail uphill. At the top of the ski lift, the path snakes to the left and you'll soon see a sign for **Pan de la Grange** (a blue run for boarders and skiers in winter). Look out for cyclists who hurtle down the mountain in summer!

**03** Take a right-hand turn to follow the GR4E trail along **Col de la Cabane**. From the flanks of the mountain you might spy **Salers cattle**, prized for their gamey meat.

WÜTHRICH DIDIER/SHUTTERSTOCK ©

**04** After half an hour of verdant trails you reach an altitude of 1775m, where **wooden steps** lead to the 1886m summit (pictured). Ignore the cable-car arrival platform – arriving on foot is far more gratifying!

**05** It takes about 30 minutes to walk up all 864 wooden steps, and the reward is a **view** of four valleys, rolling hills and the Limagne and Cézallier plateaux. If you have binoculars, this is a prime vantage point to see **wildlife**. You could see chamois (goat-antelopes) scrambling between distant ridges or marmots popping their heads up.

**06** With a spring in your step from the mind-blowing panorama, descend the wooden stairs. This time head northwest to embark on the **Pas de l'Âne trail**, just above the upper cable-car station (follow the GR30 signs).

**07** Scramble the ridge to reach the **Puy Redon pass**, the only tough section of the route. A path leads right down a series of switchbacks along the **Val de Courre** (Courre Valley).

**08** When the ground begins to level out, turn right towards the car park at the foot of the Sancy ski lifts.

Head back to the roundabout or wait for a shuttle bus to whisk you back to Le Mont-Dore for a slap-up meal.

## Take a Break

Gorge yourself on *cuisine auvergnate* at **La Golmotte** (☎ 04 73 65 05 77; aubergelagolmotte.com; rte D996, Le Barbier; s/d incl breakfast €52/65; menus €20-40; ⏱ noon-1.30pm Thu-Mon, 7-8.30pm Thu-Sat & Mon; 🚻), a rustic inn roughly 3km along the road from Le Mont-Dore to Lac de Guéry. All the regional favourites can be found here. And there are modest, good-value rooms to stay the night.

# 29

# Castles of the Dordogne

| DURATION | DIFFICULTY | DISTANCE | START/END |
|---|---|---|---|
| 5½hr return | Moderate | 18km | Castelnaud-la-Chapelle |

| TERRAIN | | Road, farm track, footpath |
|---|---|---|

This epic walk pieces together bits of many different shorter walks to create a long but exhilarating and scenically varied circular hike. It takes in some of the most famed tourist spots in the Dordogne and links them together with quiet riverside walks and ambles through oak and chestnut woodlands. There's one very short section along a busy road but otherwise it's country lanes and footpaths all the way. It's probably a bit long to be considered a family walk but otherwise it's a real classic.

## Getting Here

Castelnaud-la-Chapelle is 15km south of Sarlat; there is no public transport. Various car parks cost €3.50.

## Starting Point

The walk begins from the **Parking Tournepique** at the bottom of Castelnaud-la-Chapelle close to the bridge over the River Dordogne. In summer, though, you'll be lucky to actually get a parking space there.

**01** From the car park, turn your back to the village (a hard thing to do to such a beautiful spot) and walk over the bridge spanning the **River Dordogne**. Go past a couple of buildings on your right and one on your left. Take the **farm track** that veers off the right-hand side of the road and wanders off over the fields.

You will pass a small **waterworks** building after 200m. The cliffs of La Roque-Gageac are visible ahead. Ignore any side trails and just keep going northeast.

SIMON RIGAP/SHUTTERSTOCK ©

**02** As you draw closer to La Roque-Gageac, the River Dordogne will cosy up beside you on the right. When you reach the **campsite** entrance, turn right down to the river and follow the riverside footpath around the edge of the campsite to emerge on the D703 road. By the zebra crossing take the path going uphill to the left. There's a sign for the **Manoir de la Malartrie hotel**. There are stupendous **views** of the cliff-side village and the river from this path.

**03** You'll come to a parking area and some walk signs. Don't drop down to the river but instead carry on straight ahead and climb up towards the upper part of the village. With its honeystone houses suckled up against a multicoloured cliff face in a manner more like an organic creature than a constructed village, it's hardly a surprise to learn that **La Roque-Gageac** is considered one of the loveliest villages in France. Halfway through the village, veer up the metalled steps leading up the cliff face to visit the **Troglodyte Fort**.

**04** Go through the **gateway** and take the narrow cliffside path on the left that runs east almost at the upper level of the village houses. Follow yellow waymarkers to the **Gageac quarter**. After five minutes turn left at the fork by the **ivy-covered building**. The path turns into a trail through leafy **oak and chestnut forest**. At the signed trail junction, turn right and head downhill. After a couple more minutes turn left on reaching the small road and go along the footpath leading back into the woodland.

**05** A short but steep climb follows. Go straight over at the road. Eventually, the path levels out and runs through attractive mossy woodland. Turn right when you hit



## Château de Castelnaud

The massive ramparts and metre-thick walls of the quintessential medieval fortress of Castelnaud (castelnaud.com; adult/child €12.90/6.50) rise through the trees above the hamlet (pictured). Climb narrow stairways to a superb series of rooms displaying a fine collection of ancient weaponry. There are fantastic views from the keep's upper terrace, encompassing the Dordogne bend and Castelnaud's arch-rival, the Château de Beynac (p97), 4km to the north.

Check the website for timetables of demonstrations and family activities. Evening mystery-game tours led by costumed actors are staged four days a week mid-July to August (pre-book online).

the dirt road, which turns into a surfaced road. There are a couple of signed walk trails leading off the road. Ignore all these and stick to the road as it makes a U-shaped bend and then heads downhill. Keep going straight ahead. After passing a couple of **farms** and big houses, you will see a distant village perched on a cliff ledge ahead (this is the village of **Domme**).

**06** Turn right when you meet the main D46 road and follow it down to and over the **bridge** that crosses the River Dordogne. This is a busy road and the next few hundred metres constitutes the only slightly unpleasant part of this entire walk. Straight after the bridge, turn right onto a small road that goes past a stand-up paddleboard and kayak **rental place**. The turn-off is immediately past the Cénac town sign.

**07** Follow the red and white GR trail markers past a waterworks. Turn right at the junction and continue along a **farm track** that bends down towards the river. A long, peaceful stroll down along the river now follows. Turn left away from the river when you come to the **green walk sign** with a scallop shell symbol (indicating that you are now on one of the medieval pilgrimage routes to Santiago de Compostela in northwest Spain).

**08** The farm track traces a line along the base of a low cliff. At the point where it bends 90 degrees to the left, a **walk track** veers off right (signed with green, red and white markers). Take this and amble uphill through woodland. When you hit the road go right, then right again by the first houses and continue into pretty **St-Julien** village. As you enter the village there's a parking area on the left and a very sharp left turn. Take this turning and drop downhill. The surfaced road soon turns to a dirt road and dives into dense **deciduous woodland** full of birds.

**09** After 10 minutes a tarmac road leads off the track to the left. Ignore this; it's a private road. Instead, continue along the woodland path with red and white GR markers. There are fleeting glimpses through the trees of the river just below. Go right at the trail junction a few minutes later. A long, leisurely walk through the **woods** now follows. In the autumn in particular, when the trees alight in red and oranges, it's an absolute delight of a walk. Castelnaud-la-Chapelle will appear ahead, but then the trail bends and the village will be behind you. When you reach the fields of the valley floor, turn right and follow the trail to a small tarmac road.

**10** Cross a **bridge** over a small, clear and utterly still stream where the trees are reflected like a mirror and turn right. Just before the main road, a **cycle path** drops down to the right. Walk along this for a few minutes back into Castelnaud-la-Chapelle. Remember to allow time to explore this beautiful village and its huge castle before leaving.

## La Roque-Gageac

La Roque-Gageac's row of amber buildings, built into the cliff face along the River Dordogne, make it one of the most photographed villages in the central Dordogne Valley (pictured).

The village is a pleasure to explore (though in high summer it's often oppressively busy). The cliff that hangs above the village is incised with caves that once formed medieval defensive positions known as the Troglodyte Fort. The village is also a prime spot to hit the river waters in a kayak or on a river cruise. There are masses of summertime operators.

## Take a Break

If you set out on this walk early enough then you will have time to stop for a long lunch at **La Belle Étoile** (☏ 05 53 29 51 44; hotel-belle-etoile-dordonge.fr/le-restaurant; D703; menus €38-58; ⏱ 12.30-1.30pm Tue & Thu-Sun, 7.30-9pm Tue-Sun, closed Nov-Mar) in La Roque-Gageac. Sophisticated French food is served in a vine-shaded upper terrace with fine views across the Dordogne.

# Also Try...

JULIAN KUMAR/GETTY IMAGES ©

## Meandering Around Cadouin Abbey

| DURATION | DIFFICULTY | DISTANCE |
| --- | --- | --- |
| 2½hr return | Easy | 9.2km |

Completely dominating the butter-coloured stone village of Cadouin (38km east of Bergerac), the Unesco-listed Cadouin Abbey, which houses cloth said to have been torn from the shroud that covered Christ (since proven to be a fake), has been drawing pilgrims since the 11th century. Today, the abbey continues to bring the faithful, but also attracts walkers who relish strolling the attractive woodlands surrounding the village.

This circular walk follows yellow waymarkers. Head east away from the abbey (pictured) and into chestnut woodland. You will pass the hamlets of Les Gavachoux and St-Blanchot. Cross through the Peyre forest and work your way towards and beyond the hamlet of Soulety before bending back around to Cadouin.

## Vézère Panoramas

| DURATION | DIFFICULTY | DISTANCE |
| --- | --- | --- |
| 6hr return | Hard | 14km |

There's a bit of everything on this walk: viewpoints, pauses in a dreamy riverside village and explorations of cliff-side cave dwellings that date back as far as 50,000 years ago.

The walk begins from the car park at La Roque St-Christophe. With traces of human habitation dating back 50,000 years, the kilometre-long cliff here is dotted with around a hundred rock shelters raised some 80m off the ground. The site reached its pinnacle of habitation during the Middle Ages and guided tours bring some of the site alive. Leaving the past behind, the route crosses the River Vézère, climbs onto cliff ledges with great views and makes its way through woodland before descending down to the oh-so-pretty village of St-Léon-sur-Vézère. Crossing back over the river again, it's a countryside ramble back to the start point.

MARGOUILLAT PHOTO/SHUTTERSTOCK ©

## Monbazillac Vineyards

| DURATION | DIFF. | DISTANCE |
| --- | --- | --- |
| 2hr return | Easy | 6km |

Famed countrywide for its sweet white wines, the small village of Monbazillac is built around the large château of the same name.

This short walk enables you to admire the architecture and stroll through the tapestry of vineyards. And remember, tasting the wine while walking is considered acceptable! From the château car park, follow yellow waymarkers in a figure-eight pattern around the village via Le Tonibru, Les Croux, La Cattie and Péroudier. For the whole way, you'll walk on quiet country roads and farm tracks through a countryside ribbed with vines.

## Lac Pavin

| DURATION | DIFF. | DISTANCE |
| --- | --- | --- |
| 3½hr return | Moderate | 13km |

Deep in the Auvergne countryside, the dark, forest-fringed and near perfectly circular Pavin lake is something of a place of legend.

Locals whisper that the lake (pictured) was created by the devil's tears. Scientists, somewhat less romantically, say it was created through volcanic actions. Whichever story is true, nobody can deny that this ethereal, 93m-deep lake is a magical hiking goal. The walk begins from the village of Besse-en-Chandesse and follows the red and white waymarkers of the GR30.

## Le Cézallier

| DURATION | DIFF. | DISTANCE |
| --- | --- | --- |
| 4hr return | Moderate | 14km |

This high, windy grassland plateau offers a very different kind of Auvergne walking experience than that of the volcanic craters dotting the landscape elsewhere in this region.

Walking here is about big horizons, flower meadows and cattle. An excellent half-day walk takes in the lakes d'En Haut and d'En Bas and the rounded summit of La Motte.

Tain l'Hermitage
Tournon-sur-Rhône
Valence
Chabeuil
Romans-sur-Isère
St-Nazaire-en-Royans
Parc Naturel Régional du Vercors
Mont Aiguille
Bourg d'Oisans
Les Deux Alpes
Barre des Écrins (4102m)
Villeneuve-la-Salle
Briançon
Cesana Torinese
Sestriere
Pinerolo
Torre Pellice
Cavour
Montviso (3841m)
ITALY
Isère
Drac
Le Mure
Parc National des Écrins
Parc Naturel Régional du Queyras
Loriol-sur-Drôme
Crest
Die
Saillans
Privas
Rochemaure
Montélimar
AUVERGNE-RHÔNE-ALPES
Rhône
A7
A49
Gap
Embrun
Durance
Lac de Serre-Ponçon
Barcelonnette
Tête de Siguret (3032m)
31
37
Demonte
Cime de la Bonette (2860m)
Mont Mounier (2817m)
Grignan
Valreas
Nyons
Pierrelatte
St-Paul-Trois-Châteaux
Pont-St-Esprit
Bagnols-sur-Cèze
Vaison-la-Romaine
Mont Ventoux (1910m)
36
33
Reserve Geologique de Haute Provence
Lac d'Allos
Parc National du Mercantour
Colmars-les-Alpes
St-Sauveur-sur-Tinée
Valberg
St-Martin-Vésubie
Roquebillière
A51
Sisteron
Volonne
Peyruis
Digne-les-Bains
St-Andre-les-Alpes
Annot
Guillaumes
Utelle
Orange
Carpentras
Sorgues
L'Isle-sur-la-Sorgue
Roussillon
Sault
Banon
Forcalquier
St-Saturnin-lès-Apt
Gordes
Apt
Cereste
PROVENCE-ALPES-CÔTE D'AZUR
Barrême
Moustiers-Ste-Marie
Castellane
Lac de Castillon
Puget-Theniers
St-Martin du Var
Var
OCCITANIE
Avignon
A9
Rhône
Châteaurenard
Cavaillon
Durance
Bonnieux
Parc Naturel Régional du Luberon
Oraison
Valensole
Riez
Rougon
Lac de Ste-Croix
Bauduen
35
Comps-sur-Artuby
Vence
Nice
Cagnes-sur-Mer
Grasse
Antibes
A7
Tarascon
St-Rémy de Provence
Cadenet
Pertuis
Manosque
A51
Parc Naturel Régional du Verdon
Montmeyan
Aups
Bargemon
Fayence
Lac de St-Cassien
Cannes
Îles de Lérins
St-Gilles
Arles
Parc Naturel Régional des Alpilles
Salon-de-Provence
St-Cannat
Rians
Draguignan
A8
Îles de Lérins
St-Martin-de-Crau
Miramas
Istres
Aix-en-Provence
St-Maximin-la-Ste-Baume
Barjols
Sillans-la-Cascade
Carcès
Lorgues
Le Muy
Les Arcs-sur-Argens
Fréjus
Agay
Theoule-sur-Mer
A54
A7
A51
Trets
A8
Brignoles
St-Raphaël
34
Méjanes
Parc Naturel Régional de Camargue
Fos-sur-Mer
Étang de Berre
Rognac
Martigues
Vitrolles
Marignane
Gardanne
A52
Roquevaire
Gonfaron
Le Cannet des Maures
St-Maxime
Golfe de St-Tropez
A57
Cogolin
St-Tropez
Stes-Maries-de-la-Mer
30
Étang de Vaccarès
Golfe de Fos
Port St-Louis du Rhône
Port de Bouc
Carry-le-Rouet
Rade de Marseille
Marseille
Aubagne
Cuers
A50
Cavalaire-sur-Mer
Parc National des Calanques
Cassis
La Ciotat
Le Beausset
Le Lavandou
Côte d'Azur
32
Bandol
Sanary-sur-Mer
Le Brusc
Cap Sicié
Toulon
La Seyne-sur-Mer
Giens
Hyères
Porquerolles
Île de Porquerolles
Port d'Hyères
Îles d'Hyères
Île du Levant
MEDITERRANEAN SEA
N
0        50 km
0     25 miles

Abbaye Notre-Dame de Sénanque (p131), Gordes

# Provence & the Côte d'Azur

# Provence & the Côte d'Azur

Fields of lavender, ancient olive groves, maquis-cloaked hills, snow-tipped mountains and France's deepest canyon. No wonder it sometimes feels as if Provence and the Côte d'Azur was purpose-built for walkers. And that's before we even mention the Mediterranean itself, a bright mirror of blue reflecting craggy cliffs and endless skies.

## Arles

Roman treasures, tree-shaded squares and plenty of culture make Arles a seductive stepping stone for walks in the watery world of the Camargue.

## Cassis

The charm of this fishing village, impeccably poised amongst the *calanques* (coves), has hardly been dented by its great popularity. Yes, you're more likely to rub shoulders with crisply dressed Marseillais than sun-creased fisherfolk, but Cassis is so beautiful – and so well stocked with good bistros, bars and boutiques – that really you couldn't ask for a more ideal base for walk number 32.

## Roussillon

Home to artists' and ceramicists' workshops, Roussillon is a red-tinged beauty of a village and a lovely place to finish off the countryside ramble described in walk number 33.

## Cannes

Glamorous Cannes sets camera flashes popping at its film festival in May, when stars pose on the red carpet in tuxes and couture gowns. But the glitz doesn't end there. Throughout the year, as you walk among the fashionable bars, designer shops and palaces of La Croisette, the wealth and glamour of this city cannot fail to impress. The city is an ideal base for walk 34.

## Moustiers Ste-Marie

Pushed up tight against giant rock stacks and cliffs, attractive Moustiers Ste-Marie is the standard base for those taking on the challenges of the Verdon Gorge. Despite its small size, there are plenty of places to eat and sleep.

## Barcelonnette

At the far northern edge of the Parc National du Mercantour, which covers a great swathe of the Alpes de Haute-Provence, the small ski and hiking resort of Barcelonnette is well endowed with places to stay and eat, and forms the perfect base for walks number 31 and 37.

## Gordes

Gordes is stunning, a jumble of terracotta rooftops, church towers and winding lanes, and a classic image of rural Provence. There are good tourist facilities and lots of wonderful places to stay after an exhausting day completing walk 36.

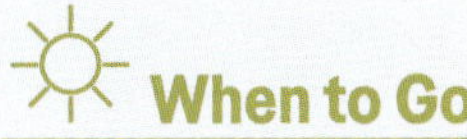

## When to Go

The climate in Provence and the Côte d'Azur is typical of the west Mediterranean, so you can walk somewhere at any time of the year.

Winter (November to February) along the coast and in the Luberon region can be warm sunshine one week and torrential rain the next. Real cold (or snow) is rare though. By contrast, the northern mountains in winter are purely the domain of skiers.

Spring (March to early May) is by far the most unpredictable and often the wettest period of the year. Snow will keep mountain trails off-limits until at least early May.

Summer (June to September) is uniformly hot, dry and sunny. July and August are often too hot for all but the high mountain routes. The heat can make many coastal walks very trying. June, though, can be a lovely time. The tourist crowds are yet to arrive, the days are long and the wildflowers blossom across both coastal and mountain slopes. For the lavender fields of the Luberon, the only option is July and August, when the entire countryside radiates a purple-blue colour.

Autumn (mid-September to October) is a superb time to walk almost anywhere here. The weather will still be settled, the sea is warm and the light beautiful and clear. As you get deeper into October, the autumn colours appear on the woodland trees and the mountain summits get a covering of fresh snow. It all looks magical at this time.

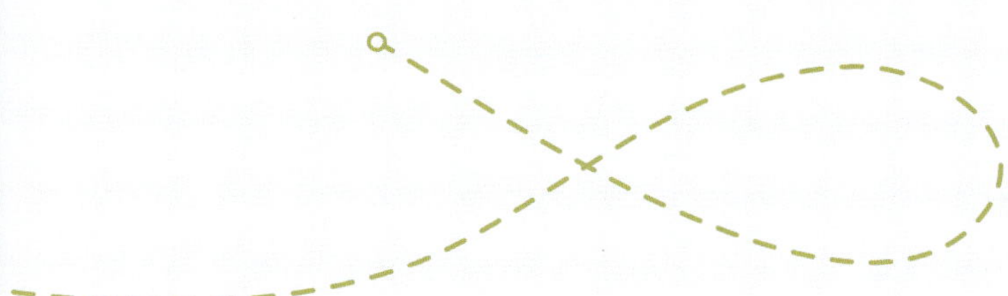

## Where to Stay

Provence and the Côte d'Azur have a huge and varied range of accommodation, from cosy rural cottages to swish pamper pads. It's wise to book well ahead everywhere in summer (online is easiest); prices are at their highest in July and August.

## What's On

**Skiing** (Dec-Apr) Provence and the Côte d'Azur's ski resorts are excellent: small, family-friendly, dotted with trees, sunny and easily accessible.

**Pèlerinage des Gitans** (24-25 May) Roma from Europe pour into remote seaside outpost Stes-Maries-de-la-Mer to honour their patron saint.

**La Transhumance** (Oct) Sheep and their shepherds descend from their summer pastures and crowd the roads of Haute-Provence, from the Verdon to Col d'Allos. The same happens in reverse in June.


## Resources

**Provence–Alpes–Côte d'Azur Tourisme** (decouverte-paca.fr) The first port of call, with a wealth of info on what to do, where to go, where to stay and much more.

**Tourisme Alpes Haute-Provence** (tourism-alps-provence.com) Guide to the mountains.

**Parc National du Mercantour** (parc-mercantour.eu) Offical website of the Mercantour National Park.

**Rando Alpes Haute Provence** (rando-alpes-haute-provence.fr) Hundreds of route suggestions, pictures, maps and tips.

## Transport

Public transport in Provence and the Côte d'Azur is generally good between bigger towns (especially along the coast), but limited to nonexistent in rural areas. A car gives maximum freedom, especially in rural parts, and is often the only way to reach trailheads. Cars can be hired in most larger towns and cities.

High-speed TGVs connect major cities; smaller towns are served by slower TER trains, sometimes supplemented by buses. Buses are useful for remote villages that aren't serviced by trains, but timetables revolve around school-term times; fewer services run on weekends and school holidays.

# Wetlands of the Camargue

| DURATION | DIFFICULTY | DISTANCE | START/END |
| --- | --- | --- | --- |
| 3½hr return | Easy | 12.5km | Parking Station de Pompage |

| TERRAIN | | Walking trail, dirt road |
| --- | --- | --- |

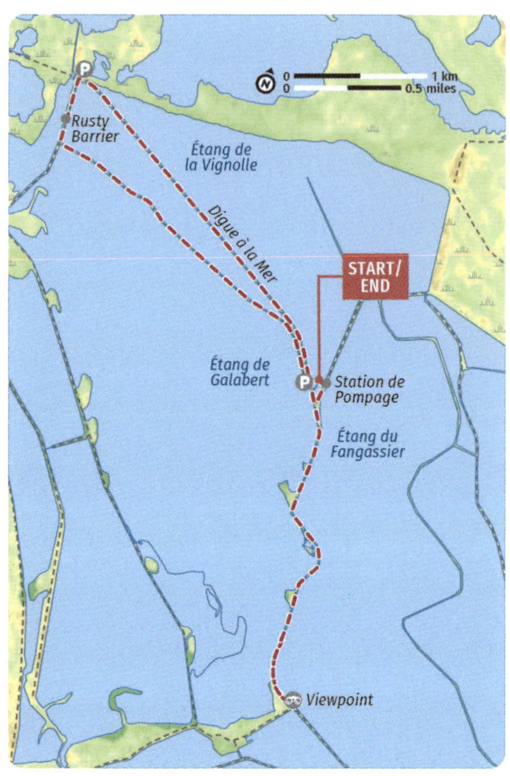


Taking in empty horizons, blue lakes and pink flamingoes, this simple walk reveals the best of the wetland wilderness of the Camargue. It's a figure-of-eight-style walk, with the start point being the middle of the eight. This means that it's easy to just do one half of the walk if you wish. Combined with it being absolutely pancake flat and with a whole host of wildlife interest, it's an ideal family walk. Do, however, avoid very windy or hot days as there's no shelter at all. Finally, make sure you bring some binoculars.

The hardest part of this walk is getting to the start point. It's 15km west of Salin-de-Girud on a tiny dirt road that crosses the Étang du Fangassier and Étang de Galabert. There's an old **water pump station** here, a bird hide and a small parking area. To start, follow the wide trail signed **Phare de la Gacholle** (Gacholle Lighthouse).

The trail goes arrow straight between the two *étangs* (brackish lagoons). The one to your north (Étang du Fangassier) is a near-guaranteed place to see **flamingoes**. Approach them quietly; they're very timid and won't let you get too close. At the parking area, after 3km, turn left, pass a **rusty barrier** and then 100m later go left again following a very minor, **unsigned footpath**. It will return you to the start point.

Then, head south away from the car park, along a narrow dirt road again sandwiched between the same two *étangs*. After 40 minutes reach a **viewpoint** over a whole web of waterways. Retrace your steps back to the car.

Best for
WILDLIFE

# 31

# Lac du Lauzanier

| DURATION | DIFFICULTY | DISTANCE | START/END |
|---|---|---|---|
| 3hr return | Easy | 10.5km | Parking au Pont Rouge (Col de Larche) |

| TERRAIN | | Walking trail, smooth track |
|---|---|---|

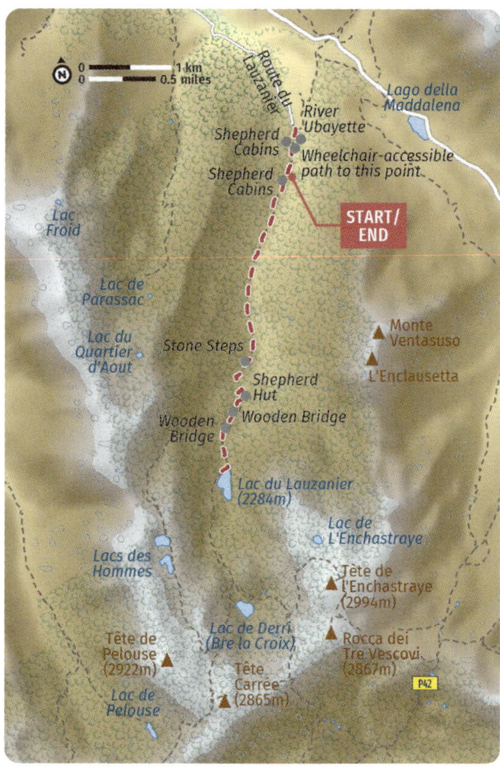



This is mountain walking at its best. An idyllic valley filled with wildflowers and comical marmots leads to a spectacular lake surrounded by glacial mountain peaks. Not only is this walk (min/max altitude 1907/2284m) visually breathtaking, but it's also short and easy, making it a superb family walk.

Follow the wheelchair-accessible path south. You'll likely pass a multitude of very **tame marmots** playing around the grass verges (don't feed them). After around 500m the trail narrows and becomes distinctly less wheelchair accessible. It's then simply a case of following the gently rising path in a straight line pretty much all the way to the lake. Pass a couple of **shepherd cabins** surrounded by

herds of sheep being watched over by guard dogs who are distinctly less friendly than the marmots (give the dogs a very wide berth and never allow a child to approach one).

The scenery is everything an alpine mountain valley is supposed to be and you half expect a French Heidi to come skipping down the trail towards you.

About an hour from the start and the trail starts gaining altitude as it climbs up **stone steps** and steep slopes. Come up onto a plateau with another shepherd hut and then cross two **wooden bridges** over the fledgling River Ubayette. Then it's one last haul up over another ridge and the glistening lake stands in front of you with a wall of 3km-high peaks reflected in its waters. Return by the same route.

Best for
WILDLIFE

# 32

# Port-Miou, Port-Pin & En-Vau

| DURATION | DIFFICULTY | DISTANCE | START/END |
|---|---|---|---|
| 4hr return | Moderate | 10km | Parking de la Presqu'île |

| TERRAIN | | Footpath, dirt road |
|---|---|---|

With their light-shifting geometry, rich plant and animal life, and idyllic hidden coves, Les Calanques are the adventure playground of the Marseillais, and a wonderful walking – and beach-hopping – destination for everyone. Just remember to bring your swimming things! Note that, in summer, the trail is sometimes closed because of the high risk of forest fire.

## Getting Here

The walk begins at the parking at the far southwestern edge of Cassis. From the town, follow road signs to Calanque.

## Starting Point

Parking costs €8 for the day (the nearby streets are metered at the same rate). Don't leave anything of value in the car.

**01** Walk back up **av Notre Dame**. Immediately after a **cube-shaped house** turn left down a footpath. Go left when you hit the road and drop down towards the fjord-like *calanque*.

**02** Walk along the west bank of the **Calanque de Port-Miou** (pictured). When you near the end of the *calanque* you will be offered a choice of an upper path and a lower one. Take the upper path, which leads to a dirt road.

**03** Near the top of the hill, where the road bends right, a footpath veers off to the left (straight ahead). Take this trail and then, a few metres later at the fork, take the upper right-hand track. You will come to a **trail junction**. The main trail, signed with red-and-white trail markers, goes right. Instead, take the smaller path that continues straight ahead and onto the **Presqu'île de Cacau** headland.

PAVEL SZABO/SHUTTERSTOCK ©

**Best for**

**COASTAL VIEWS**

**04** Work your way down to the end of the sunburnt headland. The **coastal views** are marvellous. Return back to the main trail.

**05** Drop down onto the beach at the head of the **Calanque de Port-Pin**. With its jewel-blue waters, this is everything a Mediterranean beach is supposed to be.

**06** From the far end of the beach, there's a choice of two trails. Take the one heading southwest along the headland. It's signed for the **Sentier Panoramique** and follows blue waymarkers.

**07** The trail bends around the end of the headland and starts to climb more steeply. At one point, you will pass an **old refuge** (mountain hut). After a fair bit of huffing and puffing, you'll find yourself at a spectacular **vantage point**.

**08** Continuing along the cliff-top path you'll come to another **viewpoint**. Just beyond this is a junction. Go right. At a major signed meeting of junctions go left towards the **Calanque d'En-Vau**. The descent to the beach is very steep and can be slippery. The **beach** here, squashed between sheer cliff faces, is one of the region's finest.

**09** Return back to the signed trail junction. This time take the path signed for Cassis. It drops back to the beach at the Calanque de Port-Pin. Take the wider trail cutting straight over the headland to the Calanque de Port-Miou and back to the parking.

## Take a Break

It's a pleasure to discover that none of the beaches have been marred by bars or restaurants. Bring a picnic.

# 33

# Roussillon Ramble

| DURATION | DIFFICULTY | DISTANCE | START/END |
| --- | --- | --- | --- |
| 3½hr return | Moderate | 11km | Parking St-Michel, Roussillon |

| TERRAIN | | Road, farm track, footpath |
| --- | --- | --- |

Roussillon is one of the prettiest villages in France. The houses, all of which are painted faded blushing red, look out over countryside ribbed in vineyards and dotted with strangely contorted cliffs. This family-friendly route reveals it all.

## Getting Here

The walk starts from the Parking St-Michel, which is by the roundabout at the end of the D227, a few hundred metres north of Roussillon centre.

## Starting Point

You have to pay for all the car parks all around Roussillon. There are no walker facilities here except a toilet block.

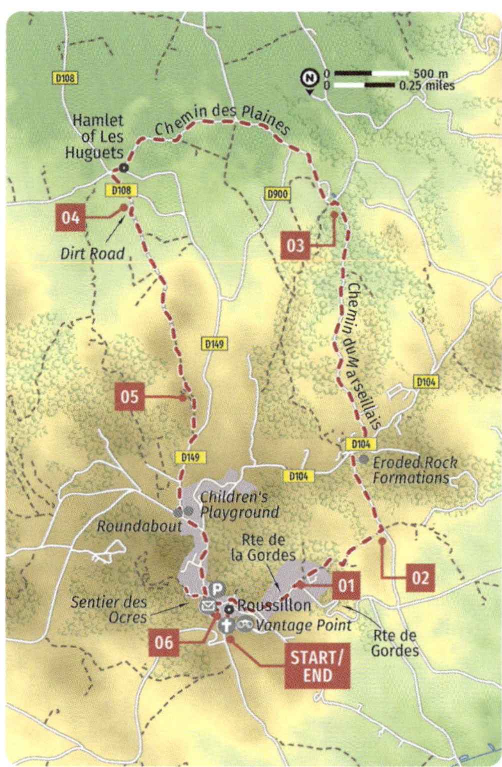


**01** Follow the road up the hill and into the village centre. Turn right and then right again down **rue des Bourgades**. At the edge of the village go left down **rte de la Gordes**. You will come to a junction known as **Ribas**. There are some hiking route signposts. Turn left down a small road that quickly becomes a walking track that descends through **pretty oak woodlands**. There are red-and-white trail markers.

**02** When you reach a road at the **Cabiscol junction**, head left (direction Pie Conil). After a few minutes' uphill climb, you'll pass some weird **eroded rock formations**. A moment later, on reaching the road junction with the D104, turn right. Eighty metres later leave the road for a track on the left signed Goult. Pass some houses and then walk gently downhill along a farm track hemmed by vineyards, patches of woodland and a few lavender fields. The red-and-white waymarkers are now largely replaced with yellow ones.

# Sentier des Ocres

This hike doesn't come to an end when you stroll back into Roussillon. Oh no, in fact one of the highlights of the walk awaits.

The **Sentier des Ocres** (Ochre Trail; adult/child €3.50/free) consists of two circular trails, taking 30 or 50 minutes to complete, which twist through mini-desert landscapes on the edge of the village (pictured).

MARKETA1982/SHUTTERSTOCK ©

**03** At the bottom of the hill you'll come to a large, peach-pink stone house on a junction signed as **la Petite Verrerie**. Go left and pass a farm and vineyard, where you can buy a tipple for your picnic. At the road junction take a right (going straight ahead). A **beautiful vista** of vineyards and hazy hills spreads out before you. At the next junction continue straight into the hamlet of **Les Huguets**, a delightful place of cream-pink stone houses.

**04** At the junction with the D108 turn left, then, 120m later, just before the road bends, a small dirt road leads off north (straight ahead).

It's signed Les Mas des Iris and Le Jas. Head up this road, following the yellow waymarkers. You'll pass a peaceful succession of **vineyards** and patches of **woodland**. The path starts to climb quite steeply. On a hot day this can be the hardest part of the whole walk but, fortunately, **oak trees** provide some shade. After a five-minute climb, things level out and oak turns to pine.

**05** Reaching a **trail fork** there's a house entry on the left and a gateway on the right. Go through the gateway and at the point where the track bends right, take the discreet turn-off marked in faded yellow paint on a boulder. Follow this

route through pine woods. Turn right at the road junction and left at the roundabout (next to a **children's playground**). Continue straight and arrive back in the old part of Roussillon.

**06** Before leaving, take the time to explore the village. Walk up to the oh-so-pretty **village hall** and carry on up to the **church** from where there's a superb **vantage point**.

## Take A Break

There are lots of touristy restaurants in the village. Market day is Thursday morning. Time your visit for this and stock up on picnic treats.

# 34

# Cap Roux

| DURATION | DIFFICULTY | DISTANCE | START/END |
|---|---|---|---|
| 4½hr return | Moderate | 11km | Pointe de l'Observatoire/ Pointe du Cap Roux |

| TERRAIN | Footpath, dirt road |
|---|---|

The Massif de l'Esterel is a great pile of sunset-tinged boulders and rock pinnacles hugging the shores of the Mediterranean. The walk (min/max altitude 0/454m) described here is one of the classics of the massif, and even though Cap Roux offers Oscar-winning views across the Côte d'Azur and down onto the millionaire villas of Cannes, the Massif de l'Esterel is a world apart from the Hollywood glam of the Côte d'Azur. Indeed, you're far more likely to stumble into a wild boar in the mountain woodlands than a Hollywood star. In summer the trail is sometimes closed because of the high risk of forest fire.

## Getting Here

The walk begins from the small parking area by the Pointe de l'Observatoire/Pointe du Cap Roux on the main Corniche de l'Estérel road (D5559). From central Cannes it's 22km. From St-Raphaël it's 18km. While buses do pass by the start point, it's much easier to have your own vehicle.

## Starting Point

At the start point, there are a couple of walking and fire-risk information panels. Don't leave anything of value in your vehicle.

**01** Turn left out of the parking area and walk 50m down the road. Just after the **railway bridge**, there's a turn-off right leading uphill. Follow this dirt road up through herb-scented scrub. Ignore the yellow waymarked turn-off after 15 minutes and carry on uphill. You will pass some **information panels** on the massif's plant life.

STUART BUTLER/LONELY PLANET ©



**02** Where the dirt road bends sharp right in front of a huge rocky outcrop, take the **pebble track** on the right. There are yellow paint slashes. Thirty minutes on you will come to the **Col du St-Pilon** (281m), a low pass. Turn right.

**03** Bending around to the cooler northern side of the massif, the woodland becomes denser and damper. At the fork go left. Turn right at the big trail junction next to a **natural water source**. The trail crosses two big **rockfall zones** but otherwise remains in deep forest. You then come to a third, larger, rockfall area. The path zigzags up the side of it.

**04** Two hours from the start, emerge from the forest. At a pass a couple of minutes later, turn right and after 100m reach the summit of **Cap Roux** (454m). On a clear day the entire coastline will be visible (pictured). Looking the other way, the southern Alps will shimmer in the haze.

**05** Return to the main trail and go right. After 15 minutes reach the **Col du Cap Roux** (404m) at the base of two sugarloaf fingers of rock. Go left, then left again and over a huge rockfall. Twenty minutes later, at another junction, turn sharp right and go downhill into a **forest**. After a long descent you will come to a wide trail junction. Go right here. At the point where the trail starts rising again, there's a small turn-off left with steps and a yellow cross painted on the rock. Turn down here and then left 200m later back onto the dirt road you walked up earlier. A moment later, you'll reach the car park.

**06** Walk 100m across the low headland by the car park for **sea views**. You can also drop down to a small cove **beach**.

## Take a Break

There's nowhere to buy food and drink on the trail. Bring a picnic and a *lot* of water.

# The Blanc-Martel Trail

| DURATION | DIFFICULTY | DISTANCE | START/END |
|---|---|---|---|
| 6hr return | Moderate | 13km | Chalet de la Maline/ Auberge Point Sublime |

| TERRAIN | | Footpath, steep cliff-face ladders |
|---|---|---|

The Blanc-Martel trail along Europe's 'Grand Canyon' is one of the iconic walks of France. It's a long and tiring walk, but with cliff-face bolted ladders to descend and long, dark tunnels to negotiate, there's always something of interest. And that's before we even mention the natural beauty of the glowing blue river waters and soaring rainbow-tinged canyon walls. The trail is very clearly waymarked all the way along. Bring a torch for the tunnels.

## Getting Here

The walk begins from the Chalet de la Maline, 8km from La Palud-sur-Verdon, and ends at the Auberge Point Sublime on the edge of the hamlet of Rougon. A **navette** (☎04 92 77 32 02) runs from La Palud-sur-

Verdon to the Chalet de la Maline and another from the Auberge Point Sublime back to La Palud-sur-Verdon. Or you can leave a car at the end point and get a taxi to the start point, but taxi numbers are limited, so book at least a week in advance.

## Starting Point

There are walk information panels and toilets at the Chalet de la Maline. Food and drinks with a view are also served here.

**01** Follow the GR4 sign down past the **Chalet de la Maline** along a clear trail through mixed woodland. After 40 minutes you'll reach a trail junction. Go left. Five minutes later you'll reach the banks of the **River Verdon** and the bottom of the gorge.

**02** A long, easy amble follows. Sometimes you'll be walking very close to the river and at other times the path rises upward and away from the waters.

STUART BUTLER/LONELY PLANET ©

**03** After 1½ hours things will start to get a little harder. Handrails will help ease you up a steeper bit of rocky terrain and then you cross a landslip area via a set of steps with an **excitingly airy view** down to the river below.

**04** Fifteen minutes later you'll pass by a big cave, the **Baume aux Bœufs**, where the bones of prehistoric cattle were found. The path continues to climb sharply up the gorge walls until, a few minutes later, you reach a junction. Go left for the main trail, but we highly recommend taking the 15-minute (one-way) detour down to **La Mescla** (pictured). It's a small, low headland above the meeting points of the Verdon and the Artuby rivers, and the mingling of **luminous turquoise waters** here is simply magical. Return back to the main trail.

**05** After a few minutes of steep climbing you'll come to the **Brèche d'Imbert** (710m), a small gap in the rock face. Immediately beyond this is the most infamous section of the entire trail. **Metal ladders** fall almost completely vertically all the way back down to the river far below. There are handrails to help you down, but even so, it's a little hair-raising.

**06** It's now a three-hour walk along the gorge floor. You'll pass the **Plage des Fères**, where most people are tempted to swim.

**07** Some five hours from the start you'll reach a series of tunnels known as the **Couloir Samson**. The second is around 1km long and you'll need a torch to navigate it. You come out into the bright light of day close to the **Auberge Point Sublime**.

## Take a Break

There's nowhere to get food or drink in the gorge, so bring a picnic and plenty of water – however, a cool beer awaits at Auberge Point Sublime!

# 36

# Gordes Loops

| DURATION | DIFFICULTY | DISTANCE | START/END |
|---|---|---|---|
| 6hr return | Moderate | 20.5km | Parking Gendarmerie, Gordes |

| TERRAIN | Road, farm track, walking trail |
|---|---|

Arguably the scenic queen of the Luberon's hilltop villages, the tiered village of Gordes seems to teeter improbably on the edge of the sheer rock faces of the Vaucluse plateau from which it rises. And that same plateau is blanketed in fields of lavender and broadleaf woodlands, and scarred with small gorges. All of which are encountered on this walk, which also takes in a famed abbey, sterling views of Gordes and an interesting historical site. Although the walking itself is easy, this is a very long walk. The good news though is that because the route makes a very neat figure-of-eight shape, with the start and end point being the middle of the eight, it's easy, and in many ways advisable, to split the walk into two shorter days.

## Getting Here

ZOU! Bus line 17 (€2.60, four daily July to September, one daily Monday to Friday October to June) stops in Gordes on its way from Apt to Cavaillon. It also stops in Roussillon along the way. The walk begins from the car park in front of the gendarmerie at the bottom of the old part of the village.

## Starting Point

There are no facilities for walkers at the start point (unless, of course, you happen to need a police officer). All parking in Gordes is metered.

**01** Leaving the car park, walk a few metres down the D15 away from the old village. Pass an **old water source** on the right and straight afterward go right, uphill along a small track. Hitting the D177 road go right, then 150m later, at a dead-end sign, turn left down a little country road. There are now both red-and-white GR trail markers and yellow waymarkers. Fifty metres later go right at the walking signs and follow the trail that runs between **two old dry-stone walls**.

**02** The path rolls lovingly between the dry-stone walls with olive groves and patches of woodland on either side. After 15 minutes turn right and then immediately left when you hit the wider path. A few minutes further on, you'll meet the **D177**. Turn left and follow the road around the sharp bend.

**03** After 200m leave the road for a footpath on the left that drops downhill through woodland to the large **Abbaye Notre-Dame de Sénanque**, which is surrounded by lavender fields (pictured p115). From this quiet, elevated position it looks an absolute treat. Allow at least an hour (not included in walk times stated here) to explore the abbey, but be careful not to trip over one of the selfie-seeking tourists standing among the lavender fields.

**04** Return to the sharp bend in the D177 road via the same footpath. Follow the sign and yellow waymarkers south in the direction of Les Dilais on a narrow forest trail. The path wends along the lip of the **Gorges de la Sénanque**, although for the most part you can't see down into the gorge because of all the trees.

**05** After 20 minutes turn right by a grey house gate and a walking sign marked Senancole (1.2km). The path sweeps steeply (in places very steeply) down along the gorge. The trail heads back up the gorge a short way, crosses a

## Abbaye Notre-Dame de Sénanque

Surrounded by fields of lavender, the Cistercian Abbey Notre-Dame de Sénanque (senanque.fr; guided/unguided tour €8/9.5) is one of the most photographed sites in Provence.

Founded in 1148, the abbey is still home to a small monastic community, members of which conduct guided tours (in French) throughout the year. You can also take an unguided tour. Reservations are essential, as are conservative dress and reverential silence.

The abbey is closed on religious holidays.

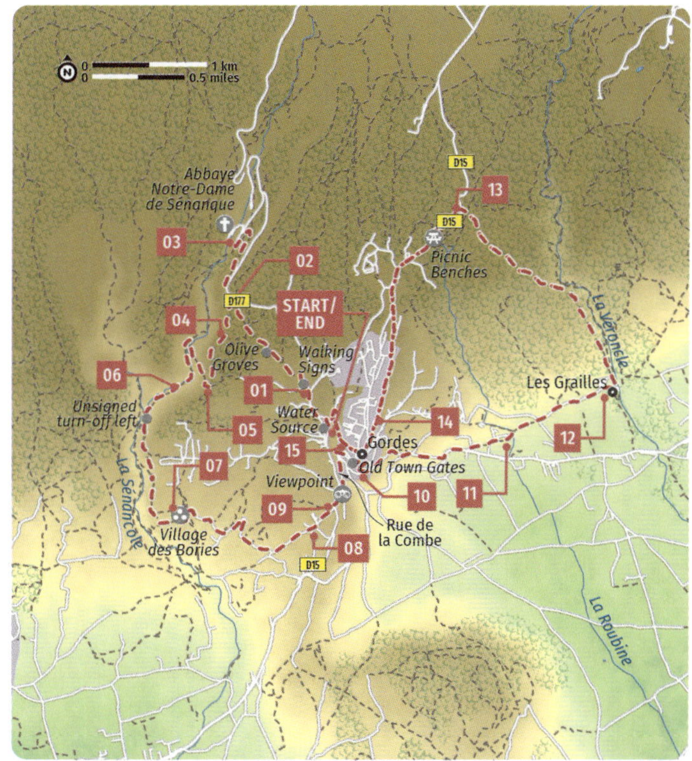

rock face and reaches a junction. Heading straight on will take you back to the abbey. Instead, spin around and head south down the **gorge**. Ignore the yellow crosses saying you've gone the wrong way.

**06** After 100m of very steep and slippery descent (take great care here), you'll bump down onto the floor of the gorge by a meeting of trails. Go left (south) down the gorge on a clear trail next to a normally dry riverbed (be careful of flash floods after heavy rain). Compared to the dry, scrubby woodlands up on the gorge slopes, what you're now walking through seems more like the Amazon jungle!

**07** After 15 minutes go straight on towards the Village des Bories at the signed junction. A few minutes later there's a discreet, unsigned turn-off left. Take this and 20 minutes later roll into the **Village des Bories**, a series of beehive-shaped stone huts (pictured) used by shepherds for hundreds of years.

**08** Leave the site via the car parks and follow the signed route along a road to **Les Grangiers**. It's now just a relaxing walk along country lanes. At the next junction with walking signposts go left. When you reach the busy road (D15), take the small road on the left next to some **large cypress trees**. Thirty metres later continue straight ahead and then straight over the main road again.

**09** Next up is a walk highlight, an epic **viewpoint of Gordes** framed between trees. Follow the path down to the base of the village and then head up into the old quarter via a wide cobbled road, which passes through the old town gates and emerges just behind the château. You can now either call it a day and return to your car or continue with the second, marginally shorter, part of the walk.

**10** From where you stand behind the **château** head downhill towards the signed *belvédère* (viewpoint) looking over the farming plains of Provence. Drop down a stone stairway to the right then follow red-and-white trail markers left (southeast). At the bottom of the hill follow the sign for Le Touron. You'll pass an **old water source** (not drinkable) and reach the busy D2 road. Go left along the road for 75m then turn left and almost instantly right onto a grassy trail in front of a big stone house.

**11** A clear, flat trail runs for 10 minutes through farming countryside and past big houses. Cross the quiet D102 and carry straight on. Do the same at the next junction.

**12** You'll come to the hamlet of **Les Grailles**. Go left by the walking trail junction and follow a stony path uphill along the lip of Les

## Village des Bories

Beehive-shaped *bories* (stone huts) bespeckle Provence, and the **Village des Bories** (adult/child €8/4) is an entire village of them, which can be explored. Constructed of slivered limestone, *bories* were built during the Bronze Age, inhabited by shepherds until 1839, then abandoned until their restoration in the 1970s.

Grailles. After 10 minutes, ignore the trail sign saying to go right and instead carry on straight ahead (north) along the edge of the gorge. A long upward slog awaits, during which you'll gain 250m in height in just 45 minutes. There's no shade so be prepared to get hot!

**13** Finally, after a long, sun-exposed climb, you'll come to the D15 road. Turn left and walk along the road verge. You'll pass some **picnic benches** after a few minutes. A short while later the road bends right. A small road goes off to the left of this bend (there are some road bollards next to it). Head down this road, which runs between dry-stone walls and houses.

**14** At the road junction continue straight ahead on a smaller track. It's now downhill all the way and there are stunning views eastward over a patchwork of vines, lavender, oak and honey-stone houses. The track becomes a footpath, but the views don't change. Pass by the **cemetery** at the edge of Gordes.

**15** Go through a small car park and follow rue St-Pons to the château in the heart of the village. After exploring the old village follow **rue de la Combe** for five minutes from the front of the château downhill and back to your car.

### Take a Break

There's nowhere to get food and drink out on the trail so bring a picnic and plenty of water.

At the end of your walk treat yourself at **Le Mas** (☎04 90 04 03 57; lemasrestaurantgordes.com; chemin de St-Blaise les Imberts; menu lunch/dinner €27/49; ⏱12.30-2pm & 7.30-9.30pm Jul-Sep, 7.30-9.30pm Thu, 12.30-2pm & 7.30-9.30pm Fri-Mon Oct-Jun). Heavy on Provençal flavours, it's one of the region's culinary highlights. Expect lots of stuffed aubergines, slow-roasted tomatoes, and lashings of olive oil and *herbes de Provence*. It's 3.5km south of Gordes off the D2.

# 37

# Les Eaux Tortes

| DURATION | DIFFICULTY | DISTANCE | START/END |
|---|---|---|---|
| 5½hr return | Hard | 17.5km | Abbaye de Laverq |

| TERRAIN | | Mountain trail |
|---|---|---|

Les Eaux Tortes is a water-logged plateau of meandering streams set at the foot of a huge cirque of 3km-high glacier-coated mountain peaks. En route to the plateau, this popular trail (min/max altitude 1640/2400m) carries you through rich scenic variety: woodlands, sheep pastures and a soul-satisfying mountain valley.

## Getting Here

The Église St-Antoine de Laverq is a long way from anywhere. From Barcelonnette take the D900 west for 14km to Le Martinet. Head south on a minor mountain road past the hamlets of St-Barthélémy and Les Clarionds. The road deteriorates into a bumpy track for the last 2.5km to the abbey. There's no public transport to the start point.

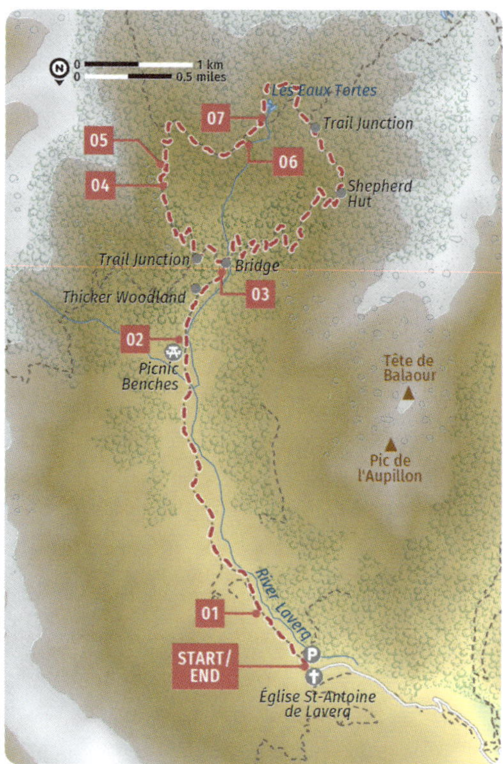


## Starting Point

There are walk information panels and, in summer, shepherds set up shop selling cheese and other mountain delights. At the time of research a big new mountain lodge was under construction and it's likely that food and drink will be available here when completed.

**01** From the abbey, follow the dirt road south. There are red-and-white waymarkers. After 20 minutes pass the parking de Plan Bas. Continue in the same direction, ignoring any turn-offs. The route climbs gently upwards alongside the **River Laverq** through open woodland and sheep pastures.

**02** After an hour you'll pass some **picnic benches** on the edge of a deeper bit of forest. Straight after these, the path starts to climb a little more vigorously into thicker **woodland**.

## Shepherd Dogs

Mountain pastures in the Alps and the Pyrenees are often grazed by sheep, but the mountains of France are also home to a fast-growing wolf population, and there's nothing a wolf likes to eat more than a tasty lamb. To protect the flock, shepherds use huge, snowy-white Pyrenean mountain dogs (known as a *patou* in French).

From afar they might look friendly, but don't try and stroke one. These dogs don't do petting. They do biting. Give them a very wide berth and if one approaches back slowly away while talking calmly to it and holding a bag or other object between you and it.

STUART BUTLER/LONELY PLANET ©

**03** Two hours from the start you'll reach a trail junction in a small forest clearing with two cabins. Go left and gently wend your way uphill through a quiet forest. Ten minutes from the cabins, go right (south) at the **trail junction**. You're now following yellow waymarkers.

**04** After a long and increasingly hard climb, the forest starts to fade away. Shortly afterwards the trail picks its way through a rockfall area opposite a **waterfall**. With loose rock and little streams of water flooding over the path, it can be slippery and hard going.

**05** The reward for the hard work comes as you clamber up onto a simply gorgeous **mountain pasture** framed by huge mountain peaks to the south. There's a **shepherd cabin** off to your right and sheep are often grazing the pastures.

**06** Cross another stream and rise up onto another, rockier pasture. The path bends away from the cirque and makes a great looping turn past a **small lake**. The **views** of the snow peaks to the south and the stark, table-top peaks to the north will keep you transfixed.

**07** Three hours after you set out, you'll reach the green plateau of **Les**

**Eaux Tortes**. Turn left and circumnavigate the plateau in 20 minutes. When your loop is almost complete you'll come to a **trail junction** and signposts. Go right. For a while the trail remains up on a high ridge with **beautiful views** all the way. After passing another **shepherd hut** you'll start dropping down quickly through forest. One hour later cross a **bridge** and you'll be back at the forest clearing with the cabins (stop 03). Retrace your steps back to the car.

 Take a Break

Tuck into a picnic in one of the mountain meadows.

# Also Try...

NIKOLAS_PROFOTO/SHUTTERSTOCK ©

## Vallée des Merveilles

| DURATION | DIFFICULTY | DISTANCE |
|---|---|---|
| 7½hr return | Difficult | 19km |

Wedged between the Vésubie and Roya valleys, this narrow, remote canyon is famous for its amazing Bronze Age petroglyphs – ancient pictures carved into rock. In total, the valley contains more than 36,000 prehistoric carvings of figures, symbols and animals, thought to have been etched by members of a Ligurian cult between 1800 and 1500 BCE.

And the good news is that most can only be seen on foot. Access is restricted without a guide, which you can arrange through the Parc National du Mercantour visitor centres. There are many different walk routes, but the trail from the Lac des Merveilles to the Refuge des Merveilles is a favourite (pictured).

## Sentier Imbut

| DURATION | DIFFICULTY | DISTANCE |
|---|---|---|
| 5hr return | Difficult | 19km |

There's more to the Gorges du Verdon than the Blanc-Martel trail. There's also the Sentier Imbut, and most people consider it the most beautiful of all the routes. The fact that it's a loop walk that starts and ends from the same point is also a bonus and, at five hours, it's shorter than the Blanc-Martel trail. So why doesn't everyone just do this walk?

Good question. Did we mention that removing yourself from the gorge involves a heart-in-the-mouth vertical climb straight up the gorge walls on a series of iron ladders? Even those without a fear of heights get halfway up the ladders and suddenly realise that they do in fact have a fear of heights. But by then it's too late. The climb is so steep and potentially dangerous that it's actually forbidden to descend back down the ladders.

JUERGEN WACKENHUT/SHUTTERSTOCK ©

# Circuit de la Roche Trouée

| DURATION | DIFF. | DISTANCE |
|---|---|---|
| 4hr return | Moderate | 10km |

In a remote corner of the Parc National du Mercantour, this wild walk is a great one for wildlife-watchers and those with a geological bent.

The upper levels of this route bend around a giant, rocky, cirque that looks like something from the American Midwest rather than the southern Alps. The sheer needles of rock are a favourite with ibex and you can normally catch sight of a few defying gravity as they scramble from ridge to ridge. This quiet walk is well marked and not too steep but the trail is very rocky.

# Sentier du Littoral

| DURATION | DIFF. | DISTANCE |
|---|---|---|
| 4hr return | Easy | 13km |

Take a dramatic cape-to-cape walk along an unexpectedly peaceful part of the Côte d'Azur.

Starting in Roque-brune-Cap-Martin and running through to Cap d'Ail you can, with the exception of a 4km stretch through Monaco, walk this entire coastal path without seeing a car. What you will see instead are rugged coastal cliffs and some dreamy beaches that may well tempt you to forget about walking any further (pictured)!

# Lac d'Allos

| DURATION | DIFF. | DISTANCE |
|---|---|---|
| 1½hr return | Easy | 4km |

You couldn't ask for a more rewarding family mountain walk than this short and simple stroll to what's touted as the largest high-altitude lake in Europe.

The walk begins from parking du Laus, from where it's just a short scramble (100m elevation gain) to the lake and its surrounding marmot-filled meadows. Add an hour or so to your walk and you can circumnavigate the lake, admiring the way the surrounding mountains are reflected in the still waters.

Aurillac
AUVERGNE-RHÔNE-ALPES
Loriol-sur-Drôme
Privas
St-Chély dApcher
Grandrieu
Langogne
N102
Aubenas
Montélimar
A7
Rhône
Serverette
Aumont-Aubrac
A75
N106
N88
La Bastide Puylaurent
Uzer
Alba-la-Romaine
Pierrelatte
Laguiole
Ruoms
Vallon-Pont-d'Arc
Truyère
Marvejols
Mende
Ardèche
Gorge de l'Ardèche Réserve Naturelle
St-Martin d'Ardèche
Barjac
Balsièges
Mont Lozère (1699m)
Villefort
Barjac
Pont-St-Esprit
Chanac
N106
Pont de Montvert
Lot
N88
Sévérac-le-Château
Ispagnac
Tarn
Florac
St-Ambroix
D904
Bagnols-sur-Cèze
Orange
Aveyron
Rodez
Ste-Énimie
40
La Malène
Parc National des Cévennes
N106
La Grand'Combe
N88
Lac Pareloup
Le Rozier
Tarn
Mont Aigoual (1567m)
St-Jean du Gard
Alès
St-Léons
Meyrueis
D986
43
Anduze
D981
Uzès
Pont du Gard
Avignon
A75
Millau
Trèves
Valleraugue
Collias
Gard
A9
La Cavalerie
Le Vigan
D999
Ganges
St-Affrique
Roquefort
D999
Blandas
Nîmes
Tarascon
42
D986
St-Sernin-sur-Rance
Parc Naturel Régional des Grands Causses
Pic St-Loup (658m)
Vergèze
D999
D999
Hérault
Cazevieille
St-Gilles
Arles
Lodève
41
Vauvert
Petit Rhône
Grand Rhône
OCCITANIE
A75
Gignac
Montpellier
Aigues-Mortes
Parc Naturel Régional de Camargue
Mourèze
Étang de Vaccarès
Mons
39
Villeneuve-lès-Maguelone
La Grande Motte
PROVENCE-ALPES-CÔTE D'AZUR
Parc Naturel Régional du Haut-Languedoc
Palavas-les-Flots
Stes-Maries-de-la-Mer
Mazamet
38
Bouzigues
Pointe du Sablon
Béziers
Marseillan
A9
Étang de Thau
Sète
Carcassonne
Lézignan-Corbières
Narbonne
Agde
Aude
A61
MEDITERRANEAN SEA
Preixan
Étang de Bages-Sigean
Fontjoncouse
Sigean
A9
Pic de Bugarach (1230m)
Tautavel
Port Barcarès
Cucugnan
Estage
Perpignan
Tét
Canet-Plage
N116
N
0          40 km
0          20 miles

Gorges d'Héric (p142)

# Languedoc-Roussillon

**38 Gorges d'Héric**

A gorgeous gorge walk through the mountains – plus natural pools to cool off in. **p142**

**39 Cirque de Mourèze**

A fairy-tale circuit of strange rock formations, with a fine ridge walk offering views over Lac du Salagou. **p144**

**40 Roc des Hourtous**

Get a bird's-eye view on the Gorges du Tarn, and take a punt on a river barge. **p146**

**41 Pic St-Loup**

Views of vineyards unfurl from one of the region's most distinctive peaks. **p148**

**42 Cirque de Navacelles**

Follow a circuit round a huge river basin and visit a medieval mill along the way. **p150**

**43 Mont Aigoual**

Tackle this taxing trek for some of the finest views in the Cévennes (and a historic observatory). **p152**

# Explore
# Languedoc-Roussillon

Curling round the Mediterranean coast from Provence to the Pyrenees, this sun-toasted region often plays second fiddle to the glitzy glamour of the Côte d'Azur to the east. But for walkers, in many ways it's a more varied and rewarding region: a land of salt flats, dusty plains, high limestone mountains and forested hills. The hiking is equally varied – but avoid the scorching summer unless you want your boot soles to burn to a crisp.

## Montpellier

Graceful, elegant and easy-going, Montpellier offers shaded backstreets, peaceful public gardens and one of the best art museums in southwest France, the fantastic **Musée Fabre** (04 67 14 83 00; museefabre.fr; 39 bd de Bonne Nouvelle; adult/child €12/free; 10am-6pm Tue-Sun).

It's also a beach town, with several kilometres of sandy coastline. It's a transport hub, with fast TGV links to the rest of France, and has a huge range of excellent restaurants, bars and accommodation options. It's an ideal place to base yourself for walks in the Hérault *département*.

## Nîmes

Nîmes is a dynamic and lively southern city, with handsome, palm-lined streets and an old town ripe for exploring. Two millennia ago, it was also one of the most important cities of Roman Gaul and several Roman buildings can still be visited. There are plenty of hotels to choose from and no shortage of good restaurants, especially in the old town. It's easy to reach by train and is a good gateway for travel to the Cévennes.

## Perpignan

Framed against the snow-topped Pyrenees, Perpignan is a sultry, sun-baked town with a distinctly Spanish flavour. Palm-shaded squares and winding lanes characterise the attractive old town, dotted with good regional restaurants and lively backstreet bars. It's easily reached by train or car, and is a good launch pad for hikes in the Haut-Languedoc and the lower Pyrenees.

## When to Go

The summer in Languedoc-Roussillon seriously simmers, with scorching temperatures, so it's far from ideal for comfortable hiking. Spring and autumn are much better times for walking, with cooler temperatures and fewer crowds. Snow falls on the mountains and higher hills in winter, so hiking at elevation is only for the experienced.

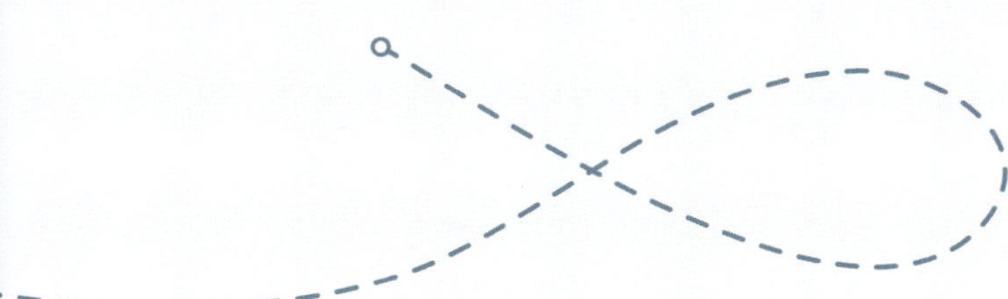

## Where to Stay

Accommodation options are ample and varied in this region. Unsurprisingly, the larger cities, particularly Montpellier, Nîmes and Carcassonne, offer the largest choices, from boutique hotels and five-star establishments to budget ventures and chain hotels. Book well ahead in summer, both inland and along the coast.

Having your own wheels opens up the region's rural landscape and the choice is even greater, with charming rural retreats and bijou bed and breakfasts.

## What's On

**Carnaval de Limoux** (limoux.fr; Jan-Mar) One of the region's biggest carnivals runs over several weekends.

**Les Grands Jeux de Nîmes** (arenes-nimes.com; Apr) Nîmes' amphitheatre hosts this Roman-themed extravaganza, complete with staged gladiatorial battles and a triumphal street parade.

**Montpellier Danse** (montpellier danse.com; Jul) Dance, both classical and contemporary, is celebrated in Montpellier.

**Embrasement de la Cité** (carcassonne.org; Jul) Bastille Day culminates with a knockout fireworks display over Carcassonne's medieval city.

**Joutes Nautiques** (tourisme-sete. com/joute-nautiques-fete-tradition. html; Aug) Water jousting tournaments take place on Sète's canals, where rival teams attempt to knock each other out of their boats using long poles. Bonkers and brilliant.

## Transport

The main airports in Languedoc-Roussillon are in Montpellier, Nîmes and Perpignan, which are served by a number of regional low-cost carriers from many French and European cities, including easyJet, Volotea, Air France, Transavia and KLM.

Getting here by train is straightforward: frequent, fast services run across the Spanish and Italian borders, and from Paris, which has onward connections to the UK, Germany, the Netherlands and other northern European countries.

Montpellier is a hub, with fast TGV trains all over France. The TGV Midi-Méditerranée links Paris' Gare de Lyon with Montpellier's two stations (central St-Roch and the new Sud de France station outside town) in just over three hours.

Local buses can be tricky to navigate, as there are multiple companies and timetables often revolve around school term times. Having a car makes exploring rural areas much easier.

# 38

# Gorges d'Héric

| DURATION | DIFFICULTY | DISTANCE | START/END |
|---|---|---|---|
| 3hr return | Easy | 9km | Gorges d'Héric car park |

| TERRAIN | | Paved |
|---|---|---|

You don't always have to bust a gut to enjoy big views. This lovely canyon trail is easy-going, paved all the way (so suitable for wheelchairs and push-chairs), involves a gentle climb (min/max altitude 785m/1100m) and even has a cute seasonal cafe at the end – and the mountain views are absolutely majestic.

The route begins at the gorge car park, just outside the village of Mons (arrive early in high season, as this is a popular walk and the car park's often full up by 9am). From here, the tarmac trail winds up straight into the gorges, and, before too long, you'll find yourself framed on either side by seriously high mountains, with **thickets of chestnuts** and green oak carpeting the lower slopes. Signed panels provide information on local nature and wildlife.

The path ascends gradually, following the right bank of the river. As you walk, you'll pass plenty of **natural plunge pools** filled with crystal-clear mountain water (pictured): they're perfect for cooling off in on a hot day, but take care climbing down as the rocks can be slippery and it's easy to twist an ankle.

The mountains get ever higher as you climb further into the **Massif du Caroux**. These mountains are home to some of Haut-Languedoc's classic climbing routes, so keep your eyes peeled for rock-bunnies picking their way up the sheer cliffs.

After about 1½ hours, the trail climbs around a sharp bend and eventually arrives at the tiny hamlet of **Héric**, little more than a cluster of stone farmhouses and slate-roofed barns. In summer, there's a little cafe here where you can refresh yourself with a drink and a snack before retracing your steps back down the valley.

# Cirque de Mourèze

| DURATION | DIFFICULTY | DISTANCE | START/END |
|---|---|---|---|
| 3hr return | Easy | 9km | Gorges d'Héric car park |

| TERRAIN | | Paved |
|---|---|---|

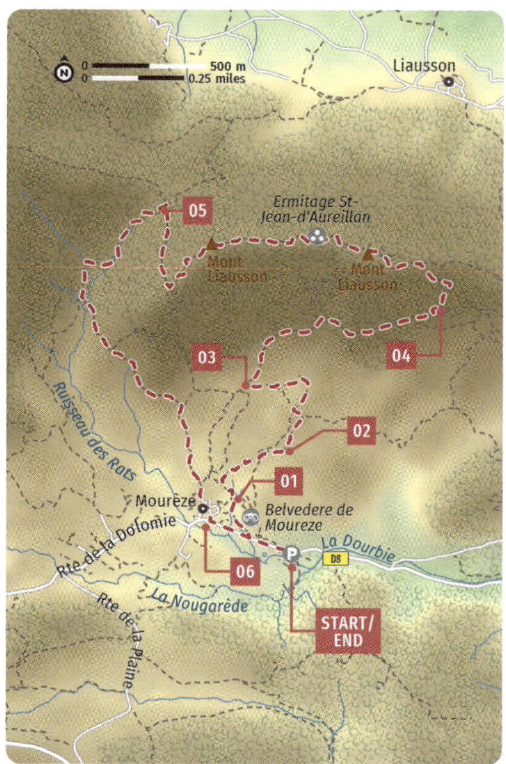



This hike (min/max altitude 200m/535m) explores a strange amphitheatre of limestone peaks, then climbs onto a rocky ridge for wonderful views of the Lac du Salagou and the surrounding Languedoc landscape.

## Getting Here

The walk is directly accessed from the village of Mourèze. There are regular buses from Montpellier (line 663 or 685, 45 minutes; six daily Monday to Saturday, three on Sunday). See herault-transport.fr for timetables.

## Starting Point

The village car park is on the edge of Mourèze and clearly signposted. There is also limited parking available along the roadside if the car park is full.

**01** From the car park, follow trail signs for the cirque (bring extra water and a hat, as the cirque acts like a cauldron on hot summer days). You'll climb up a short staircase and then enter the amphitheatre proper. **Dolomite peaks** appear immediately, carved out into all kinds of weird shapes by aeons of erosion. Before long you'll pass a viewpoint, the **Belvédère des Courtinals**, which offers a panoramic view of the cirque, and the rooftops of Mourèze beyond. Many of the rocks are said to resemble things – see if you can spot the Sphinx, the Camel and the Grand Manitou.

**02** There are several trails to follow through the cirque. They're well signed, but it's quite easy to miss the markers, so keep your eyes open. The trail dips and dives between the **rock pillars** and **towers**; it's not too tough, but can be dusty and slippery underfoot. You'll pass thickets of **garrigue**, the hardy, fragrant shrubs that are about the only things that can grow in the Languedoc's dry land-

HUANG ZHENG/SHUTTERSTOCK ©

## Lac du Salagou

Created in 1968 by damming the Salagou River, this reservoir is popular for hiking, horse riding and summer picnics.

Covering 750 hectares, it's known for its crimson-orange rock and strangely shaped islands, making it look rather like a lake might on Mars. It's 48km northwest of Montpellier.

scape: rosemary, heather, juniper and arbutus. During the Middle Ages the cirque was used by local shepherds as a natural pen for their sheep flocks, which kept the vegetation in check.

**03** After a while you'll see signs for the **Circuit des Charbonniers**, which is the next route to follow. It meanders gradually up to the edge of the cirque, then climbs sharply up into a forest of stubby green oaks that provide some very welcome shade.

**04** The uphill, winding section through the trees is steep and tough work – about 300m of ascent –

so take your time, and as many breathers as you need.

After about 20 to 30 minutes of climbing, you'll emerge on a rocky ridge called the **Mont Liausson**. It affords an impressive outlook south over the cirque, and also north across the Lac du Salagou. There are also the ruins of a medieval hermitage of **St-Jean-d'Aureillan**, but these are off-limits. The ridge is a perfect place for a picnic lunch, if you've brought one: there are plenty of shaded spots to choose from. When you've fuelled up, follow the path west along the ridge, then downhill: this section is rocky and rubbly, so watch your step.

**05** You'll reach a junction – the **Col de Portes** – turn left, following it south back into the cirque. You'll pass rock formations before eventually rejoining the Sentier des Courtinals.

**06** From here, it's easy walking to **Mourèze** (pictured), where there are several cafes. The **medieval church** is also worth a look before heading off.

## Take a Break

For lunch, **L'Art de la Flamme** (☎ 04 67 96 08 11; art-de-la-flamme.fr) on the edge of Mourèze is a decent spot.

# 40

# Roc des Hourtous

| DURATION | DIFFICULTY | DISTANCE | START/END |
|---|---|---|---|
| 4hr return | Moderate | 9.5km | La Malène |

| TERRAIN | Rocky paths, steep woodland trail |
|---|---|

The Parc National des Cévennes offers hundreds of superb walks. This one (min/max altitude 560m/915m) takes in a panoramic view over the Tarn valley and the moonscape of the Causse Méjean.

## Getting Here

Your own wheels are the best way to explore the gorges. In July and August there are daily shuttle buses between Florac, Ste-Énimie and Le Rozier, but none of these go to La Malène.

## Starting Point

There is a large public car park along the banks of the river in La Malène, but there's no village shop.

**01** From the car park, cross the **bridge** over the river (pictured) and turn right. Soon, you'll see a trailhead ascending up the steep hillside to your left. Take it, and follow it as it switchbacks steeply up the cliff. There are a couple of excellent viewpoints along the way, offering super views over the valley, the clattering river and the rooftops of La Malène.

**02** It's initially steep-going as you climb, but eventually the trail starts to level off as you reach the top of the cliff. After about an hour of climbing, you'll eventually come to the pretty little hamlet of **Rieisse**, with its stone farm buildings, chicken coops and the occasional puttering tractor.

If you wish, there's a detour trail from the village that leads north to the top of the **Roc du Serre**, where there's an orientation table that helps interpret the view. It's about 50 minutes there and back if you choose to take it.

## On the River

Right up until the early 20th century, the Tarn was still used to carry goods and passengers between the surrounding valleys. Historically, boatmen would have used flat-bottomed barges known as barques, but nowadays canoes and kayaks are a much more common sight on the river.

If you'd prefer to experience the river the traditional way, **Les Bateliers de la Malène** (gorgesdutarn.com; per 4 people €100; Apr-Oct) will punt you down an 8km stretch of the gorge from La Malène in an authentic old-fashioned barge, then drive you back. The journey time is one hour, depending on river conditions.

ROGERMECHAN/SHUTTERSTOCK ©

**Best for**

**ESCAPING THE CROWDS**

**03** Continue west from Rieisse. As you leave the village, look out for a cross and signs to the **Roc des Hourtous**, which you'll reach after about 20 minutes of walking.

There's a cafe and a car park at the Roc where you can stop for refreshments if you wish, with a grassy picnic area and tables looking directly out over the valley. Continue northeast along the rocky ridge line along the cliff edge, skirting through the trees. There are several **viewpoints** along the way where you can look out over the chasm, and stare down to the river several hundred metres below.

**04** After about 800m, signs lead down off the ridge – they're easy to miss, so stay alert. From here, the trail descends very sharply on the steep cliff face beneath the Roc des Hourtous. The trail is very rocky and slippery at times, but is at least fairly easy to follow – walking poles might come in handy. Just be grateful you're climbing down rather than climbing up...

**05** Eventually, you'll reach the end of the downhill path and emerge onto the south bank of the **Tarn**. Follow the path as it leads right (east), looping round the base of the **Rocher de Montesquieu** before returning to the start point at La Malène.

## Take A Break

There are several places to eat in La Malène, but the 13th-century, turreted **Manoir de Montesquiou** (04 66 48 51 12; manoir-montesquiou. com; d €82-152, 4-person apt €160; menus from €18; Apr-Oct; P ❄ 🛜) is the pick. The attractive restaurant has a plane-tree-shaded terrace overlooking the river and La Malène's old stone bridge, and serves excellent, locally inspired dishes.

# 41

# Pic St-Loup

| DURATION | DIFFICULTY | DISTANCE | START/END |
| --- | --- | --- | --- |
| 2hr return | Moderate | 5.5km | Pic St-Loup car park |

| TERRAIN | |
| --- | --- |
| | Rocky paths |

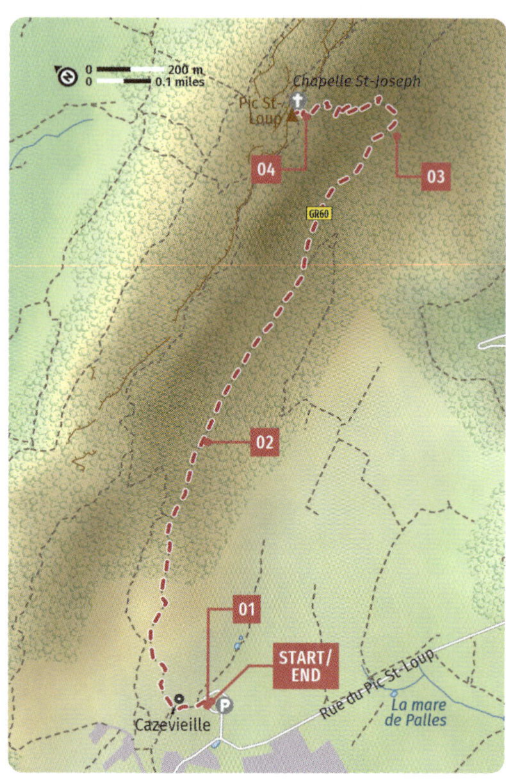


Another of the Languedoc classics, this uphill hike (min/max altitude 220m/658m) ascends to the summit of one of the region's most distinctive peaks – the shark-fin-shaped Pic St-Loup, topped by a medieval church.

## Getting Here

The village of Cazevieille is a 25km drive from Montpellier. Public transport is a pain: the nearest bus runs as far as Les Matelles, 9km from the village.

## Starting Point

The car park for Pic St-Loup is signposted from Cazevieille.

**01** From the car park, follow the signposted trail uphill, passing a small stone shelter and bearing right up the stony path. Dead ahead, you'll see the distinctive pyramidal profile of **Pic St-Loup**, one of the most famous geological features in the Languedoc – not least because it graces countless local wine labels. The path climbs gradually through fragrant **garrigue** and stands of holm oak, boxwood and juniper – the only trees hardy enough to survive in this dry, sunbaked environment. The ecosystem is delicate, so stick to the trail to avoid erosion.

**02** The path continues on a gentle incline for about 1.5km. The mountain remains ever in view. It was formed some 190 million years ago during the Jurassic period, when the entire landscape around was covered by sea, and tectonic movements shifted the seabed, forming the chain of mountains stretching from Provence to the Pyrenees. Around 65 million years ago, the waters receded and the peak of St-Loup was, for many millennia, a 1000m-high island. Forty-five million years ago the seas retreated further, and a long process of erosion pared the summit down to its current height of

PHOTOPROFI30/SHUTTERSTOCK ©

## The Legend of Pic St-Loup

The Chapelle St-Joseph is involved in the medieval legend that gave the peak its name. Three brothers (Loup, Guiral and Clair) all fell in love with the same girl before going off on a holy crusade. When they returned, they were distraught to discover that their beloved had died. Heartbroken, they resolved to become hermits, and each chose a solitary summit on which they would build a fire in her memory every year. Loup (Wolf) also built the chapel on the mountaintop. He was the last of the three brothers to die; in their honour, local villagers named their peaks after them – Mont St-Guiral, Mont St-Clair and Pic St-Loup.

658m, carving out its sheer sides in the process. It's been a protected site since 1978.

**03** You'll reach a junction: ignore the path descending to the right, and continue through a tunnel of holm oaks. Not too far along you'll reach another junction, known as the **Crossroads of the Croisette**. Turn left (uphill). Here's where the trail gets steep: it winds through a series of switchbacks, ascending fairly sharply up the hillside. At times the path is narrow and rubbly, and a bit unstable underfoot – after periods of rain, it can be slippery. It's a stiff climb to the summit, 300m or so further up.

**04** It's easy to know when you've reached the top – it's marked by the medieval **Chapelle St-Joseph**, which was restored in 1995 but is probably built on a much older sacred site. The summit has also clearly been a holy place for many centuries: the surrounding area is covered with many tumuli and ancient remains. Nearby, a striking iron cross reaches skyward, and a **belvédère** opens out onto a stunning view over the surrounding valley (pictured). The ridge of **Col de Fambétou** lies dead ahead; on a clear day you can make out the summits of **Mont Lozère** and **Mont Aigoual** in the Cévennes to the northeast and, way off to the east, is the snow-dusted hump of **Mont Ventoux**, Provence's queen of mountains. The valley below is filled with vineyards; wine was first grown here by the Phoenicians, and has been a vital part of the economy ever since. When you've enjoyed the views and had a picnic, retrace your steps back to the car park, about 2.7km downhill.

 Take a Break

Cazevieille is tiny, so there's not much choice for sustenance – most people pack a picnic and eat it at the summit beside the Chapelle St-Joseph (real connoisseurs might even pack a bottle of local Pic St-Loup wine).

# 42

# Cirque de Navacelles

| DURATION | DIFFICULTY | DISTANCE | START/END |
|---|---|---|---|
| 3½hr return | Moderate | 10km | Cirque de Navacelles car park |

| TERRAIN | Well-signed stone paths |
|---|---|

This amazing natural amphitheatre looks like a crater from an ancient meteorite strike. In fact, it's the result of nothing more devastating than aeons of natural erosion.

## Getting Here

The cirque is a 77km drive from Montpellier, between the villages of St-Maurice-Navacelles and Blandas (if you're using sat nav, don't get confused with the other Navacelles, which is miles away in the foothills of the Cévennes). Buses (line 108) run from Montpellier to the nearby village of Le Vigan, from where there are shuttle buses in summer.

## Starting Point

There are a couple of car parks down in the village, but they fill up quickly in summer – arrive early to be sure of a spot.

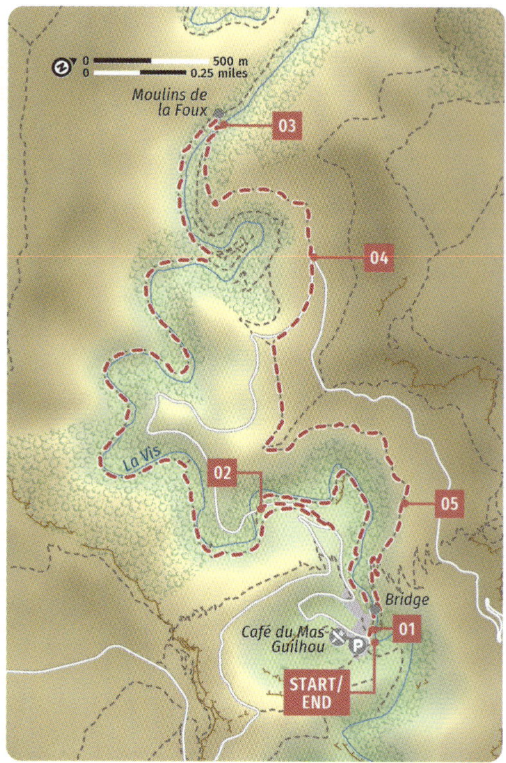


**01** From the car park on the riverbank, follow the river until you get to the handsome **arched stone bridge** that crosses the Vis, but don't take it; for the first section of the walk you'll be tracing the right riverbank. It's a pleasant walk through **woods**, with the clattering **Vis** a constant presence on your right.

**02** The trail loops back on itself and eventually you'll reach a junction with the road (D130E). Turn left and walk uphill on the road for about 400m; where the road branches, you'll see a trail on your right heading away from the road to the southeast. Take it, and follow it downhill as it meanders back down towards the river. The trail becomes **increasingly wooded** as you continue; some sections can be slippery after rain, and a few points near the river occasionally get flooded (signs will indicate if this is the case). Follow the path all the way to the Moulins de la Foux.

## The Source of the Vis

Even though local folk tales say that the Vis is bottomless, several cave-diving expeditions have tried to find the source.

The deepest dives were made in 2006 by divers from the European Karst Plain Project, who penetrated 2.3km at a depth of 104m, an epic dive that lasted six hours and 19 minutes.

A subsequent dive the following year managed a further 600m, reaching as far as the village of Vissec on the Causse du Larzac – but so far, the true source remains a mystery.

RUDMER ZWERVER/SHUTTERSTOCK ©

**03** The **medieval mill** marks the rough halfway point of the walk, so it's a good place for a picnic. It's perched beside a rushing, roaring cascade (the word *foux* comes from the Occitan word *fos* meaning spring). Thanks to the force of water, there's been a mill here since the late 11th century; the present buildings were built in 1629 – although one was swept away by a massive flood in 1741 – and continued working until 1907. The mills were carefully restored in 2000. You can walk inside, and at times gaze down through the stone floor into the foaming tumult below. During very dry periods and very hot summers, the river occasionally peters out to a trickle, and sometimes disappears altogether – so to see it in full flow, it's best to come in spring or early summer, after there's been a day or two of rain.

**04** Cross over the bridge next to the mill and follow the trail on your left as it climbs up. After a while you'll reach a junction with the D713. Follow it downhill for a while, then take the trail left.

**05** Before long you'll find yourself quite a distance above the valley floor, with steep scree slopes tumbling down to your right – a bit daunting if you're wary of heights, but offering **impressive views**. The path continues like this all the way to a series of zigzagging switchbacks that lead back down the hillside and into the village. Cross the bridge and you'll be back where you began.

### Take a Break

The **Café du Mas Guilhou** (06 47 62 77 23; masguilhou.fr) is a convivial place for lunch, serving salads, tartines and sharing platters. It also offers B&B rooms and *gîte*-style bunks if you feel like staying overnight.

# Mont Aigoual

| DURATION | DIFFICULTY | DISTANCE | START/END |
|---|---|---|---|
| 8hr return | Hard | 24km | Valleraugue |

| TERRAIN | Mountain paths, forest trails |
|---|---|

This epic walk is also known as the Sentier des 4000 Marches (Trail of 4000 Steps) – which gives you a hint that there might be some climbing involved. The reward? One of the finest mountain views in the south of France – but boy, you have to earn it (min/max altitude 350m/1565m).

This is the classic walk of the Cévennes, a loop route via the summit of Mont Aigoual. But there's no getting around it: it's a tough, full-day proposition, with just over 1400m of ascent and mixed terrain, so definitely for hardened hikers only. Make sure you pack plenty of food and water, a waterproof jacket and proper high-ankle boots.

## Getting Here

Valleraugue is about 60km south of Florac, or 72km north of Montpellier, an easy 1½-hour drive. There is a daily bus between Montpellier and Le Vigan (line 608), and another which travels onwards to Valleraugue (line 108), but you'll probably have to overnight in Valleraugue as you'll need an early-morning start to ensure adequate time to complete the walk. See herault-transport.fr for full timetables.

## Starting Point

Check in at the Maison du Pays (which also doubles as Valleraugue's tourist office) for the latest weather forecast and route tips.

**01** Despite its name, there actually aren't that many steps on this route – and no one's quite sure how it got its moniker. There's a bit of tricky trail-finding along the way, so a good map will come in very handy: *IGN Top 25 2641ET Mont Aigoual/le Vigan/Parc national des Cévennes* is the one you want, at 1:25,000 scale.

Leaving from the Maison du Pays, turn left and walk along the rue de Luxembourg. At the bridge turn right and cross the river. Continue uphill on the chemin du Mas Mouret. After about 130m, turn right onto the chemin du Stade and walk (alongside a football pitch) for 60m until you reach a fork in the road, go left (uphill) onto the narrow, tree-lined chemin du Magnel until you reach an impressive **belvédère** where you can stop and enjoy the view before starting on the walk proper.

**02** From here, the path begins to climb. It's a reasonably sharp ascent, passing through groves of **chestnut trees** planted by villagers in previous centuries, when they relied on the trees to provide food and flour. Gradually the **views** open up as you ascend towards l'Estivel.

**03** After about 3km of climbing, you'll reach the **Estivel plateau**, a good place for a breather. Ignore any side trails on the right and continue climbing. There's some hard graft involved here, as this is where you'll be making the majority of the day's ascent, but you just have to push on and tick off the metres. It's another 4km to the top, but it'll take a while because of the gradient. You'll pass through some beech groves and eventually reach the cross-roads at **l'Hort de Dieu** and the distinctive menhir known as the **Font de Trépalou**.

**04** From here, make a left detour to stand on the **absolute summit** of the mountain at 1567m. It's impossible to miss thanks to the castle-like observatory built at the top, which is well worth a visit. Even if you don't go inside, there's a **majestic vista** from the viewpoint, encompassing the whole Cévennes and, on the very clearest days, an unbroken pano-

YANN GUICHAOUA-PHOTOS/GETTY IMAGES ©

## The Transhumance

The Cévennes is one of only a handful of places in France where the age-old spectacle known as the transhumance can be seen.

Every spring, local shepherds lead their flocks on foot up from their lowland farms to the higher mountain pastures, where they'll spend the rest of the summer, before returning them again in autumn.

It's a colourful spectacle, with the animals decorated with coloured ribbons and bells, and the shepherds dressed in their traditional finery – and a throwback to a way of life that's sustained the Cévennes for many centuries.

rama that sweeps from the Alps to the Mediterranean and the Pyrenees. It's an incredible spot, and one that makes the hard slog uphill from Valleraugue suddenly seem worth every step.

Opened in 1894, the **Mont Aigoual Observatory** (📞 04 67 42 59 83; aigoual.fr; ⏰ 10am-7pm Jul & Aug, 10am-1pm & 2-6pm May, Jun & Sep) is the last remaining mountain-based meteorological station in France (pictured). Inside, you can learn the science behind weather forecasting and cloud formation. There's also an orientation table from where you can take in the wrap-around views of the central Cévennes.

**05** After the observatory, return to the menhir and take the trail signed for Aire-de-Côte/Sentier des Botanistes. This is also a section of the GR6, GR66 and GR7 long-distance trails, and follows a ledge with **big views** over the southern valleys, and big drops off to the right: watch your step.

**06** This is where the trail map will come in handy, as there are several side trails involved here. Continue around a couple of hairpin bends, and after the second one look out for a track that leads quite steeply down into the forest. Take the next path on the right, which again tumbles down a steep slope for about 50m, then takes another turn at a stone cairn down onto a shale slope. Look out for a gap in the rocks, and follow a fence until it reaches the ridgeline, dips through patches of pine forest and eventually rejoins the main GR6/GR7/GR66 trail.

### A Sky Full of Stars

This region of central France has some of the darkest skies in the country. Not great if you're out camping without a headlamp, but ideal if you're pondering the galaxies, and if you have a telescope, super! But if you haven't got one handy, a pair of binoculars works fine on clear nights. It's possible to see the moon, Saturn, Jupiter, Mercury, Venus and Mars with the naked eye, depending on the time of year and the sky conditions. You can use an app like Night Sky or Star Walk to identify constellations and planets in the sky. Check the tourist office to see if local astronomy clubs have upcoming stargazing sessions.

HEMIS/ALAMY STOCK PHOTO ©

**07** Continue on the trail until you reach **Aire-de-Côte** at 1085m, another natural point of rest. From here, you'll be following the tarmac D100 road southeast.

**08** After about 1.5km, a trail appears on your right, heading southwest away from the road, signposted for Col du Pas. Take it and walk for about 1km.

**09** When you reach **Col du Pas** – a popular target for cyclists – you'll see another trail signed for Valleraugue. From here, the path descends quite steeply into the Vallée des Salles, switchbacking downhill into the little rural hamlet of **Berthezène**.

**10** Cross over a **bridge** spanning the River Clarou, and follow the D10 road all the way back to your starting point in Valleraugue. A tough, long day on the mountain for sure – but congratulations are due: you've just climbed up and down to the rooftop of the Cévennes.

## Take a Break

Valleraugue has a small convenience store for supplies, or stop at the simple **Café du Jardin** ( 04 67 27 37 23; cafedujardin-valleraugue.fr) on rue du Luxembourg for a pre-hike coffee hit or a post-hike fuel stop.

# Also Try...

JEROME PARIS/SHUTTERSTOCK ©

## The Canal du Midi

| DURATION | DIFFICULTY | DISTANCE |
| --- | --- | --- |
| 3hr return | Easy | 4km |

You don't necessarily need a *péniche* (narrowboat) to enjoy the delights of the Canal du Midi: its towpaths provide plenty of walking potential too (with the benefit of also being pancake-flat).

Pretty much any section is worth a wander, but an easy one is the short walk from the hilltop town of Béziers to the famous stepladder of locks known as the Écluses de Fonséranes (pictured), southwest of town. The eight locks and nine gates were built to negotiate a drop of 21.5m from the canal down to the level of the River Orb.

## Signal St-Pierre

| DURATION | DIFFICULTY | DISTANCE |
| --- | --- | --- |
| 3½hr return | Moderate | 9km |

An impressive walk along an old drovers' route leads up to another of the Cévennes' signature viewpoints, the signal point of St-Pierre at 695m.

It's a glorious place, elevated from the surrounding forest and offering a 360-degree view over the treetops: on clear days you should be able to see the Mediterranean away to the south, and the humps of the Massif Central off to the north.

The first section of the route traces the GR70, also known as the Chemin de Stevenson – the route followed by Robert Louis Stevenson and his donkey Modestine in 1878.

TRABANTOS/SHUTTERSTOCK ©

# Carcassonne: La Bastide to the Cité

| DURATION | DIFF. | DISTANCE |
| --- | --- | --- |
| 2hr return | Easy | 4km |

While Carcassonne's dramatic medieval fortress unsurprisingly gets most of the attention, there's actually another side to the town: a square *bastide* (fortified town; pictured) dating from the 13th century, with its distinctive grid of straight streets.

The walk between the two is easy and very rewarding, and en route you get to cross the pedestrianised Pont-Vieux, one of the few surviving medieval bridges in France, prized for its graceful arches and compact dimensions.

# Sommet de Finiels

| DURATION | DIFF. | DISTANCE |
| --- | --- | --- |
| 2hr return | Easy | 4km |

The highest point in the Cévennes is Mont Lozère at 1699m – or to be specific, the Sommet de Finiels.

Unlike the much tougher route to Mont Aigoual, there's a surprisingly easy way to reach the top: you can get a head start by parking at the Chalet du Mont Lozère at 1416m, with just 283m of climbing left to reach the summit. There's an orientation table at the top, and a view that takes in the Monts du Cantal, the Grands Causses and the distant Alps.

# Mont Canigou

| DURATION | DIFF. | DISTANCE |
| --- | --- | --- |
| 4hr return | Moderate/ hard | 8km |

At 2784m, this snow-capped peak is sacred to Catalan people.

The route to the top is best attempted in summer, when the weather is at its most settled. The easiest way to ascend is to get a lift by 4WD to the ski station of Les Courtalets, from where it's a two-to-2½-hour hike, followed by a 1½-to-two-hour return. Even in summer it's a proper mountain walk: wear appropriate gear, and consider employing the services of a local guide for maximum safety.

Parc Naturel Régional des Landes de Cascogne
Roquefort
Mont-de-Marsan
A65
Agen
Valence
Moissac
Caussade
A62
Garonne
N20
Aveyron
Castelsarrasin
Montauban
Gaillac
Tarn
A68
St-Suplice
Montréal du Gers
Condom
Lectoure
Beaumont-de-Lomagne
Aire-sur-l'Adour
Valence-sur-Baïse
N21
Adour
NOUVELLE-AQUITAINE
A65
Gimont
L'Isle-Jourdain
Auch
Colomiers
Toulouse
Mirande
OCCITANIE
Muret
Revel
A64
Morlas
Masseube
Villefranche de Lauragais
Pau
Arros
Mielan
Castelnau Magnoac
Boulogne-sur-Gesse
A61
Oloron-Ste-Marie
Pau
Pontacq
Tarbes
D935
N21
Trie-sur-Baïse
D929
A64
Carbonne
N20
Nay
D940
Lourdes
Lannemezan
St-Gaudens
Garonne
N134
Arudy
Cazères
Montesquieu-Volvestre
Bielle
Argelès-Gazost
Bagnères de Bigorre
Montréjeau
D117
Salat
Pamiers
Mirepoix
Bedous
Laruns
Pierrefitte-Nestalas
D918
N125
St-Girons
Le Mas d'Azil
Ariège
Chalabre
N134
Eaux-Bonnes
52
Pic du Midi (2865m)
St-Béat
Foix
Lavelanet
Puivert
Gabas
Cauterets
Barèges
53
Arreau
Pic de Maubermé (2880m)
Massat
Tarascon-sur-Ariège
Montségur
D117
46
Luz-St-Sauveur
Bagnères-de-Luchon
Mt Valier (2838m)
Seix
Pic des Trois Seigneurs (2199m)
Port de Pailhères (2001m)
Pic du Midi d'Ossau (2884m)
Balaïtous (3146m)
Bossòst
The Pyrénées
Ascou
Parc National des Pyrénées
Vignemale (3298m)
Gavarnie
48
49
Vielha
Ax-les-Thermes
51
45
St-Lary Soulan
Pic Schrader (3174m)
Pic Perdiguère (3222m)
Mt Rouch (2858m)
Pica d'Estats (3143m)
ANDORRA
Jaca
Biescas
Mt Perdido (3355m)
Bielsa
Pico de Aneto (3404m)
ANDORRA LA VELLA
Pic Carlit (2921m)
Sabiñánigo
44
Aínsa
Campo
50
El Pont de Suert
Sort
La Seu d'Urgell
Llívia
47
Rio Gállego
Puigcerdà
Saillagouse
N20
Huesca
La Pobla de Segur
Bagà
Río Noguera Ribagorçana
Benabarre
Tremp
Berga
Barbastro
Río Segre
Solsona
SPAIN
Monzón
Cardona
Binefar
Río Cinca
Balaguer
Manresa
0    40 km
0    20 miles
N
Lleida
Tàrrega

Lac Gentau (p167)

# The Pyrenees

# Explore
# The Pyrenees

The Pyrenees are something special. Sure, they might lack the height of the Alps, but the mirror-glass lakes, the picture-postcard flower meadows, the candy-green fields in the valleys, the neat stone villages and the extensive mossy forests all combine to make these snow-dusted mountains among the most beautiful in Europe.

### Eaux-Bonnes

During the 19th century, the pretty village of Eaux-Bonnes (literally, Good Waters) flourished as a spa resort thanks to its geothermal hot springs. People still come here to take to the waters, but today hiking and skiing are the mainstay of the local economy. It's an ideal base for walk 46.

### Cauterets

The delightful mountain town of Cauterets is full of fin-de-siècle character, with a stately spa and grand 19th-century residences dotted round town. Today it's a busy mountain resort serving both nearby hiking trails and ski slopes. From campsites to swanky hotels, there are plenty of places to stay and, in summer, there are minibus transfers to some of the most popular walking trailheads. Use it as a base for walks 45 and 52.

### Luz-St-Sauveur

Topped by a tumbledown old castle and hemmed in on all sides by mighty peaks, attractive Luz-St-Sauveur is a mountain resort par-excellence. With hiking shops, lots of restaurants and supermarkets and a whole host of different accommodation options, this is an ideal base for walks 44, 47, 48 and 53.

### Bagnères-de-Luchon

Bagnères-de-Luchon (or simply Luchon) is a trim little town of gracious 19th-century buildings, expanded to accommodate the *curistes* who came to take the waters at its splendid spa. It's now one of the Pyrenees' most popular walking and ski areas. In summer minibus transfers are available to some of the most popular trailheads. Base yourself here for walks 49 and 50.

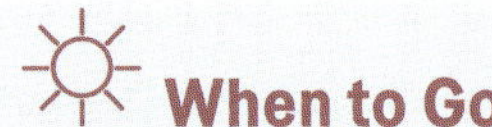

## When to Go

We'll get straight to the point. If you can, go in late September and early October. This is when the leaves of the beech trees that blanket the mountain slopes turn a flaming red and orange, and a dusting of new snow on the summits hints to the coming winter yet the weather remains stable, sunny, and just the right kind of warm.

Autumn might be the best period, but summer is naturally the most popular time to walk here. Days are long and the weather is very reliable. However, it can be too hot and afternoon thunderstorms are common.

Spring (April and May) can be hit and miss. Some years can be wonderful but others can be very wet (or snowy up high) and unsettled. Many of the higher passes remain blocked by snow.

Winter is generally a bad time to walk in the Pyrenees thanks to short days and periods of stormy weather. The snow line is often down as low as 1000m, making most walking routes impassable. That said, in recent years winters have been surprisingly dry and settled and snowfall fairly rare until after Christmas. Increasingly, skiing is giving way to walking.

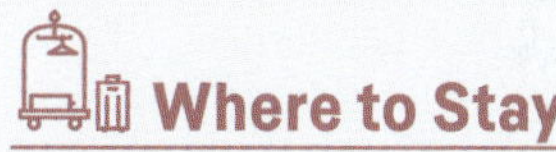

## Where to Stay

You'll find a great variety of lodging on offer in the Pyrenees, including pretty farmhouse B&Bs with mountain views and campsites near hiking spots.

There is a superb series of *refuges* (mountain lodges) deep in the mountains throughout the Pyrenees, where accommodation is generally dorm style. From May to October many of these are staffed and meals can be provided for guests and often non-guests. Although basic, they have a great atmosphere and are good places to meet up with other walkers and exchange info on the trails.

Reserve all accommodation way ahead in the summer. Outside the ski areas, rural lodging generally closes down from about November to March.

## 👍 What's On

**Le Transhumance de Lourdios** (🕑 Jun) Follow the livestock and shepherds during their annual migration to the high mountain pastures. The Vallée d'Aspe has the best known transhumance.

**Foire au Fromage** (cheese fair; 🕑 Oct) Annual fair held in Laruns in the Vallée d'Ossau that celebrates the valley's famed cheese.

**Ski season** (🕑 Dec-Apr) The ski resorts of the Pyrenees are much more low key and local than those of the Alps.



## Resources

**Parc National des Pyrénées** (pyrenees-parcnational.fr) The national park's official tourist site is full of useful info.

**Cauterets Tourist Office** (cauterets.com) Lots of information on walks close to Cauterets.

**Vallée de Gavarnie** (vallees degavarnie.com) Official website for the Gavarnie region.

**Vallée d'Ossau** (valleedossau -tourisme.com) Covering the Ossau Valley in the western part of the range.

**Pyrénées 31** (pyrenees31.com) The lowdown on the soaring peaks around the town of Luchon.

## ✈ Transport

The most convenient airport for the Pyrenees is Pau, but international flights are limited. Biarritz and Toulouse are much busier.

Buses between towns and villages in the Pyrenees are limited and to most walking trail heads they're virtually non-existent (though some tourist offices lay on summer-only minibus transfer services to the most popular walking areas). To properly explore you'll need wheels.

# Plateau de Bellevue

| DURATION | DIFFICULTY | DISTANCE | START/END |
|---|---|---|---|
| 2hr return | Easy | 5.5km | Main car park, Gavarnie |

| TERRAIN | |
|---|---|
| | Mountain trail |

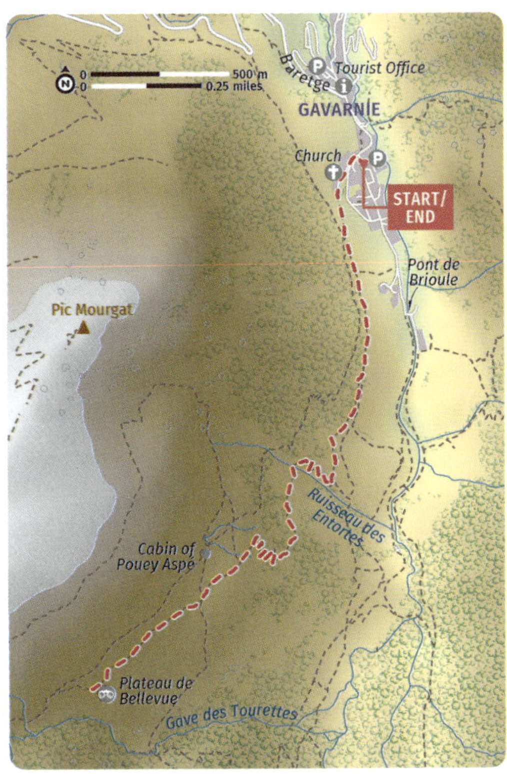


Is this the best family mountain walk in France? Walk (min/max altitude 1365/1700m) to this stunning viewpoint overlooking the famed Cirque de Gavarnie on a warm day in October, when the sky is blue, the leaves on the beech trees are golden and the mountain summits are fluffed with the white of the first winter snows, and you'll probably agree that it is.

From the main car park in Gavarnie, take the cobbled road up past the **church** and **cemetery**. Pass some walking signs and continue along a clear track that rises gently and enters a **deciduous forest**. You'll be able to see the main trail to the **Cirque de Gavarnie** below you, and if it's a nice day then chances are it will be packed with day-tripping tourists. By contrast, you'll likely be alone and tranquil.

The views of the cirque will get better as you climb. The path starts getting steeper and weaves in great curves up the slope. After a little under an hour, you'll clear the tree line and emerge onto the plateau. The small **cabin of Pouey Aspé** is off to the right.

Continue onwards for another 15 minutes until you come to the edge of the **Plateau de Bellevue**, a walk signpost and a great pile of rocks. You now have a grandstand view of the **Cirque de Gavarnie**. The peak to the extreme left is the **Casque du Marbauré** (3325m), **le Casque** (3006m) is more centre, and **Taillon** (3144m) is the biggie on the far right.

From here you can descend into the cirque, but it's a steep, long walk that's not suitable for families. Return instead by the way you came.

# 45

# Refuge des Oulettes de Gaube

| DURATION | DIFFICULTY | DISTANCE | START/END |
|---|---|---|---|
| 5hr return | Moderate | 15km | Parking du Pont d'Espagne |

| TERRAIN | Mountain trail |
|---|---|

This spectacular walk to the glaciers and soaring cliffs of the Vignemale (3298m), the highest point of the French Pyrenees, offers wild forests, sublime lakes, quiet mountain meadows and a face-to-face encounter with some of the mightiest of Pyrenean peaks. Although quite a long walk (min/max altitude 1460/2151m), and one that takes you deep into the high mountains, this is actually a pretty simple hike along a well-signed trail that can even be accomplished by children.

From the park gates head left along a path signed for the GR10 and Lac de Gaube. A couple of hundred metres later, veer left and clamber up through **mixed forest**. After an hour, you'll trip over a rise and arrive on the glimmering blue shores of the large **Lac de Gaube** (pictured). Many families make this the goal of their walk before returning back to the car (1¾ hours return).

Continue around the western shore of the lake on a clear, flat path and then carry on onward and upward. After 2½ hours pass the **Esplumouse waterfalls** on your left. There are great views back down the valley. A short time later, the path levels out at the **Plateau des Petites Oulettes** and the views of the Vignemale fill the horizon ahead.

After another half-hour, during which you climb quite sharply, you will come to the **Refuge des Oulettes de Gaube**. In front of you is a large, waterlogged plateau, at the end of which is the sheer, vertical wall of the mighty north face of the **Vignemale** (3298m) and its **huge glacier**. Return by the same route.

# 46

# Lac d'Ayous Circuit

| DURATION | DIFFICULTY | DISTANCE | START/END |
|---|---|---|---|
| 5½hr return | Moderate | 14km | Parking Lac de Bious-Artigues |

| TERRAIN | Mountain trail, very clearly signed |
|---|---|

This walk (min/max altitude 1419/2103m) is forever throwing something of interest towards you: pastures filled with docile-eyed cows and sheep; soaring fang-like pillars of rock; mossy forests; streams filled with fat trout; not to mention a dazzling multitude of lakes. But as the scenery immediately around you changes one thing remains constant: the towering presence of the Pic du Midi d'Ossau (2884m) just across the valley.

## Getting Here

The nearest village is Gabas. There's very little public transport.

## Starting Point

The walk begins from the Lac de Bious-Artigues, which is a steep 4.5km uphill drive along the D231

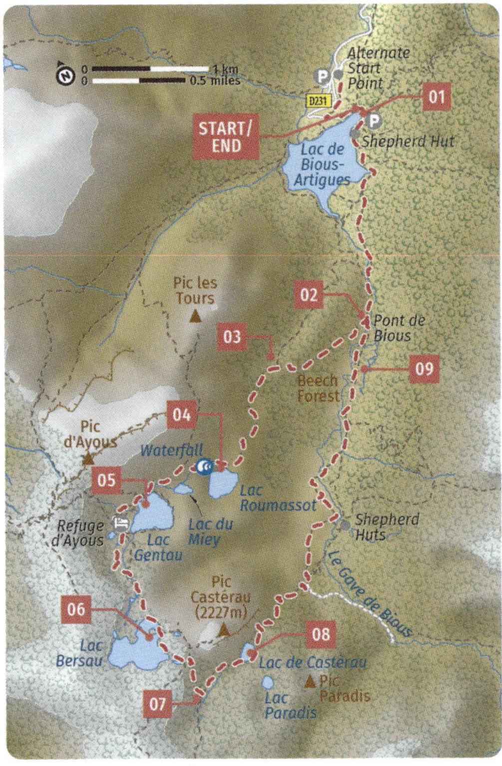


from Gabas. The upper car park (€6.50 per day) is small and fills up fast. Unless you get here early, chances are you will end up in the lower car park (€3.50 per day), which is a very steep, energy-sapping 20- to 30-minute walk to the start point of this hike.

**01** From the upper car park follow the signed path past a **snack shop**, along the eastern bank of the reservoir and uphill through mixed woodlands.

**02** After a sweaty half-hour, the trail levels out at a metal farm gate. Go through this and 100m later the woodlands peel back to reveal a vast pasture shot through by a **fast-flowing stream**. Right at the start of this pasture, the trail forks at a clear **signpost**. Go right (southwest) and uphill back into woodlands.

**03** The next half-hour involves zigzagging uphill through **beech forest** to a small **flower meadow** with **views** over to the Pic du Midi d'Ossau.

STUART BUTLER/LONELY PLANET ©

**04** The next scenic highlight is the **Lac Roumassot**, the first of a multitude of lakes you'll pass. The trail works its way past the lake and then uphill again, flirting with a small **waterfall** as it does so.

**05** Pass more small lakes and pools, then climb up and over another ridge to the spectacular **Lac Gentau** (pictured p159). On a still day, its blue waters beautifully reflect the Pic du Midi d'Ossau. On a bluff just above the lake is the **Refuge d'Ayous**.

**06** The trail works its way uphill through a rocky, desolate landscape. You will soon reach a couple of differ-ent lakes. The biggest is the final lake, **Lac Bersau.**

**07** As you leave Lac Bersau the trail forks. The obvious path carries on straight ahead (south-southwest). Do not take this one. Instead, veer sharp left (east) and downhill. In-stantly, the horizon opens out into a **memorable view** of a grand expanse of high peaks, while just to your left is the bizarre thumb-shaped rocky outcrop of the **Pic Castérau** (2227m; pictured).

**08** The path tumbles in a se-ries of sharp bends down to the **Lac de Castèrau** and then starts a long, leg-aching descent to the valley floor.

**09** Soon enough, you hit the valley floor, where there are often **free-ranging cows and sheep**. In spring the grasslands sparkle with **wild-flowers**. You will come to a rough cement road (authorised vehicles only). Follow this for 20 minutes until you reach the metal gate that first welcomed you to this upland paradise.

Retrace your steps back down-hill to the car.

## Take a Break

The **Marche au Crêpes** snack bar is a little shack, right next to where the walk starts, selling crêpes, galettes and a few other snacks.

# 47

# Brèche de Roland

| DURATION | DIFFICULTY | DISTANCE | START/END |
|----------|-----------|----------|-----------|
| 5hr return | Moderate | 13km | Col de Tentes |

| TERRAIN | Well-marked mountain trail plus a glacier crossing |
|---------|---------------------------------------------------|

Get up into the frosty realms of the high mountains on this trail (min/max altitude 2200/2807m). You'll scramble across scree slopes, tip-toe across the foot of a glacier and then, at the walk's culminating point, stand in the dramatic rock gateway of the Brèche de Roland. But there is a catch…deep snow renders this walk inaccessible for much of the year. You should only attempt this route in fine, settled weather between late July and early October. During these months, this is a very popular walk.

## Getting Here

The village of Gavarnie is an obvious base. The Col des Tentes is a spectacular 25-minute drive southwest of Gavarnie along the D923.

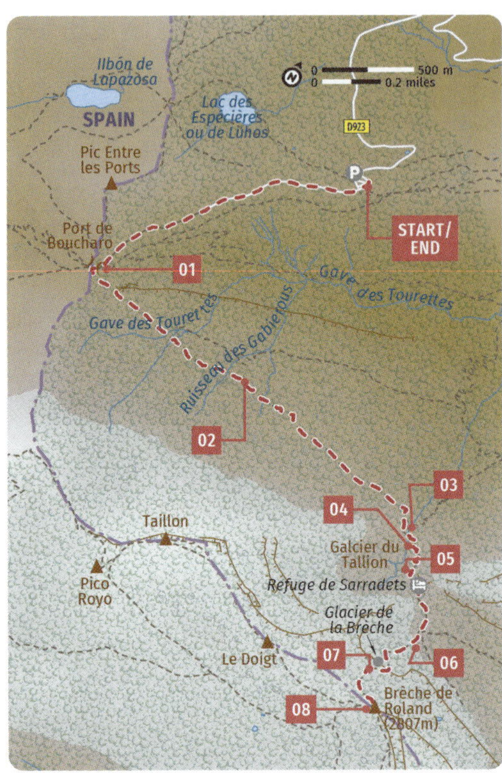


## Starting Point

The walk begins from the car park at the Col des Tentes. There are no facilities here, but there are grand views.

**01** Take the track heading southwest towards the **Port de Boucharo** (at the France–Spain border). A couple of different walk trails meet here. Our route veers sharp left (east) and climbs upward.

**02** For the next hour the trail leads gently upwards along the steep northern flank of **Le Taillon** (3144m).

**03** The first real challenge is crossing a **multifingered stream**. The waters flow fast and it's very slippery. There's no set crossing point. Just watch where other people are crossing (pictured).

STUART BUTLER/LONELY PLANET ©

**04** The trail climbs steeply for 15 minutes before popping up onto flatter ground at the foot of the **Galcier du Tallion**. Pick your way around the edge of the glacier. In July this might involve walking on the last of the winter snow. Always stick to the obvious trail.

**05** Next stop is the **Col de Sarradets** (2589m) and the **Refuge de Sarradets**. From here there's an incredible view of **Cirque de Gavarnie**. The **Grande Cascade** (Large Waterfall) is directly in front of you. For those walking with children, this is a good place to call it a day. Simply retrace your steps to make a walk of 3½ to four hours.

**06** For those carrying on to the Brèche de Roland, the way ahead is obvious if a little daunting. The trail climbs very steeply upwards along a **ridge of scree**. If you're here early (or late) in the season and the ridge is covered in snow with no obvious path through it, do not ascend any further.

**07** Cresting a ridge, the Brèche de Roland is now just above you, but between you and it lies the **Glacier de la Brèche**; a giant ice ramp that leads to the rock gateway. The trail over the ice and snow is normally obvious but still requires a lot of care and attention.

**08** Ten minutes later, you'll find yourself standing in the shadow of the **Brèche de Roland** (2807m). The views south into Spain and north over France are astounding. The Spanish side is a desert-like wilderness of empty rock scarred and wrinkled by ice. By contrast, the views over the French side lead the eye over distant fertile mountain pastures. Retrace your steps the way you came.

## Take a Break

The **Refuge de Sarradets** serves full evening meals for people staying, and drinks and snacks at lunchtime for those just passing through.

# 48

# Cirque de Troumouse

| DURATION | DIFFICULTY | DISTANCE | START/END |
|---|---|---|---|
| 4½hr return | Moderate | 12.5km | Parking de la Chapelle d'Héas |

| TERRAIN | Mountain trail |
|---|---|

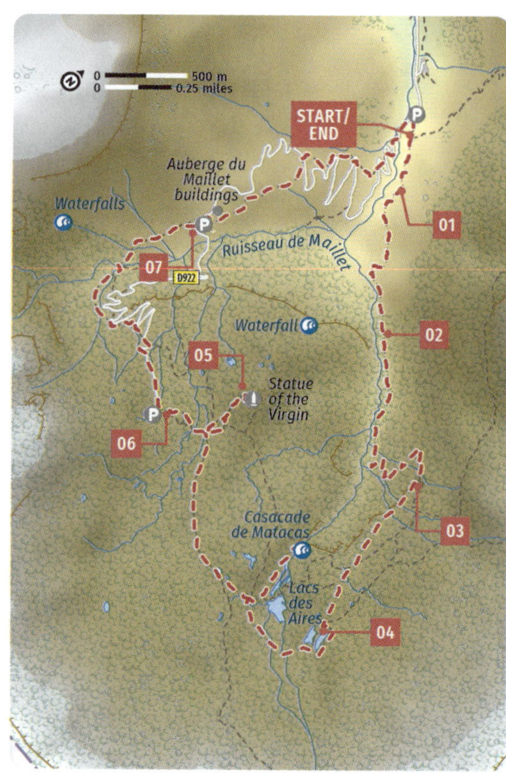


From first-time hiker to hardened mountain yeti, there's something for everyone on this fabulous circular walk (min/max altitude 1517/2135m) around the base of the Cirque de Troumouse. The cinematic landscape here is wide and wild: a huge rolling pasture dotted with small pools stands at the foot of a wall of grey-brown rock and snow-dusted peaks.

## Getting Here

The walk begins from the hamlet of Héas. To get there from the attractive town of Luz-St-Sauveur, drive south along the D921 to Gèdre, then take the minor D922 to Héas. It's 20km from Luz-St-Sauveur and 8.5km from Gèdre. When you're in Héas, park at the large car park on the right just beyond the church. There's no public transport.

## Starting Point

There are no facilities at the start point except some walk information signs.

**01** From the car park, head uphill on the clear **stone track** signed for the Cirque de Troumouse. At the junction 50m from the start continue straight.

**02** After 30 minutes, the trail flattens a little and you enter a **pasture** with views to the mountains ahead and a **waterfall** to your west. At the head of the pasture, the trail starts climbing, first slowly and then in steep zigzags. This is the part of the walk where you earn your ticket to the cirque! Allow at least 45 minutes for this climb.

**03** At the **signed junction** continue straight ahead (south) towards the wall of mountains. A few minutes later, the path levels up and you start to enter the **cirque**.

## Family Version

For a shorter, more family-friendly version of this walk (3½-hour return without stops) follow stages 01 to 04 and then simply turn around and return by the way you came.

This part of the walk is possible with young children without too many dramas – though be sure to take a whole load of snacks and leave a full day to complete.

STUART BUTLER/LONELY PLANET ©

**04** The floor of the cirque is a wide grassy basin pocked with small hills and dotted with **pools and lakes**. The path makes a slow semicircle as it traverses the floor of the cirque (pictured). The **views** just seem to get better and better with a solid line of 3000m-plus peaks forming one giant wall. There are numerous short side trails leading off the main path to **pools**, **drop-offs** and **viewpoints**.

**05** The trail works over a low ridge and bends slightly northwest away from the mountain wall.

You will come to a junction. Head straight on (north) to a table-shaped rise topped with a **statue of the Virgin**. From here, you can admire staggering **mountain views**.

**06** Return back to the main trail, cross the bridge and head towards a small car park. Descend on a trail that crosses the road multiple times.

**07** The trail leaves the road and heads towards a dramatic series of **waterfalls**, before bending back around and arriving in a lower car park. Drop down to the lower of two buildings here, cross a cattle grid and go immediately left before the stone bridge on a faint trail that follows the course of some electricity pylons. As you walk, the trail becomes clearer. A long, tiring and very steep descent now follows, during which you cross the road a couple of times. After a muscle-burning, knee-jarring hour, you will arrive back at your car.

## Take a Break

Bring a picnic and enjoy it in the quieter eastern side of the cirque.

# 49

# Lac Vert

| DURATION | DIFFICULTY | DISTANCE | START/END |
|---|---|---|---|
| 5½hr return | Moderate | 12.5km | Parking Vallée du Lis |

| TERRAIN | |
|---|---|
| | Mountain trail |

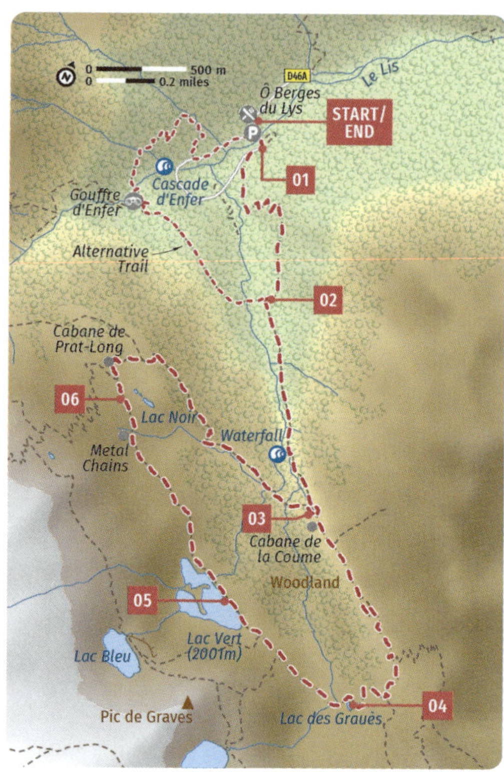


You don't have to spend long walking in the Pyrenees to realise that lakes are an essential element of any walk here. All of them are beautiful, but perhaps none more so than Lac Vert (Green Lake). High above the floor of the Lis Valley and reached via a trail (min/max altitude 1135/2010m) that wends through forests and up and down ridges, Lac Vert is a hypnotic emerald-green haze backed by dark mountain slopes and surrounded by lush meadows.

## Getting Here

From Luchon take the road (D125 and D46) towards Superbagnères, but veer off onto the D46a that leads into the Vallée du Lis (Lis Valley) before dead-ending at the large car park near the electrical plant. It's 11.5km from Luchon.

## Starting Point

There's a large car park but several classic walking routes start from here; in summer, the car park fills up early and you may have to find a parking space somewhere back along the road. Facilities include walk-information panels and a restaurant.

**01** From the parking area, cross the bridge over the **River Lis** and, around 100m later, leave the road for a signed grassy track on the left. The trail rises steeply southeast through thick beech forests and then pine. It's hard going but at least it's shaded!

**02** After a little under an hour, the path levels out and you emerge onto a summer livestock pasture with a **shepherds' cabin** (1390m). At the trail junction, take the left fork

## Family Walk

For a great family outing (2½ hours; min/max altitude 1132/1390m) take a walk up to the shepherds' cabin mentioned in stop 02.

From here, turn right and descend to the Gouffre d'Enfer (a lake and dam) and then loop down to the valley floor and the dramatic Cascade d'Enfer (Enfer Waterfall).

STUART BUTLER/LONELY PLANET ©

(straight ahead). You'll quickly be back into forest and the climb resumes. Along the way you'll pass a couple of impressive **waterfalls** that make good spots to rest and cool off.

**03** Around 1½ hours from the start, you come to a second cabin (**Cabane de la Coume**; 1715m) and the trail forks again with Lac Vert signed in both directions. Take the left fork.

**04** As you continue to climb steeply, the trees get smaller and then finally die away completely, and you will find yourself walking over grassy pastures with mountains starting to fill in the view ahead. The path zigzags upward and bends to the right (south). With a final heave, you'll come face to face with the small **Lac des Grauès**.

**05** The going is easier as the clear trail undulates over a couple of ridges before bringing you to the shores of the large, surreal **Lac Vert** (2001m). Walk along the northern shore of this almost figure-eight-shaped lake and watch how the waters change colour with the movement of sunlight and cloud.

**06** The path rises and falls along the lake and then starts a long descent. **Metal chains** are bolted to the rocky slope to ease you down a steep section (in fine weather you don't really need the help of the chains). Eventually a smaller, darker lake springs into view. This is the **Lac Noir** (Black Lake); shortly after, you pass the **Cabane de Prat-Long** where the path forks again. Turn sharp right (east) and start a tiring, long drop through forest to the junction at the Cabane de la Coume. From here, simply retrace your steps back down to your car.

# Lac d'Oo & Lac Saussat

| DURATION | DIFFICULTY | DISTANCE | START/END |
| --- | --- | --- | --- |
| 4½hr return | Moderate | 13km | Granges d'Astau |

| TERRAIN | | Mountain trail |
| --- | --- | --- |

Lac d'Oo is a huge, startling coloured sheet of water bookended by spectacular cliffs and crashing waterfalls, while the higher-altitude Lac Saussat is smaller, wilder and more intimate. The walk (min/max altitude 1139/1967m) to either of them is a non-stop succession of changing scenery and there's something in this valley suitable for all types of walker. It's no surprise then that this is one of the more popular walks in the Pyrenees. Go early or try and avoid high summer if you want a hint of peace.

## Getting Here

The nearest town – and an ideal base for this walk – is Bagnères-de-Luchon (normally just called Luchon). A *navette* (shuttle-bus service) runs from outside the tourist office in Luchon to the Granges d'Astau twice a day (adult/child return €11/5) throughout July and August. Otherwise, it's a 14km drive southwest from Luchon along the D76.

## Starting Point

There's a large car park at Granges d'Astau, with walk-information panels and places to buy snacks.

**01** The route up to Lac d'Oo is very clear. Simply follow the signed track away from the parking area and start climbing through **mixed woodland**. After a while, the wide track shrinks to a smaller footpath, but it remains obvious. The climb is generally very gentle. An hour

## Additional Trails

For a more challenging walk (8½ hours return), you can continue onwards from the Lac Saussat to the Refuge du Portillon (2570m), which sits on the often frozen shores of the lake of the same name. The vista from the refuge out across the lake to the wall of mountains piled up around it is one of the best views in the Pyrenees.

Other than the distance this isn't an especially hard walk in fine summer weather, but we would suggest overnighting at the refuge in order to fully appreciate the high-mountain ambience.

STUART BUTLER/LONELY PLANET ©

after setting out, you will arrive on the shores of the large **Lac d'Oo** (pictured). It's a marvellous spot; light woodland lines its banks, and at the far southern end a wall of rock rises up more dramatically, down which plunges a 275m-high **waterfall**. Lac d'Oo is a good goal for families with younger children.

**02** The trail, which has red-and-white GR waymarkers, makes its way along the eastern side of Lac d'Oo and, towards the far end of the lake, begins to climb more steadily. Both the trees and the crowds start to slowly thin out as you gain altitude. Pass a small waterfall and a little while later veer right at the trail fork.

**03** After a further 1½ hours you will climb breathlessly up onto the **Col d'Espingo** (1967m). From here, there are **views** to the south of a solid wall of 3000m-plus mountain peaks. Just beyond the pass is the **Refuge d'Espingo**, just off the trail to the right, and the pretty **Lac d'Espingo**.

**04** Many people call it a day at the *refuge*, but it's worth carrying on another 10 minutes to the slightly lower (1940m) **Lac Saussat**. Much quieter than either Lac d'Oo or Lac d'Espingo and with the mountains reflected brilliantly in its lime-green waters, this is an ideal place to idle a while before returning to your car via the same route (leave two hours for this).

## Take a Break

At both Lac d'Oo and Lac d'Espingo there are mountain *refuges* that serve snacks, drinks and even full meals. Many people also just picnic on the shores of one of the lakes.

# 51

# Pic du Tarbésou & the Blue & Black Lakes

| DURATION | DIFFICULTY | DISTANCE | START/END |
|---|---|---|---|
| 4½hr return | Moderate | 12.5km | Parking Pla de Mounégou |

| TERRAIN | | Mountain trail |
|---|---|---|

With a bracing summit ascent, a grandstand view of a huge swathe of the Pyrenees and an exhilarating ridge walk past a triplet of mesmerising, multicoloured lakes, this walk (min/max altitude 1920/2364m) packs a lot of punch. The scenic rewards will keep even the most hardened mountain walker content, but it's also a good bet for adventurous families.

## Getting Here

The best base is the village of Ascou, which is 12km west of the trail head at Parking Pla de Mounégou.

## Starting Point

The start point is from the Pla de Mounégou car park, a few hundred metres west and down slope of the Col de Pailhères. There are picnic tables and information panels.

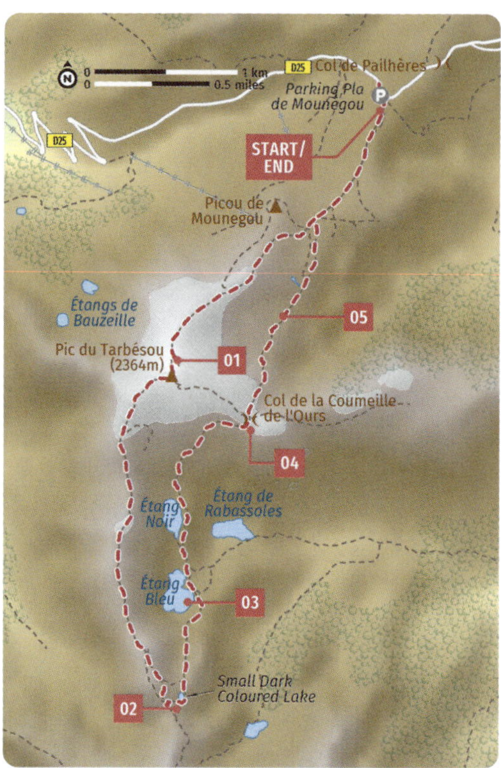


**01** Take the clear, wide trail heading south-southwest away from the parking area. After 15 minutes, a small foot trail veers off left (southwest) signed in yellow for the Pic du Tarbésou, all the time climbing steadily up the left-hand side of the mountain. After a while, you'll come to a subtle trail junction. Follow the yellow waymarkers right (southwest) and upwards.

A short while later the trail rises triumphantly onto the summit of the **Pic du Tarbésou** (2364m). The summit offers an incredible view of the main Pyrenean range to the south and foothills to the north. But the real surprise is reserved for when you walk to the southern edge of the summit for your first view over a triple crown of **multi-coloured lakes**: the **Étang de Rabassoles** and the appropriately named **Étang Bleu** (Blue) and **Étang Noir** (Black).

STUART BUTLER/LONELY PLANET ©

**02** The yellow waymarked trail drops down in a southwest direction very steeply towards the obvious **ridge**. The trail creeps along the ridge with stunning views whichever way you care to glance. From the top of the last crest, drop southeast. After a few minutes the path forks.

The main route stays high and bends around a ridge to a **small dark-coloured lake** that up until now has remained hidden from view. From a small pass just to the south of this lake, a minor trail breaks away left (north) off the main route and descends to the lake.

**03** Walk along the eastern shore of this small lake. You will now be following red-and-white GR trail markers. You will soon arrive on the eastern side of the turquoise-blue **Étang Bleu**. From the northern end of the lake, take the trail with the red-and-white GR waymarkers and not the wider, more obvious trail heading eastwards. The trail climbs up another ridge to the **Étang Noir** and passes along the eastern shore.

**04** There's now a gruelling half-hour climb up to the **Col de la Coume-ille de l'Ours**, from where you get a lingering last glance back at the lakes (pictured).

**05** It's then just a gentle half-hour amble along the plateau back to the car. About halfway through this stage, you'll meet up with the dirt road that you walked along at the very start.

## Take a Break

There are no cafes or restaurants along this trail. The meadows surrounding the Étang Bleu call out for a picnic stop.

# Marcadau Valley & the Cardinquère Lakes

| DURATION | DIFFICULTY | DISTANCE | START/END |
|---|---|---|---|
| 6½hr return | Hard | 18.5km | Pont d'Espagne |

| TERRAIN | | Mountain trail |
|---|---|---|

From the thunderous waterfall at the Pont d'Espagne, to autumnal red beech forests, highland pastures and sharp mountain spires speckled in snow, this long walk is one of the classics of the Pyrenees. With a high pass to cross, luminous lakes to linger by, gushy rivers and fields of flowers, this is a walk (min/max altitude 1460/2429m) that just keeps on giving.

## Getting Here

Cauterets is the closest base to this walk. There's a bus from the town to the Pont d'Espagne car park six times daily from July to early September and four times daily at other times. The cost is €8.50 return.

## Starting Point

The walk starts from the huge Pont d'Espagne car park (€8 per day parking fee). It's 8km from Cauterets along the steep and twisting D920. There's a park information office and walk-information panels.

**01** Kick into gear by walking to the famed **Pont d'Espagne** (Spanish Bridge; pictured), an impressive 19th-century bridge that's totally overshadowed by the incredible wedding-cake waterfalls that crash and smash behind it.

**02** From the bridge follow the signs for the chalet, **Refuge du Clot**, a few minutes' walk away. Just afterwards, the track forks. You can go either way but we start by taking the newer route and will return by the older and more interesting route. Take the left fork (south) over the bridge and walk along a driveable track through mixed forest. After around 40 minutes, the forests surrender to an open plateau where the river meanders in looping lines and cattle graze.

**03** An hour from the start you reach another signed junction. Ignore the sign pointing right for the Circuit des Lacs (we will return down this route at the end of the day) and head left (southeast), following the trail to Refuge Wallon.

The trail marches through forest and across riverside meadows. After a further hour, it bursts out into a pasture dotted with trees and giant granite boulders. At this point, the mountains really start to make their presence known. To the south is the **Grand Pic d'Arratille** (2900m) and slightly to the southwest is the **Grand Pic de Peterneille** (2764m). Turn right (west) at the trail junction and in a couple of minutes you'll be at the **Refuge Wallon** (1865m).

This is a real hikers' crossroads of the central Pyrenees and numerous day and multiday trails fan out from here. The *refuge* reopened in summer 2021 after a full refurbishment. If you're a family with smaller children, this is probably a good place to have a picnic and dip your toes in the river before returning by the same way that you came.

**04** Leaving the idyllic valley around the *refuge*, take the small trail northwest that passes behind the small stone **Chapelle du Marcadau**. Twenty minutes after leaving the *refuge* and chapel, the trail shimmies out of the forest and onto a barren grass plateau known as the **Pédet-Malh**.

## The Pyrenean Brown Bear

In 2004 the last native brown bear left in France was shot by a boar-hunter, supposedly in self-defence. The demise of the female bear, known as Cannelle to conservationists, marked the extinction of a species that a century ago was still a relatively common sight in the Pyrenees.

The species has since been reintroduced using bears imported from Slovenia. They have bred successfully, and it's thought that by 2020 there were around 60 brown bears roaming across the mountains. However, not everyone is celebrating the return of the bears. Some local shepherds and farmers see the bears as dangerous predators that pose an unwelcome threat to their flocks and livelihoods.

At a signed trail junction take the right (north) fork. The trail zigzags steadily uphill into ever more barren territory. Ahead, a sheet of steep rock rears up with a small stream and waterfall running down the side of it. Follow this stream up to the nick in the rock face to arrive at **Lac Nère** (2307m), a green-tinged lake settled into a small mountain bowl.

**05** The trail climbs for a further 20 minutes up over scree slopes to **Lac du Pourtet** (2420m). Don't forget to look behind you and take in the **stellar view** of the mountains filling in the southern end of the Marcadau Valley. Snug in a glacial cirque, and surrounded by jagged, rocky spires, Lac du Pourtet is a large, icy-blue lake that beautifully offsets the forbidding high mountain terrain that surrounds it. It can be cold and windy here even in high summer.

The route picks its way around the eastern side of the lake and in places is narrow and with a sheer drop to the waters below. An abrupt right (east) turn at the far end of the lake rewards with a view of the trail cartwheeling down to a **chain of jewel-blue lakes** far below. It's one of the best viewpoints on the walk.

**06** The next hour of walking, during which you will lose some 400m of height, is simply delightful. The path is easy to follow, and not too steep (pictured). As it drops, it passes lake after glorious lake. These are the **Embarrat Lakes** and there are at least four of them, plus some minor pools and marshes. The first lake is surrounded by the detritus of rockfalls and avalanches, but then, with each lake passed, the landscape gets greener and more lush.

**07** Dragging yourself away from the lakes, you enter a different habitat. Just beyond the far end of the final lake, the **Lac Inférieur d'Embarrat**, the trail turns sharp left (north) and moves away from the river. Trees start to make a return to the scene and there are views across folds of mountains and down into the Marcadau Valley that you walked up earlier in the day. Soon you reach an **avalanche area**. Pick your way gingerly over the rocks.

As you near the end of the rockfall area, look for an indistinct fork in the trail that turns sharply back on itself and drops downhill to the right. Take this. Do not carry on straight ahead. It's easy to overlook this junction.

**08** The trail now drops steeply through increasingly **thick and varied woodland** for the next 50 minutes. The last half-hour, in particular, is especially steep. You'll be glad you're heading downhill here and not up! Eventually, you arrive on the valley floor and meet a trail junction and signpost. You're now back by the river (**Gave du Marcadau**) that you followed on the way to the Refuge Wallon. However, instead of crossing over the river and following this same trail back to the car, we are going to take the old path back to the Refuge du Clot by staying on the left (west) side of the river.

**09** For the next 45 minutes, the path undulates along the edge of **boggy pastures** – sometimes it runs close to the river; sometimes it moves further away. Sheep and cows graze here and the clanging of cow bells is a musical accompaniment to the final stages of your walk.

When you reach the Refuge du Clot, simply follow the path back downhill past the Pont d'Espagne to the car park.

## Take a Break

The meadows around the Refuge Wallon make for a delightful picnic spot. The *refuge* itself also sells basic meals and snacks to non-guests.

# 53

# Col & Pic de Madamète

| DURATION | DIFFICULTY | DISTANCE | START/END |
|---|---|---|---|
| 7½hr return | Hard | 18km | Pont de la Gaubie |

| TERRAIN | | Clear mountain trail; snow can block pass until late June |
|---|---|---|

Sitting north of the main ridge of Pyrenean peaks, the Réserve Naturelle de Néouvielle contains some epic mountain scenery. This circular hike to the Col (pass) and Pic de Madamète (2657m) combines silky blue lakes, bucolic meadows, glacial tarns, soaring mountains and a dramatic crossing of a high pass followed by a scramble to a lofty summit, making for a spectacular day out.

But beauty comes with a sting. This is a very long and demanding hike (min/max altitude 1538/2657m). Walking at a solid pace and without stopping, it will take you at least seven hours. But because you will want to stop and admire the lakes and viewpoints and dawdle through the meadows, then really you should set aside 10 or 11 hours.

## Getting Here

The nearest town is the small ski resort of Barèges. However, only a few minutes' drive further down-hill is Luz-St-Sauveur, an attractive and bustling little town with lots of places to stay and eat. From either of these towns take the D918 uphill towards the Col du Tourmalet. At the *télésiege de Caoubère* (Caoubère chairlift, 10km from Luz-St-Sauveur and 3km from Barèges), there's a small turn-off to the south. Drive 1.5km down this to the Pont de la Gaubie.

## Starting Point

There are only a very limited number of parking places (six or seven) at the Pont de la Gaubie. Unless you're here very early, you will need to park in the huge car park at the *télésiege de Caoubère* and walk from there (add a total of 25 minutes to your overall walk time).

**01** The first half of the trail to the Col de Madamète follows the GR10 long-distance trail. Signage is exceptionally clear and easy. Just follow the obvious trail with the red-and-white waymarkers painted at frequent intervals on rocks and trees. After about eight minutes, there's an unmarked junction. Turn right (south). Twenty minutes later, at another fork in the trail, take the left-hand trail. You will be returning much later in the day via the other trail.

**02** Fifty minutes from the start of the walk, during which you have been ambling over pastures with many cows and sheep, you arrive at a dreamy little **meadow** with a clear **stream**. At the end of this meadow take the left-hand trail fork and cross over the stream. The trail dips back into woodland and continues on its gentle, but steady, uphill climb.

**03** Around two hours from the start of the walk, you'll reach a small meadow with a **marshy lake**. Follow a ridge line above the lake and gawp at the big mountains that are increasingly ganging up at the head of the valley.

**04** After a further half-hour, the **Lac de Coueyla-Gran** appears. It's a wonderful spot to rest for a while and admire the reflections of the mountains in its still, cold waters.

**05** Things toughen up when you leave the lakeside. The trail veers back on itself slightly and then sets a high course for the head of the valley. After a sharp 30-minute climb up a rocky slope, you reach **Lac de Madamète**, a pretty, green-blue lake filled with fat trout. Behind the lake, you can clearly see the Col and the Pic de Madamète. A sign indicates that it's an (optimistic) 45 minutes to the pass.

## Snow & Trail Breaks

Snow can be an issue on the Col de Madamète and – even more so – on the summit of the Pic de Madamète and the ridge that follows between late October and late June. If the route is blocked by snow, you will need to retrace your steps back the way you came.

If possible, we suggest breaking this trek into a leisurely two-day affair. **Refuge d'Aygues-Cluses** opened in 2023 and is a modern, welcoming *refuge* to spend the night at. Half-board from €55, homemade dinner and organic, homemade bread.

Many families walk to the Lac de Coueyla-Gran for a picnic and then return the way they came (leave 4½ hours without stops).

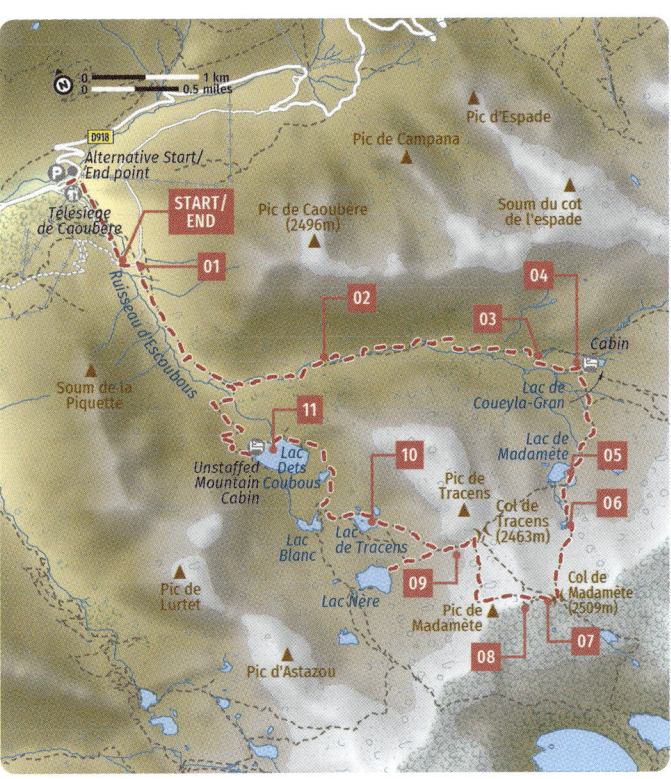


STUART BUTLER FR/LONELY PLANET ©

**06** The trail climbs again and passes a whole flurry of **little lakes**. You're now in the high mountains and the scenery (pictured p182) is very different from the gentle green valleys and pastures that you started the morning in. With each successive lake, the landscape becomes more barren and broken and the higher lakes often remain covered in ice until early summer.

**07** After a final, brisk 10-minute haul, you'll stand atop the **Col de Madamète** (2509m). The views from this lofty vantage point will make you catch your breath. Looking back the way you came, the numerous lakes you sauntered past lie scattered like glowing jewels over the stark landscape. But the real treat is the view south. The land drops steeply away from the pass to a series of large lakes (Aumar, Aubert, Orédon and Cap de Long) and around them massive mountain hulks and glaciers, including, just to the southwest, the eternal snow-covered **Pic de Néouvielle** (3091m).

**08** For an even better view (pictured), scramble for 25 minutes up the zigzag trail to the 2657m-high summit of **Pic de Madamète** (the rounded peak immediately to your right – west – when standing on the pass looking south). The summit and the ridge you'll be following afterwards are often snowbound until much later in the season than the Col de Madamète. If you're in any doubt, do not continue – instead return to the car the way you came (leave three hours). If the snow has cleared, then drop down from the summit to the ob-

HEMIS/ALAMY STOCK PHOTO ©

vious ridge to the northwest and then onto the **Col de Tracens** (2463m).

**09** Beyond the Col de Tracens, a torn-up landscape of **giant boulders** cast aside by ancient glaciers awaits. The trail-finding can be a little complicated but just keep heading northwest. The 20-minute (return) detour to **Lac Nère** is recommended.

**10** Around 45 minutes after leaving the summit, the trail, which by now is becoming much clearer and easier to follow, passes by **Lac de Tracens**, where grass and stunted trees return. This is followed a few minutes later by the beautiful **Lac Blanc**.

**11** Continue downwards and across a marshy plateau. Finally, the last, and largest, lake of the day, **Lac Dets Coubous**, looms into sight. There's a small cabin here and the northern end of the lake has been dammed, but it's still an attractive parting shot.

You may now think that you're home and dry, but there remains one final challenge. A leg-searingly steep descent zigzags downwards to the trail junction you passed much earlier in the day. From here, it's a simple but exhausting half-hour walk back to the car, retracing the route you took at the start of the day.

## Take A Break

While the lakes make perfect picnic spots, if you're looking for something heartier, visit the **Refuge d'Aygues-Cluses** for an omelette.

# Also Try...

YVON52/SHUTTERSTOCK ©

## Cirque de Gavarnie

| DURATION | DIFFICULTY | DISTANCE |
| --- | --- | --- |
| 3½hr return | Easy | 11km |

The family-friendly walk into the belly of the stunning Cirque de Gavarnie is easily the single most famous day walk in the Pyrenees. And for good reason: when you reach the end of the path, you will stare in awe at this bowl-shaped wall of glacier-covered rock. From the valley floor to the summit peaks is a vertical 1.5km and down the sheer sides crashes the highest waterfall in France. It's like being in nature's very own Colosseum.

But on a walk like this, you can't expect to walk alone and, in high summer, thousands of people trudge the trail every day. If you can, come out of season. The walk begins from Gavarnie village and is just a gentle uphill stroll along a clear, smooth trail (the first part is wheelchair accessible) to the Hôtellerie du Cirque (pictured).

## The GR10

| DURATION | DIFFICULTY | DISTANCE |
| --- | --- | --- |
| 52 days one way | Hard | 86km |

Long-distance walks don't come much more epic than the GR10, or the Grand Traversée des Pyrénées.

Starting wth your boots in the Atlantic Ocean in Hendaye, this near two-month-long traverse of the mountains ends when you rush headlong into the Mediterranean in Banyuls. During this marathon hike, you will climb and descend some 48,000m, but the reward for this effort is a straight-line sweep through the very best of the Pyrenees (and you'll have legs of steel afterwards). And, when you've done it one way, you could spin around and walk the GR11, which also traverses the Pyrenees but this time on the Spanish side of the border.

HEMIS/ALAMY STOCK PHOTO ©

## The Néouvielle Lake Circuit

| DURATION | DIFF. | DISTANCE |
|---|---|---|
| 3 days return | Hard | 45km |

In a remote corner of the Parc National du Mercantour, this wild walk is a great one for wildlife-watchers and those with a geological bent.

Day one sees you walking from the Lac d'Orédon to the Refuge de la Glère via a high pass crossing. Day two swings through wild countryside to the Cabane d'Aygues-Cluses and on day three you skip your way back to the start point via another high pass and a handful of lakes.

## Pic des Trois Seigneurs

| DURATION | DIFF. | DISTANCE |
|---|---|---|
| 5hr return | Moderate | 10km |

Walkers familiar with the wild peaks of the Ariège region tend to talk about this fabulous circular hike in excited tones of wonder. From the achievable summit of the Pic des Trois Seigneurs (2199m), a huge view opens out that takes in most of the great mountains of the eastern part of the Pyrenees.

This diverse walk begins from the car park at Port de Lers and swings through lakes, meadows, rivers and rocky passes on its way to and from the summit (pictured).

## Puig Carlit

| DURATION | DIFF. | DISTANCE |
|---|---|---|
| 6hr return | Hard | 15km |

This exciting but challenging ascent of Puig Carlit (2921m) is the classic walk of the far-eastern part of the Pyrenees. You have to be prepared for a very steep final ascent, with snow likely even in high summer. But along the way, you'll get to enjoy a sprinkling of jewel lakes surrounded by summer flowers.

The walk begins from the car park at Barrage des Bouillouses at the end of the D60 road and the route is well marked.

N
0    20 km
0    10 miles
Ligurian Sea
Barcaggio
Îles Finocchiarola
56
Centuri
Macinaggio
Pino
Luri
Canari
Marine de Pietracorbara
Cap Corse
D80
Golfe de St-Florent
Erbalunga
D80
Patrimonio
Miomo
Bastia
Désert des Agriates
St-Florent
Étang de Biguglia
D81
Oletta
T11
Île Rousse
Murato
Algajola
Belgodère
T30
Calvi
Cateri
Felíceto
Ponte Leccia
Morosaglia
Monte San Petrone (1767m)
Moriani-Plage
Calenzana
D81
Galéria
Haut Asco
59
57
Cervione
T20
T10
Réserve Naturelle de Scandola
Girolata
Monte Cinto (2706m)
Calacuccia
Corte
D84
Col de Verghio (1477m)
Vallée du Tavignano
Vallée de la Restonica
Golfe de Porto
Porto
Ota
Évisa
Venaco
Capo Rosso
58
Piana
60
Monte Rotondo (2622m)
Vivario
Tavignano
Étang de Diane
D81
Monte d'Oro (2389m)
Vizzavona
T50
D70
Cargèse
Sagone
Bocognano
Ghisoni
D344
T10
Cateraggio
54
Golfe de Sagone
Étang d'Urbino
D81
T20
Bastelica
Parc Naturel Régional de la Corse
T10
Ghisonaccia
Ajaccio
Zicavo
Travo
Pointe de la Parata
T40
D83
Solenzara
Îles Sanguinaires
Golfe d'Ajaccio
Porticcio
D69
D268
Col de Bavella (1218m)
Portigliolo
Verghja
Aullène
Quenza
Favone
Conca
Capo di Muro
Petreto-Bicchisano
Zonza
Ste-Lucie de Porto-Vecchio
D155
Abbartello
Olmeto
Levie
Porto Pollo
Ste-Lucie de Tallano
L'Ospédale
Golfe de Porto-Vecchio
Golfe du Valinco
Propriano
D268
Porto-Vecchio
Campomoro
Sartène
Bocca Del l'oro
D48
Tyrrhenian Sea
Tizzano
D859
T40
Pianottoli-Caldarello
T10
MEDITERRANEAN SEA
Bonifacio
Cap Pertusato
Îles Lavezzi
55

Cala Genovese (p197), Sentier des Douaniers

# Corsica

# Explore

# Corsica

Jutting from the Mediterranean like a rock fortress, Corsica has astounding geographical diversity. Set out on a walking trail here and, within an hour, the landscape can see-saw spectacularly from glittering bays and fabulous beaches to sawtooth mountain ridges and dense forests. All of which makes Corsica a wonderfully rewarding place for hikers.

## Bonifacio

Protected by vast smooth walls, the southern town of Bonifacio stretches along a narrow, top-heavy promontory, undercut by creamy-white limestone cliffs hollowed out by centuries of ceaseless waves. The old city, though, is what truly lingers in the mind, a ravishingly romantic web of alleyways lined by ramshackle medieval houses and chapels with faded pastel plasterwork.

There's a huge array of tourist accommodation in and around Bonifacio as well as an equal number of restaurants and bars. All this makes it the perfect base for walk 55.

## Macinaggio

A port since Roman times, Macinaggio, high up along the barren but beautiful Cap Corse peninsula, today centres on a pleasure marina used by summer excursion boats. To explore the coastline north of town, you've got no option but to strike out on foot, which is exactly what we do on walk 56. Macinaggio has places to stay and eat for when you return back to town.

## Piana

Teetering above the Golfe de Porto, the village of Piana makes a useful launching pad for hiking Capo Rosso. It's also ideal for exploring Les Calanques (Calanche) de Piana.

## Corte

Blessed with a stunning natural setting, circled by jagged peaks at the confluence of several rivers, the mountain stronghold of Corte is as forbidding as it is spectacular. Home to Corsica's only university, its strong youthful energy is boosted in summer when hikers, bikers and climbers flock in to explore the nearby valleys.

It's the perfect base for walks 54, 57, 59 and 60.

## When to Go

Corsica is the quintessential Mediterranean island and has about the most forgiving climate in France. Between May and the end of October you can near-enough guarantee endless long sunny days, and even in winter there are enough crisp, clear days to make the island's coastal trails inviting.

Winter (November to February), though, is a very mixed affair. Some years can be an endless succession of storms interspersed with a few sunny periods, but in other years the settled periods vastly outnumber the wet spells. In fine weather, all the coastal routes can be walked. Mountain routes though are often blanketed in snow.

Spring (March to early May) is by far the most unpredictable season and is often the wettest period of the calendar. Snow can also remain a problem on higher routes.

It hardly needs saying that summer (June to September) is uniformly hot and sunny. Often too hot even for the high mountain routes. The heat can make many coastal walks very trying indeed, but there's invariably a beach to cool off at somewhere along the way.

This leaves autumn (mid-September to October), with still largely settled, sunny weather, warm coastal waters, beautiful clear light, and perhaps the first frosts and light snow dustings on the mountain summits, as far and away the best time of year to walk almost anywhere in Corsica.

Corsica's tourism is heavily seasonal. Most hotels, restaurants and even sights open only from Easter to October, so winter visitors will need patience.

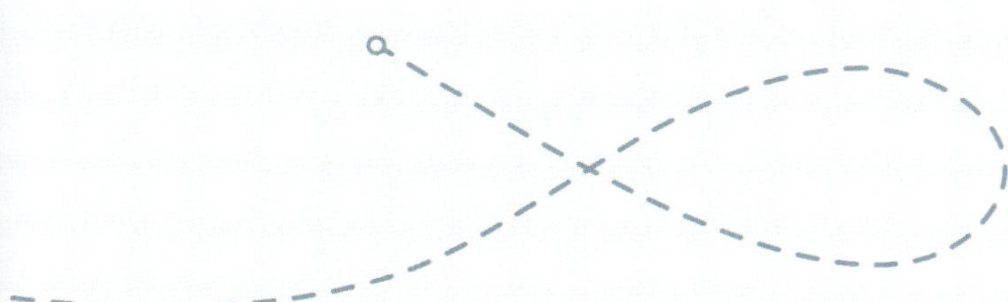

## Where to Stay

From seaside hotels with sweeping Mediterranean views to mountain retreats that invite you to cosy up by the fireside, Corsican accommodation is generally comfortable and of high quality. Budget travellers will find campgrounds island-wide, and simple *refuges* (huts) along the high mountain trails.

## What's On

**Semaine Sainte** (◷ Mar & Apr) Elaborate religious processions march through the streets of Bonifacio, Corte and other towns.

**Cavall'in Festa** (◷ early Jun) The mountain town of Corte celebrates the humble horse with processions, dressage shows and other events.

**Corsica Raid** (en.corsicaraid.com; ◷ early Jun) Held in locations throughout Corsica, this event mixes canyoning, trail-running, kayaking and mountain biking.

## Transport

By far the best way to get around Corsica is by car, and many trailheads can only be

## Resources

**Visit Corsica** (visit-corsica. com) Tourist-board website that includes hiking suggestions.

**Corte Tourisme** (corte-tourisme. com) Covering Corte and surrounding mountain regions.

**Bonifacio Tourisme** (bonifacio. fr) Gives the lowdown on this cliff-side town.

**Bastia Tourisme** (bastia -tourisme.com) Information on Bastia and Cap Corse.

**Ouest Corsica** (ouestcorsica. com) Covering the jagged, mountainous west of the island.

reached by a private vehicle. Public transport only connects the larger towns and cities, from which local explorations can continue on foot or by bike or scooter (both readily available for hire).

Corsica's only train line, the Chemin de Fer de la Corse (cf-corse.corsica), is an attractive if limited option, running across the stunning mountainous interior between Bastia and Ajaccio, with a branch route to Calvi and L'Île-Rousse. The bus network is more comprehensive but often there's only one bus per day, and none on Sunday.

Corsica Bus & Train (corsicabus.org) is a one-stop website displaying up-to-date bus and train timetables, island-wide.

# 54

# Cascade des Anglais

| DURATION | DIFFICULTY | DISTANCE | START/END |
|---|---|---|---|
| 1½hr return | Easy | 6.5km | Gare de Vizzavona |

| TERRAIN | | Road, walking trail |
|---|---|---|

While many of the mountain walks in Corsica are a bit tough for children, this charming walk through thick beech forest to a pretty series of cascades and rapids is the ideal Corsican mountain hike for families. It's true that in high summer it gets busy, but the shade, cool freshwater and sense of peace that comes with being in the forest make it worthwhile. If you can, walk this route (min/max altitude 915/1100m) in October, when the leaves on the beech trees are the colour of the setting sun.

From the tiny train station, walk uphill along the road signed for the cascades, pass a huge, **ruined house** and then the **Casa di a Natura** (park information office). Follow red-and-white GR trail signs along a track lined by a dry-stone wall and into a beech forest.

Cross a bridge over the **River Agnone** and turn right immediately afterwards; then shortly after that cross another bridge and start marching uphill to a wide, dirt road. Turn left here and follow the road through the forest.

When you get to a road junction go straight over and then, a few minutes later, veer left off the **dirt road** by the signpost. After 50 minutes, the path moves slightly away from the river before returning and crossing a **bridge** at the bottom part of the **Cascades des Anglais** (pictured).

Continue up the trail, which clambers around rocks among the forest, passing numerous magical **waterfalls** and **pools of rapids**. When you reach the top of the last of the waterfalls, turn around and retrace your steps back to where you started.

# 55

# Capu Pertusato & Bonifacio

| DURATION | DIFFICULTY | DISTANCE | START/END |
|---|---|---|---|
| 3hr return | Easy | 9.5km | Port de Bonifacio |

| TERRAIN | | Road, walking trail |
|---|---|---|

From the tourist hustle of Bonifacio, you only have to walk a short way to discover a world of secret beaches, breezy headlands and woodlands full of birdsong. This ideal family walk also takes in an exciting cliff walk and the chance to snap that clichéd photo of Bonifacio perched atop the cliffs. Don't forget your swimsuit!

## Getting Here

The walk starts from the main port in Bonifacio. From the old town, simply walk or drive down the hill to where the boats to the Île Lavezzi depart.

## Starting Point

There are large car parks just behind the port and the whole area is awash in bars and restaurants, but there's nothing walker-specific here.

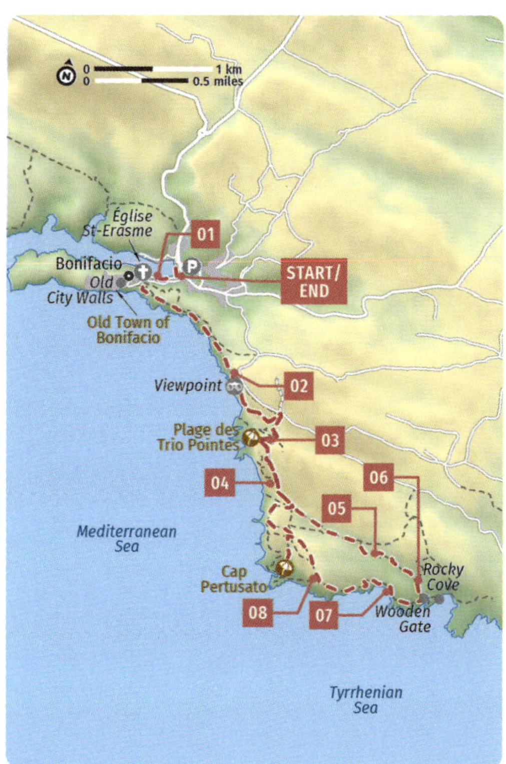


**01** Walk along the eastern side of the port and take a left to the **Église St-Erasme**. To the left of this, a wide set of steps rises up. Emerging at the top of these steps you will find yourself facing the **old city walls**. Cross the road and go up the cobbled road. Turn left and start off along high cliffs.

**02** It's now an easy walk along a footpath that scrapes along the edge of chalky white cliffs. After around 15 minutes, you will reach a **viewpoint** that offers that classic postcard view of Bonifacio hanging on its cliffside perch (pictured).

**03** The trail moves away from the cliff edge and meets a road. Turn right, drop downhill, pass a ruined building and go past a parking area.

**04** Continue along the dirt road past a **military control tower**. Drop downhill and at the junction, veer left (east) down a track.

STUART BUTLER/LONELY PLANET ©



**05** After 15 minutes look for a discreet path on the left marked with **rock cairns**. The turn-off is about 25m before an entrance to a private property.

**06** The trail wends through a brushy forest and passes through a gateway. Go right when you reach a junction with another trail. A moment or so later, you will reach a small, **rocky cove**. Turn sharp right and go through a **wooden gate**.

**07** The trail now heads westwards along low **ruddy-coloured cliffs** with the **clear, blue sea** just below. A few minutes later, you will come to the most thrilling part of the walk: a **narrow ledge** etched into the cliff face underneath a big overhang of rock. It's only around a hundred metres – and is perfectly safe – but it will still keep you on your toes!

**08** Afterwards, the path goes back into woodland and climbs. It takes about 20 minutes to reach the **Pertusato lighthouse**. Follow the wider path back northwards until you see a trail veering off left signed 'Plage'. Take this and drop down to a spectacular **desert-like beach** of chalky-white sand, with cliffs and rock stacks eroded into bizarre shapes.

Return to the junction, turn left and, a couple of minutes later, you'll be back on familiar ground. Retrace your route back along the cliffs to Bonifacio.

## Take a Break

There's nowhere to get refreshments when you leave Bonifacio. In summer, you will need a lot of water. Make a reservation in town at the popular **Mama Gina** (04 95 53 77 41; 3 Mnt Rastello, 20169 Bonifacio; mains from €15, pizzas from €8.50; midday-2.30pm & 7-11pm), where the real star of the restaurant is the gnocchi with bread baked over the bowl.

# Sentier des Douaniers

| DURATION | DIFFICULTY | DISTANCE | START/END |
|---|---|---|---|
| 3½hr return | Easy | 12.5km | Parking Port de Macinaggio |

| TERRAIN | | Footpath |
|---|---|---|

The Sentier des Douaniers (Customs Trail) is a glimpse back in time to how much of the Mediterranean coastline must have looked before the arrival of mass tourism. This superb family walk, along a clear footpath, enjoys stunning sandy beaches, extraordinary blue seas and a wild, wooded hinterland. Although you can do the walk in half a day, we would recommend bringing your swimming things and a picnic and making a day of it.

## Getting Here

The small town of Macinaggio, close to the end of the Cap Corse peninsula, is 37km and an hour's drive north of Bastia along the D80. There are one or two buses per day (€8, one hour, no Sunday service).

## Starting Point

There are a couple of car parks close to the port in Macinaggio. This walk starts from the most northerly one.

**01** Head north past the pleasure boat marina and then onto **Macinaggio beach**, a long, broad sandy expanse. Head towards the low headland at the far end of the beach.

**02** A clearly signed trail leads off the beach and onto the headland. Straight away go right at the **trail junction**. Follow the path to the tip of the headland and past the **old cannon**. At the next junction go right, continuing around cliffs.

**03** Follow a dirt road to **Plage de Tamarone** (pictured), a gorgeous stretch of sand backed by fields.

## To the End of Corsica

You can continue on northwards from Cala Francese (stop 06) to the small town of Barcaggio and its magnificent beach, which is about another 1¾ hours.

You can then either walk all the way back again (total 6¾ hours) or catch a summertime water taxi (sanpaulu.fr/navette-maritime).

Best for

COASTAL VIEWS

STUART BUTLER/LONELY PLANET ©

**04** Make sandy footprints all the way up to the northern end of the beach. At the trail junction go right and follow the trail around the headland. At one point you'll climb up quite steeply but from the top of the headland there are wonderful **coastal views**.

**05** Stroll through tough, sun-blasted scrub until coming to a third beach, **Plage des Îles**. As the name suggests, just off the northern end of the beach are three small, **rocky islands**. Continue up to and around the headland to the north. You'll come to a turn-off to the left for the Chapel Santa Maria. Ignore this and continue on down to the next beach, which has a semi-restored **Genoese tower** built on a tiny rock outcrop.

**06** Over another headland and a big decision awaits. Two gorgeous **silver-sand beaches** – Cala Francese and Cala Genovese (pictured p189) – are separated by a swathe of greenery and massaged by glowing turquoise waters. But at which one will you choose to take a break?

**07** To return retrace your steps back past the Genoese tower and its beach and then, instead of following the headland around, cut down past the dour **Chapel Santa Maria** and take the inland path heading straight south. The path runs through pretty Mediterranean scrub that smells of the sun and emerges onto Plage de Tamarone. At the southern end of this, again take the inland trail rather than the headland trail. There are two turn-offs on the left. Ignore the first but take the second one, which quickly drops you back to **Macinaggio beach**.

### Take a Break

On Plage de Tamarone there's a little **wooden beach shack** selling drinks and snacks in summer only. Otherwise bring a picnic and plenty of water.

# 57

# Vallée du Tavignano

| DURATION | DIFFICULTY | DISTANCE | START/END |
|---|---|---|---|
| 5½hr return | Easy | 13km | Corte |

| TERRAIN | | Rough paved trail |
|---|---|---|

The mountains of Corsica are shot through with vertically inclined narrow valleys and gorges through which rivers crash and smash. This compelling walk (min/max altitude 450/760m), which follows the course of an old mule path, slinks along the sheer northern side of the valley and rewards with views of the river surrounded by thick forests and the ever narrower valley walls crowned with jagged rock spires on either side.

## Getting Here

The walk begins from Corte town, which makes it a good one for those reliant on public transport. From the town centre, walk or drive to the small (pay) car park at the end of rue St-Joseph.

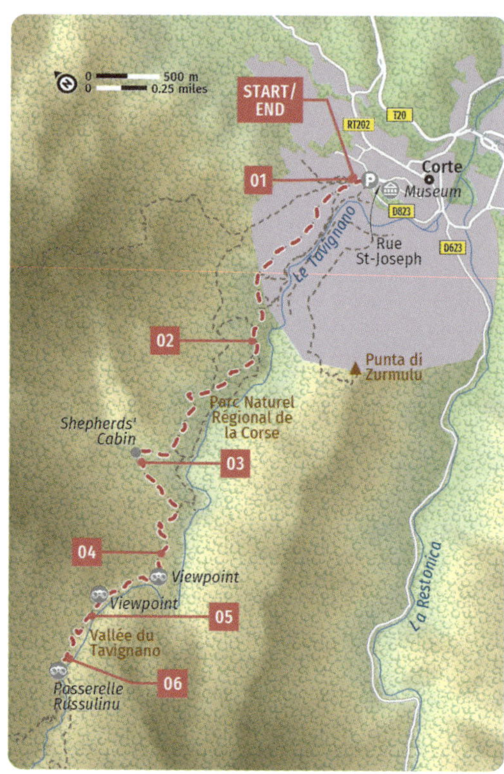


## Starting Point

Just past the car park there are a number of different walking route signposts. Look for the one that reads Passerelle Russulinu.

**01** From the car park, head down the footpath and through a gate. You're now at the start of the **Mare a Mare** long-distance hiking trail, which is very well marked with orange paint splodges.

**02** The trail climbs up gently through heathland and passes a **small white shrine** (although because of its positioning in relation to the trail you might not notice it until you return back along the trail at the end of the day).

**03** Gradually the trail descends towards the river and the trees – a real mixed bag of high mountain pines and lower altitude

## Family Walk

This is a very simple walk with little elevation gain and no possibility of getting lost. However, if you walk all the way to the bridge at the Passerelle Russulinu, it does make for quite a long day. Because of this, even though the views get better the further along the valley you walk, many people don't get this far and turn around when they've seen enough.

This makes it quite a good family walk (though be careful near cliff ledges and avoid hot days when the valley can turn into a furnace), as you can just walk as far as the little ones' legs will carry them.

STUART BUTLER/LONELY PLANET ©

Mediterranean oak and chestnut – start to close in. After around 1¼ hours, the trail reaches a small side stream that you will need to hop across to a stone **shepherds' cabin**. There's also a water source here.

**04** Thirty minutes on from the shepherds' cabin, the trail forks. Turn right and go uphill, still following the orange waymarkers. A few minutes later, the trees clear to reveal the first of a number of **impressive viewpoints**. Looking further up the valley, you will see a giant grey wall of tortured and torn rock (pictured) and,

looking the other way, you'll be able to spy Corte in the valley floor.

**05** The valley walls now close in tight around you, the cliffs fall steeply away and the river becomes much fuller, crashing over the boulders. You will pass another couple of **viewpoints** with sheer drop-offs.

**06** Cross another small stream and, rounding a corner a moment later, you will come to a **bridge** spanning the **Tavignano River**. There's also another water source here. This is the **Pas-**

**serelle Russulinu**. Although the Mare a Mare route continues over the bridge and along the river (eventually coming to the source of the river at Lac de Nino), this is where we turn around and retrace our steps back to Corte.

## Take A Break

While there are many restaurants, cafes and bars in Corte, there's nowhere to find food along this trail. In summer the valley can get uncomfortably hot so bring plenty of water.

# 58

# Capo Rosso

| DURATION | DIFFICULTY | DISTANCE | START/END |
|---|---|---|---|
| 3½hr return | Moderate | 9.5km | Parking Capo Rosso |

| TERRAIN | | Walking trail |
|---|---|---|

Standing next to the 16th-century Genoese Tower on the tip of Capo Rosso (Capu Rossu), a vertical-edged lump of rock protruding deep into the Mediterranean, you'll feel like a gull soaring on the breezes. This short coastal walk to the most westerly point of Corsica offers one of the most extraordinary views on the entire island – if you're brave enough to peer over the cliff edge, that is!

## Getting Here

The best base for the walk is the small town of Piana. Despite its diminutive size, there are plenty of tourist facilities. From Piana take the D824 for 6km in a westerly direction towards the Plage d'Arone. At the point at which the road makes a sharp bend to the left, there is a small car park. The walk starts here.

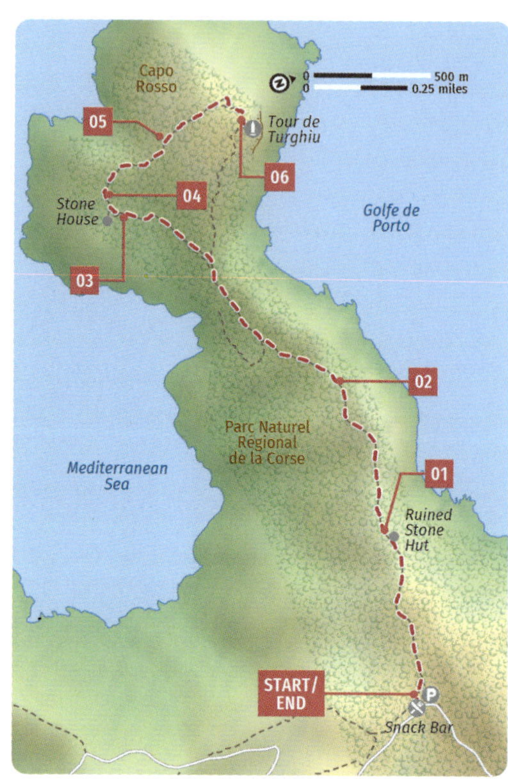


## Starting Point

There's a walk-information sign and a snack bar.

**01** Follow the clear footpath northwest out of the car park and then go left a moment later at the **dry-stone wall**. Start descending. A short while later, you will pass a **ruined hut**, with **sea views** opening out to the south.

**02** Go left at the junction among stumpy, weathered trees and giant heathers but, before you do, pause to take in the **view** down cascading cliffs.

**03** When you reach the level plateau, take the right fork signed for **Capo Rosso Torra di Turghju**. The trail continues to dip down towards sea level, before coming to a **stone house**. Head right here.

STUART BUTLER/LONELY PLANET ©

## Genoese Towers

Looking like squat lighthouses, the Genoese towers that dot the Corsican coast in some ways serve a similar purpose, except they weren't warning approaching ships of danger but, instead, they were warning frightened Corsican coastal communities that ships were approaching. Pirate ships!

In the 1500s, Corsica was controlled by the Genoese, but Turkish corsairs sailed the western Mediterranean in ships rowed by captured Christian slaves, and the coastal villages of Corsica were a favourite hunting ground. In order to help protect them, the Genoese built around a hundred defensive towers, and many of them remain standing today.

**04** At the **walk signposts** 50m later, go straight on and start to climb. At first, it's a gentle climb but it quickly becomes much steeper. The trail then mellows again as it nudges ever closer to what, from this angle, appears to be a sheer-sided, rust-orange cliff face that you somehow will have to negotiate.

**05** The answer to how you get up this cliff reveals itself a few moments later: a hidden **rock stairway** carved discreetly into the cliff face. The climb is relatively short but with the sun likely pounding down onto your back, you do have to work for it a bit. When the steps stop, the trail continues upward over an exposed red-rock slope. It can be a little tricky to make out the proper path. Keep an eye out for **rock cairns**.

**06** Two hours after you set out, you will find yourself standing triumphantly on the summit (pictured) next to the **Tour de Turghiu**, a Genoese tower. But of course we know you didn't walk all the way out here to look at an old building. Go on then, walk towards the edge of the cliff and peer over. Now that is a view! You might only be at an altitude of 331m but the sheer violence with which the rock sheers away below you gives the impression that you're actually standing atop a mountain. The sea is a deep, glittering blue and rugged cliffs stretch off northwards up the coast. It really is one of the **best viewpoints** on the island. To return simply retrace your steps (leave 1½ hours for this).

## Take a Break

There's a small seasonal (April to October) **snack bar** in the car park with a breezy terrace and sensational sea views. Otherwise, picnic with a view next to the Tour de Turghiu.

# Lac de Nino

| DURATION | DIFFICULTY | DISTANCE | START/END |
|---|---|---|---|
| 4½hr return | Moderate | 11.5km | Maison forestière de Poppaghia |

| TERRAIN | |
|---|---|
| | Mountain trail, rocky terrain |

When first viewed after clambering up the steep, rocky slope, Lac de Nino and its surrounding pastures come across like a vision of a mountain paradise, and the lake is quite rightly considered one of Corsica's most beautiful. But as well as the goal of the lake, this enjoyable and popular hike (suitable for older children; min/max altitude 1076/1762m) also offers a melodic amble through stately forests where semi-wild black pigs forage, and there are glorious views across to Corsica's highest mountain.

## Getting Here

The walk starts from the Maison forestière de Poppaghia, which is around 11km east of the Col de Verghio on the D84 between Calacuccia and Évisa. You'll need your own car to get here.

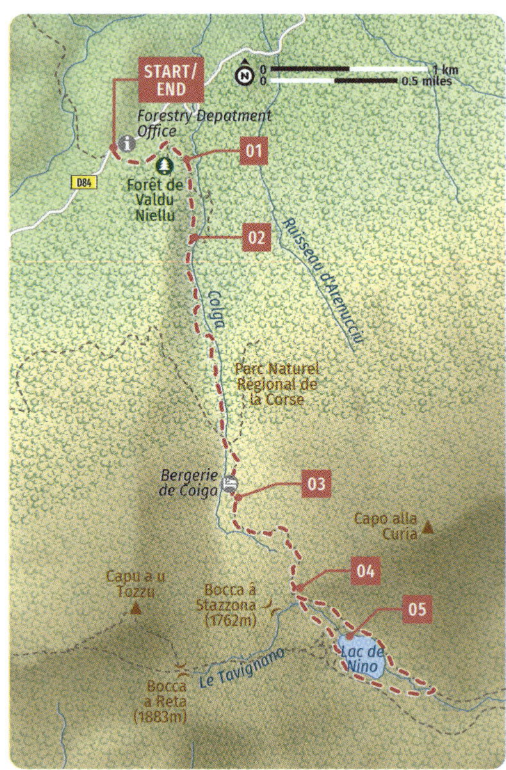


## Starting Point

There's a parking area, picnic benches and a small *accrobranche* (tree-climbing centre) next to the Maison forestière de Poppaghia. There are also information boards giving that day's forest-fire risk level. At times of heightened alert, you might be forbidden from walking here.

**01** Follow the yellow paint splodges uphill away from the forestry office and into the impressive **Forêt de Valdu Niellu**. Made up predominately of Corsican black pine, this is the largest montane forest in Corsica. Some of the magisterial trees found here can be 30m high and 300 years old. If you see shadows moving in the undergrowth that will be the **semi-wild pigs** and cattle that wander at will through this forest.

PETER GIOVANNINI/GETTY IMAGES ©

**02** After around 20 minutes, you will come to a forestry road. Cross straight over and continue marching gently up through the trees. Ten minutes later hop across a small stream.

As you gain altitude the trees slowly start to die away and, behind you, views will start opening out across the valley to mighty **Monte Cinto** (2706m), the highest mountain on the island.

**03** The trail, which starts to become a little rockier, crosses over a couple of streams (look for suitable rocks to hop on to) and then emerges onto a small rocky plateau where you'll find the semi-abandoned shepherds' huts known as **Bergerie de Coiga**, 1¼ hours from the start.

**04** This next part is where the hard work begins. For the next hour and a bit, the trail climbs steeply up a rocky slope. At times, you might need to use hands and feet to scramble over some of the rocks. Be careful in wet weather as they can be very slippery. Finally, you'll emerge onto the **Bocca â Stazzona** pass (1762m), from where you'll catch your first view of the lake just below (pictured).

**05** Descend from the pass to **Lac de Nino**. After the rocky, barren country on the last half of the climb up here, the piercing green pastures, laced through with streams and marshes, are a welcome surprise. Do a complete circuit of the lake, admiring how the colours change with the light, before climbing back up to the Bocca â Stazzona and retracing your route back to the car.

## Take a Break

There's nowhere to get food on the trail. Bring a picnic and tuck in with the view over the lake from the Bocca â Stazzona.

# 60

# Lac de Melo & Lac de Capitello

| DURATION | DIFFICULTY | DISTANCE | START/END |
|---|---|---|---|
| 4hr return | Moderate | 6.7km | Parking Bergerie de Grottelle |

| TERRAIN | | Mountain trail |
|---|---|---|

If we had to pick one mountain walk in Corsica that simply cannot be missed then it would be this superb day hike to Lake Melo and its higher altitude twin, Lake Capitello. Although it's relatively short, you will traverse a fascinating range of habitats, from grand old-growth woodland to alpine pastures, before finally arriving in the high-altitude rock and scree wastes of the mountains. It's in this zone that the two lakes can be found. The lower of the two, Lac de Melo, is saucer round and a peaty-black colour, while Capitello, some 200m higher up, is a richer blue that reflects the stark surrounding mountains.

With some short steep sections, and even a few rock-bolted chains and ladders to haul yourself up, there's just enough challenge in this walk (min/max altitude 1370/1930m) to make it feel like you've achieved something, but it still remains easy enough for children to make it to at least the first of the lakes. All up, if you want to see why Corsica has earned such high regard in the eyes of walkers the world over, then this spectacular walk will show you.

## Getting Here

The best base for this walk is the lovely mountain town of Corte. There's every possible kind of tourist facility here and much of it is aimed at walkers (there are some decent hiking shops). From Corte, the trailhead is a 15km drive along the D623; a very narrow and tortuous drive (and very busy in summer) to the very end of the Restonica Valley.

In July and August, a shuttle service operated by **Autocars Cortenais** (autocars-cortenais.fra) runs from the information point at Chjarasgiolu (4km from Corte) to the trailhead. Return tickets are €15 and departures are at 8am, 9am, 10.30am and noon. Return services are at 1.30pm, 2.30pm, 4pm and 5.30pm. Make sure to reserve in advance.

## Starting Point

Begin at the Bergerie de Grottelle, which sits at the very end of the road that winds up the Restonica Valley. There's a large car park here (car/motorcycle €6/3) and a huddle of shepherds' huts that sell drinks, cheeses and snacks.

**01** This is a well-marked and popular trail so in general route-finding is simple. From the parking, follow the clear but rocky trail heading southwest further up the valley. The icy-blue **Restonica River** will be crashing over the rocks on your left.

**02** After 30 minutes, you'll pass a couple of **stone shepherds' huts**. In July and August, the shepherds will whip you up a delicious omelette and sell cheese, coffee and cold drinks.

**03** A short way from the shepherds' huts, you'll pass the first of a couple of small **waterfalls** on the opposite side of the river. Look for the shepherd's livestock grazing on the slopes around here.

**04** After an hour, the trail, which has been pretty forgiving up until this point, suddenly lurches upwards over giant boulders and bare rock face. These can be very slippery so, at one point, some **chains** were attached to an especially steep bit of rock (pictured). You're only really likely to need them in icy or wet conditions. Just after this, a series of **fixed ladders** run up the rock face next to a waterfall. These you will have to use but there's nothing dangerous about it and the kids will love it.

## To Higher Ground

An exciting add-on to this walk is to go from Lac de Capitello up onto the mountain ridge directly behind the lake, hook up with the famed GR20 route and then drop back down on a steep trail to Lac de Melo. This semicircular route adds around 2½ hours more onto your overall walk time and takes you to an altitude of 2133m.

In snow-free, clear conditions the route isn't too taxing and there's clear waymarking (look for the yellow waymarkers). From the top, you could even carry on eastward past the Col de Rinoso to descend back down to the valley floor almost opposite the stone shepherds' huts you passed on the way up.

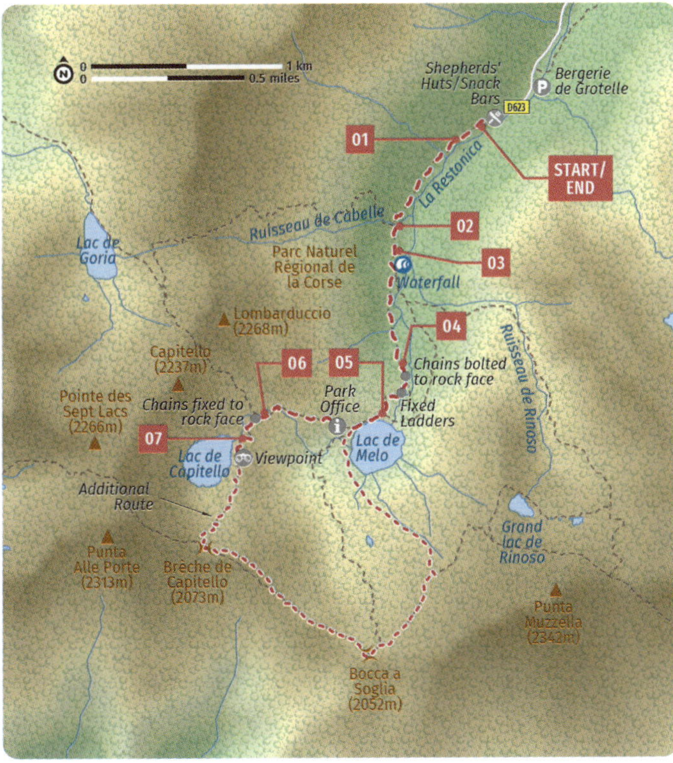

**05** Wobble off the last of the ladders and there in front of you is the first of the lakes, **Lac de Melo** (1711m). Lodged between great shafts of soaring rock, this dark-coloured lake is quite a sight. For hiking families, this is a good endpoint to your adventure and the grassy pastures around the lake make for an ideal picnic stop. Leave one hour to return to the car (total 2¼ hours).

**06** For everyone else follow the path around to the right, skirting around the side of the lake. Walk past a small park office on your left and start climbing; at first only gently but then much more steeply as you aim for a gap in the cliff face below shark-tooth peaks (pictured). There's a fair bit of scrambling over rock and boulder and, once again, there are a couple of **chains** bolted to the mountain in places to help ease you up the trickier and steeper sections (but again these aren't normally strictly necessary). The trail is always clear and obvious, though.

**07** Two and a half hours from the start and with a final heave-ho, you'll emerge onto a platform of rock, in the centre of which lies the deep blue **Lac de Capitello** (1930m) framed against a ridge of mountains of around 2400m. Be sure to walk to the eastern edge of this small plateau to check out the startling view to Lac de Melo almost directly below.

To return simply retrace your route back to the parking (leave at least 1¾ hours for the descent).

STUART BUTLER/LONELY PLANET ©

## Tackling the GR20

The GR20 long-distance walking path has gained almost mythical status among hardened hikers. Running from north to south across almost the entire length of Corsica's jagged spine, this 180km walk takes an average of 15 days to complete and is considered the hardest of all the GR trails in France.

With near-endless steep ascents and descents and punishing summer sun, it's perhaps no surprise to learn that the majority of people who set out on the trail don't complete it. It's even said that up to 40% of people who start out on the GR20 give up before the end of day one.

If you do want to attempt it, then early June and September are considered the prime periods.

## Take a Break

There's nowhere to buy food and drinks around the lakes but shepherds set up seasonal cafes both in the car park and around a third of the way along the trail. Even so, it's wise to bring a picnic.

# Also Try...

BEBOY/SHUTTERSTOCK ©

## Calanche

| DURATION | DIFFICULTY | DISTANCE |
| --- | --- | --- |
| 4½hr return | Easy | 11km |

Just outside the small town of Piana, melted mountains of orange-red granite have created a bizarre landscape of strange rock creatures and faces overlooking a shimmering Mediterranean. It's one of the most memorable landscapes in Corsica and is a very popular place for an easy walk (some might say it's a bit too popular!).

There are three standard, signed walks here, all of which are very short but by easily linking them together, you can come up with a satisfying half-day walk. Start off by following the Chemin de la Châtaigneraie trail, which is the quietest, longest and wildest of the three routes. From this, you can link straight into the Chemin du Château-Fort trail, which takes you to an impressive coastal viewpoint (pictured). Finally, clamber through the Chemin des Muletiers, which heads through a landscape of surreal rock formations.

## Îles Lavezzi

| DURATION | DIFFICULTY | DISTANCE |
| --- | --- | --- |
| 1½hr return | Easy | 4.5km |

So perfect are the white-sand beaches fringed by giant granite boulders, that sailing into a bay on the Îles Lavezzi, a group of small islands off the south coast of Corsica, you could well be forgiven for thinking you'd arrived in the Seychelles.

This walk, which meanders lazily around the main island, might be super short and easy, but it'll likely take you all day to complete because of having to continuously stop and test the waters at each and every beautiful beach. There's a web of sandy trails around the car-free island and walking arrows guide you in the right direction but, in truth, this is one place where it really doesn't matter if you're on the right trail. Just walk. Swim. And enjoy.

WILLEMA/SHUTTERSTOCK ©

## Monte d'Oro

| DURATION | DIFF. | DISTANCE |
| --- | --- | --- |
| 9hr return | Hard | 45km |

At 2389m, Monte d'Oro isn't the highest mountain on the island but the circular route to the summit of the mountain is arguably the most spectacular.

Starting from the Gare de Vizzavona, follow trails through dense beech woodland higher and higher until trees turn to mountain meadows and mountain meadows turn to rock moonscapes. The thrilling route runs along a ridge to the Bocca di Porco, then up to the summit before a whirlwind steep descent on the other side and back through more woodland via the Cascade des Anglais.

## Monte San Petrone

| DURATION | DIFF. | DISTANCE |
| --- | --- | --- |
| 5hr return | Moderate | 13km |

East and slightly away from the main knuckle of Corsican mountains, Monte San Petrone (1767m) has wonderful views from the summit. On a clear day they take in much of the east coast of the island, the fortress-like central mountains and most of the Cap Corse peninsula.

The walk begins from the Col de Prato and spends much of the time in the shade of Mediterranean woodland and, higher up, beech forest, before arriving at the rocky summit topped by a big cross. It's a good goal with older children.

## Monte Cinto

| DURATION | DIFF. | DISTANCE |
| --- | --- | --- |
| 8hr return | Hard | 16km |

At 2706m, Monte Cinto is the summit of Corsica.

There are a couple of routes up the mountain. All are long and very challenging, but perhaps the most satisfying, varied and manageable for the average mountain walker is the southeast route starting from close to the small village of Lozzi. You can also shave a good 2½ hours off the walk by starting from a parking area, Capella a sa Lisei, at the end of a long bumpy piste, but doing so means you miss out on some delightful scenery (pictured).

# Arriving

The main points of entry in France are Paris and Nice. RER B connects both Charles de Gaulle (CDG; pictured) and Orly (ORY) airports in Paris to the city centre. From Nice, it's possible to take Tram 2 into the centre. If you're arriving in France from a non-EU country, build in time for passing through customs.

## Travelling with Hiking Gear

On planes, most hiking equipment can be carried in a backpack as hand luggage, as long as the bag is in accordance with size restrictions. Some items that may not be accepted include pocket knives, tent poles, hiking poles and camping stoves/gas. In this case, look into checking your tent in as 'sports equipment', which usually costs less than a regular checked bag. However, airline agents may be picky about you putting other forbidden hand-luggage items in the bag with the tent (such as knives or hiking poles). In this case, your best bet is to check in your whole hiking pack.

As long as it fits in the luggage compartments, there are no special rules about taking hiking gear on trains. Bear in mind that if you're carrying an instant-pop-up tent, there may be rules about bulky luggage.

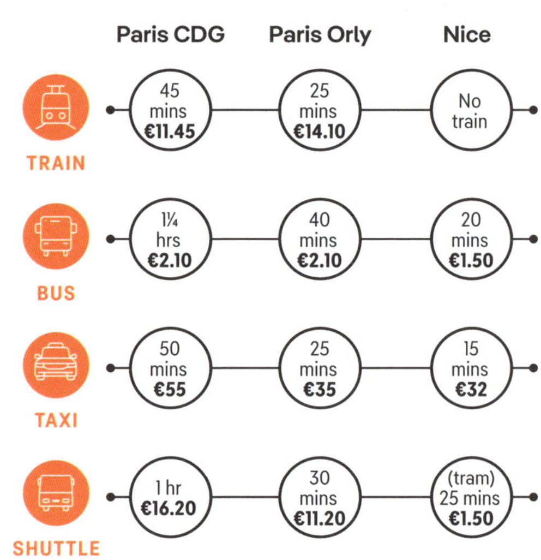

|  | Paris CDG | Paris Orly | Nice |
|---|---|---|---|
| **TRAIN** | 45 mins €11.45 | 25 mins €14.10 | No train |
| **BUS** | 1¼ hrs €2.10 | 40 mins €2.10 | 20 mins €1.50 |
| **TAXI** | 50 mins €55 | 25 mins €35 | 15 mins €32 |
| **SHUTTLE** | 1 hr €16.20 | 30 mins €11.20 | (tram) 25 mins €1.50 |

### WI-FI & SIM CARDS

Wi-fi is common in train stations, cafes and hotels. If you're an EU resident, your phone will work in France. It's possible to buy local SIM cards in cities, or at large airports.

### VISAS

Around 60 non-EU nationalities don't need a visa for a tourism visit of less than 90 days in France. If you do need one, check with your consulate at least 3 months before travelling.

### CASH

Withdraw cash at major banks: BNP Paribas, Crédit Agricole, CIC or Société Générale. Use an online bank that supports multiple currencies to avoid extra fees. Change money at a bureau de change.

### BORDER CROSSINGS

Land borders with France are usually unregulated, except for occasional stops to enter Switzerland (which requires a special sticker to drive on the highways) and Andorra.

# Getting Around

## DRIVING INFO

Drivers must give way to vehicles on the right.

On highways it's forbidden to pass other cars on the right.

### .05

Blood-alcohol limit in France is 0.05%.

**CITY BREAK?**

Out for a multiday hike but need to stash your pack while in a city? Most medium-sized cities have luggage storage in stations or in shops near the stations. Usually about €9 to €15 for 24 hours, this is a great option to lighten your load for a day. Some hotels also offer luggage drop-off prior to check-in – give them a call or email prior to your arrival.

## Low-Carbon Travel

Reduce driving time and enjoy the scenery by using France's wide train network to reach medium-sized cities before renting a car. Or, consider using car-share programmes like Blablacar (blablacar.fr). Try Roastr (roadstr.fr) or Ouicar (ouicar.fr) for private rental from a local.

## Bus Lines

Most bus lines change schedules during the school holidays – autumn break, Christmas, Easter and July/

August. Interregional buses leave from the *gare routière* (bus station). Some buses have special places for bicycles. A good intercity option is Flixbus (flixbus.com).

## Parking at Trailheads

Popular hikes usually have designated car parks and spots fill up early. Some are free, others charge a day rate. If your hike doesn't have a designated parking area, copy locals and park on the roadside, away from traffic.

## Speed Limits

Highway speed limits are 130km/h, with regional roads 110km/h and urban areas 50km/h unless otherwise noted. Pedestrian areas are usually limited to 30km/h. Speed radars dot the highway and high-traffic roads, and speeding tickets will catch up with you.


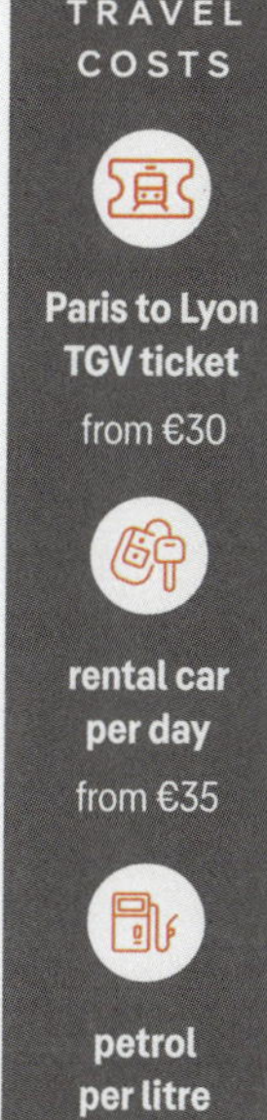

## TRAVEL COSTS

**Paris to Lyon TGV ticket**

from €30

**rental car per day**

from €35

**petrol per litre**

approx. €1.95



LEFT: MILA CHE/SHUTTERSTOCK ©, RIGHT: V_E/SHUTTERSTOCK ©

# Accommodation

**GÎTES D'ÉTAPE**

A *gîte d'étape* is a type of rustic B&B specifically designed for overnight stays, usually catering to hikers. Often located in villages or hamlets not far from popular long-distance hiking routes, these are affordable stopovers that offer all that's needed for hikers to get a good rest. The average price is about €30 per person. Dorm-style sleeping arrangements are the norm, but some also offer 4- or 6-bed rooms. Usually it's possible to wash clothes, get directions and have a hot meal. A pretty comprehensive list is available online at gites-refuges.com.

**HOW MUCH FOR A NIGHT IN...**

*refuge* (half-board)

from €55

**a campsite**

from €12

**a château**

from €140

**a *gîte d'étape***

€30

## Refuges (Mountain Huts)

The classic hiking and mountaineering accommodation, *refuges* range from quite luxurious to simply a shelter from the elements. Those run by the Club Alpine Français are typically affordable and have a simplified booking system online, but are often oriented towards mountaineers more than hikers. You're still welcome, but don't be surprised that it's lights out by 10pm!

## Camping

Many campsites offer special pricing for hikers – sometimes up to 50% less than if you arrive by car. On average, this comes to about €12 to €14 per night, instead of €25+. And, these campsites – or *'campings'* – know what you need: a hot shower and to wash some clothes, and they can recommend a warm dinner somewhere nearby.

## Farmhouses

If you're in Provence and are looking for a typical place to stay, book a night in a *mas* (farmhouse). Usually, they're built with low-cost materials like locally sourced clay, wood or stone. Several buildings often make up a *mas* as in bygone days each one served a purpose on the farm.

## Chateaux & Manors

Revisiting imperial days with a stay in a French castle or manor is a fun way to feel like royalty. Many châteaux and manors rent B&B-style rooms. Stretching from the countryside outside Paris down through the Loire Valley, you'll find the highest concentration of chateaux. Prices start from €140 per night.

### WORKING FARMS

Different to staying in a farmhouse, lodging that carries the label *'Bienvenue à la ferme'* means booking a stay at a working farm. It's an easy way to meet locals in the countryside, who may share their secret hiking spots or homemade goat's cheese with you. Plus there are usually some animals around; fun for kids (or kids at heart!).

# On the Trails

### Gear Rental

Luckily, hiking is an activity where you don't need much gear! Renting gear in France is hit or miss, depending on what you're looking for. You should generally come with your own clothes and shoes, though heavy mountaineering boots can be rented in some hiking-centric towns like Chamonix. This may be a good option if your walk still has some snowy patches, or if you don't want to invest in boots for a single-day hike.

It is more common to rent camping gear – many shops rent tents, sleeping pads and bags. Decathlon offers a rental service for all things camping and outdoor. Some hotels may loan you a pair of hiking poles, or a backpack, but don't count on it.

### Trail Etiquette

Trail etiquette in France is very friendly! Hikers are expected to say *'bonjour'* when they cross paths with others. Except in high-altitude (mountaineering) situations, it's rare to see cairns. Do not construct them on your own as too many cairns disrupt flora and fauna, and can also be misleading to hikers. You'll need to carry your rubbish out – when stopping at *refuges,* unless there is a road nearby where a car can pick up rubbish, keep it with you.

*Refuges* have a rich cultural history in France, and that comes with some rules. The main ones are that shoes must be taken off inside (there are usually slippers or crocs available for your use), dinner is at 7pm, and if you're staying overnight, you should pay after dinner. Remember to bring cash as often there isn't any phone service in the huts, so cards are not accepted.

## USEFUL RESOURCES

### refuges.info

Find mountain springs for drinking water, cabins and mountain huts.

### visorando.com

User-populated hiking database with thousands of routes.

### meteofrance. com

The most reliable weather service; especially useful in the mountains.

LEFT: MAREK CECH/SHUTTERSTOCK ©, RIGHT: PETR POHUDKA/SHUTTERSTOCK ©

# Health & Safe Travel

## INSURANCE



Basic travel insurance should do the trick for hiking in France, as hiking is usually included in the activities covered. To be safe, confirm that your insurance covers all recovery and evacuation – if you find yourself stuck on a ledge in need of helicopter rescue, the bill is steep without insurance!

## Drinking Water

In the mountains, there are numerous springs where it's safe to drink the water, especially during spring and early summer. Later in the season, drink with care, as livestock can spoil the water supply. In villages, you'll usually find a fountain in the main square. Or ask at a cafe, or a local resident – this is a great way to meet people too!

## Wildfires

Avoid lighting campfires except in designated places, and do not leave cigarette butts on the trail (lit or unlit!). Some national parks restrict

access to hikers during summer months to reduce the risk. Others forbid the use of hiking poles with metal tips, which could create sparks against the rock. Do your research before heading out.

## Blisters

Some people use very hydrating cream on their feet for a week leading up to a big hike, or just before putting on their socks. The thickness and texture of the socks you wear are key – if you only invest in one hiking-specific piece of gear, good socks are worth their weight in gold!

## Sheepdogs

Sheepdogs (patous) can pose a risk to hikers. If you walk through a pasture and see a patou, keep your distance from the animals that they're watching over. Avoid eye contact, don't swing your poles at them or throw rocks, and remain calm. Do not reach out to pet them, even if they are fluffy!

### IN CASE OF EMERGENCY

Call 112 for emergencies: ambulance, fire, police. In the mountains, ask for the *'secours en montagne'* and give the region to reach the local mountain-rescue service.

# Responsible Travel

## Climate Change & Travel

It's impossible to ignore the impact we have when travelling, and the importance of making changes where we can. Lonely Planet urges all travellers to engage with their travel carbon footprint. There are many carbon calculators online that allow travellers to estimate the carbon emissions generated by their journey; try resurgence.org/resources/carbon-calculator.html. Many airlines and booking sites offer travellers the option of offsetting the impact of greenhouse gas emissions by contributing to climate-friendly initiatives around the world. We continue to offset the carbon footprint of all Lonely Planet staff travel, while recognising this is a mitigation more than a solution.



### WWoofing

*wwoof.fr*
Stay/volunteer at organic farms.

### Ecovoyageurs

*ecovoyageurs.com*
Great eco travel plans (in French).

### Rando sans voiture

*rando-sans-voiture.fr/*
Connects public transport to hiking departures.

## SUPPORT LOCAL

Local produce tastes all the better when it's prepared in an environmentally and socially responsible way. Check out Ecotable (ecotable.fr) to find establishments that are engaged in eco-responsible dining.

## TRUSTWORTHY GREEN LABELS

For hotels, check out Clef Verte – the EU eco-label – and EarthCheck. When dining, Michelin flags green choices with a clover leaf. And visit Mr Goodfish (mrgoodfish.com) to avoid eating overfished seafood species.

LEFT: TOMMY LAREY/SHUTTERSTOCK ©, TOP RIGHT: CARLOS YUDICA/SHUTTERSTOCK ©, BOTTOM RIGHT: BARMALINI/SHUTTERSTOCK ©

# Nuts & Bolts



## CURRENCY: EURO (€)

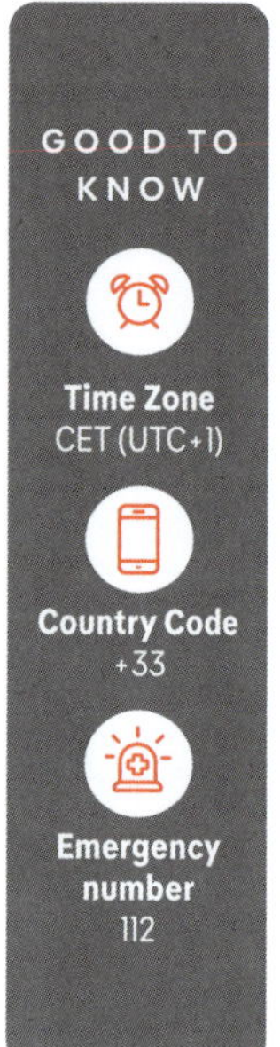

**GOOD TO KNOW**

**Time Zone**
CET (UTC+1)

**Country Code**
+33

**Emergency number**
112

### Contactless & Card Payments

Known as *'sans contact'*, paying by touch with a card or a phone is on the rise in France. It's also possible on toll roads and for train tickets. For businesses, the fees for this technology are high, so small shops may not have a card reader.

Paying by card is fine in restaurants and shops, and for train tickets, hotels etc. But in markets, bars and small shops, cash is appreciated (and sometimes obligatory). At mountain huts, it's almost always obligatory – no phone service usually means no card reader!

## ELECTRICITY 230V/50HZ

**Type E**
**220V/50Hz**

### Tipping

Tips are included in the service fee in France at restaurants. For other services, like taxis or food delivery, tipping is customary but not required. Usually, this is simply a question of rounding up, so providers don't have to give change.

### Opening Hours

Many shops close between noon and 3pm. In small towns, many shops may only be open in the afternoon.

Sundays and Mondays are common days of rest for businesses.

### Toilets

Public toilets are available in most towns, usually near the town hall or car parks. Bring toilet paper.

### Smoking

Keep your cigarette butts with you and dispose of them properly once you're off the trail.

**HOW MUCH FOR A...**

**hike parking charge**
from €3

**bottle of water in a *refuge***
from €4

**short-haul bus fare**
€1.80–4

**museum entry**
€5–16

# By Difficulty

# Index

Trails 000
**Map Pages 000, 000**

Trails 000
**Map Pages 000, 000**

# THE WRITERS

This is the 2nd edition of this guidebook, updated with new material by Ashley Parsons. Writers on the previous edition whose work also appears in this book are included below.

**Ashley Parsons**

Ashley is a travel and adventure writer who splits her time between Provence and the French Alps. She's cycled from France to Uzbekistan and crossed Albania (750km) and Kyrgyzstan (1600km) on horseback, unguided. Her first film, *En Selle: The Kyrgyz Ride,* follows her childhood dream to gallop across the steppe and mountains of the old Silk Road to learn how to live as a modern nomad. When travelling, she always lets a question or topic guide her journeys -- that's how she ended up running 100 miles around Mont Blanc on the quest for the best beer on tap in a mountain hut! Follow her travels on horseback, bike, foot or by train on Instagram @enselle.voyage.

**Contributing Writers**

Oliver Berry, Stuart Butler, Steve Fallon, Anita Isalska, Nicola Williams.

## SEND US YOUR FEEDBACK

We love to hear from travellers – your comments keep us on our toes and help make our books better. Our well-travelled team reads every word on what you loved or loathed about this book. Although we cannot reply individually to your submissions, we always guarantee that your feedback goes straight to the appropriate writers, in time for the next edition. Each person who sends us information is thanked in the next edition.

Visit **lonelyplanet.com/contact** to submit your updates and suggestions or to ask for help. Our award-winning website also features inspirational travel stories and news.

Note: We may edit, reproduce and incorporate your comments in Lonely Planet products such as guidebooks, websites and digital products, so let us know if you are happy to have your name acknowledged. For a copy of our privacy policy visit **lonelyplanet.com/legal**.

## BEHIND THE SCENES

This book was produced by the following:

**Commissioning Editor**
Darren O'Connell

**Production Editor**
James Appleton

**Book Designer**
Virginia Moreno

**Cartographer**
Katerina Pavkova

**Assisting Editors**
Soo Hamilton, Kate Mathews, Mani Ramaswamy, Fionnuala Twomey

**Cover Researcher**
Ania Lenihan

**Thanks to**
Ronan Abayawickrema, Gwen Cotter, Fergal Condon, Alison Killilea

**Product Development**
Amy Lynch, Marc Backwell, Katerina Pavkova, Fergal Condon, Ania Lenihan

## ACKNOWLEDGMENTS

**Cover Photograph**
Chemin des Chèvres, Puy de Dôme; Hervé Lenain/Alamy Stock Photo ©